British *Greats*

British *Greats*

CASSELL&CO

Introduction

The vexed question of Britishness continues to preoccupy us. Who are we? Are we really a 'we' at all or merely a loose affiliation of geographically proximate, highly distinct cultures? By British do we really mean English? And how European are we? You will perhaps be relieved to discover that this book has no intention of addressing these questions. While they may lurk between the lines, or occasionally signal from the horizon, they are very much part of the subtext. The book's aim is to celebrate events, inventions, concepts, pastimes, achievements – rejoicing in the surfeit of choice, the necessary omissions, the inherent eccentricity – that an outsider might deem unmistakably British.

But celebration doesn't come easy to us. Towards the end of his gloriously funny journey, *Notes from a Small Island*, Bill Bryson makes a serious point:

> What an enigma Britain will seem to historians when they look back on
> the second half of the twentieth century. Here is a country that fought
> and won a noble war, dismantled a mighty empire in a generally benign
> and enlightened way, created a far-seeing welfare state – in short, did
> nearly everything right – and then spent the rest of the century looking
> on itself as a chronic failure.

As so often, it takes an outsider to state the obvious. There is plenty to celebrate. Bryson goes on to participate in what may be a quintessentially British parlour game: the making of lists. Whenever British culture or our character is discussed, lists follow – from Orwell and Betjeman to Jeremy Paxman and Nick Hornby, we cannot resist setting down our preferences.

And what you have here are the enthusiasms of contemporary great Britons, most of them commissioned, some spontaneously offered. Reviewing all 78 contributions, one is immediately struck by the serendipitous connections to be made. John Elliott on the Armada is linked to Len Deighton on the Battle of Britain less by the fact of victory against impossible odds than by the sense of the heroic growing organically out of the homely: a game of bowls interrupted; pints left standing on the bar as the pilots scramble. And there's an element in both these pieces, as in many others, of the cult of the amateur or the underdog where character and integrity mean almost as much as the end result.

This deeply ingrained refusal to systematise and the trust in the slow accumulation of tradition is often remarked upon in British institutions, but we are very practical in our idealism and when we decide we want something – the abolition of slavery, the welfare state – we go about it with a briskness and a disregard for bureaucracy which is admirable. Indeed, for all our patience and oft-cited stoicism, we have produced a remarkable succession of revolutionary ideas – Newton's laws, the Industrial Revolution, Darwin's *Origin of Species*, the Cavendish Laboratory – and an astonishing line of inventions from the longbow to penicillin, the miniskirt to the corner shop.

At the heart of our capacity for innovation and invention is a bias towards the utilitarian – we are good at making things that people need – and when Stephen Bayley describes the

London taxi as 'eccentric, decent, convenient, safe, comforting' the adjectives seem to fit very snugly for a whole range of British enterprises. But we are odder than that. We are obsessive – 'in love with the preposterous' as Julie Burchill demonstrates in her encomium to pets. Alongside pets we might add comics, the weather, or, as Michael Palin has it, the Saturday ritual of the football results. According to Len Deighton, the British are successful precisely because of 'a healthy mistrust for uniforms and authority' and this includes those who wear the uniforms and wield the authority. Andrew Graham-Dixon sees the familiar red telephone box 'confessional' as expressing the 'secret yearning' of the British to 'return, miraculously, to their repressed Catholic origins'. And then there is our peculiar sense of humour, in which Howard Jacobson discerns Baudelaire's 'sustained note of fury'. This 'uncultivated' note sounds through Shakespeare and Dickens, in the Beatles' best work and the rude energy of punk, and it is reprised, perfectly, in 'the barely suppressed rage' with which the traditional British publican greets his customers.

Here, as elsewhere, high and popular culture are mixed indiscriminately. All the best British artists from Chaucer through Robert Burns and Wordsworth and Coleridge to W H Auden have, to borrow the quotation from Joseph Brodsky that appears in the essay on Auden, 'ladled from every puddle'. Great art is built from scrupulously observed details of everyday life and speech. Taken too far, our bias towards the populist runs the risk of that misunderstood British vice, philistinism – giving people only what they say they want – but where else would you find festivals as accessible, well-attended and at the same time as ground-breaking in their content as the Edinburgh Festival and the Proms? And for all its problems, the BBC still has a record of programme-making unmatched anywhere in the world.

There are many more connections to be made browsing these pages and that is, I hope, one of the principal pleasures of the book. Like good whisky – which also finds a place here – it should be sipped slowly. It is offered in the same spirit that Norman Davies commends at the end of his magisterial history of Britain, *The Isles*:

> The most pertinent contributions to the present debate about Britain
> were the ones that betrayed the least anxiety. We live in a fortunate and
> relatively gentle part of the continent.

Amen to that. The absence of anxiety here has less to do with blindness to the seismic shifts Britain is undergoing than a confidence that we will survive and prosper regardless. Like Alexander Fleming's petri dish, British culture has a proven knack for growing strange and beautiful blooms from the most unpromising circumstances. Who knows what such a list will look like in a hundred years time? We are living in a vibrant, multicultural broil where new ideas and modes of living are invented and communicated at unprecedented speed. What is certain is that we will still be sitting down and making lists of things that matter to us. And that is how it should be. If this book provokes you into setting down your own list of British Greats, it will have more than served its purpose.

John Mitchinson, *Cassell & Co*

The Defeat of the Spanish Armada
John Elliott

Great victories – and great defeats, too – sometimes become defining events in the shaping of a nation's image of itself. So it was with the defeat of the Invincible Armada. The Spanish galleons moving in stately formation up the Channel for their rendezvous with the Duke of Parma's army; Sir Francis Drake finishing his game of bowls on Plymouth Hoe; the fireships wreaking havoc among the vessels anchored off Calais; Elizabeth's speech to the troops at Tilbury; and the storm that dispersed the great ships and littered the shores of Ireland with the wrecks of the defeated Armada as it limped home to Spain – these scenes were replayed in the nation's collective consciousness for generation after generation, and helped keep alive the memory of 1588 as a providential year in English history.

'The magnitude of the catastrophe', wrote James Anthony Froude nearly three centuries later, 'took possession of the nation's imagination.' Yet at the time, many weeks were to pass before the scale of the disaster that had overtaken the Spanish fleet came to be realised. Although a sermon was preached at St Paul's on 20 August, praising God 'for our great victory by Him given to the English nation', no major public thanksgiving was ordered until late November, when it was timed to coincide with the 30th anniversary of the Queen's accession. There followed a week of services, sermons and processions, with lighting of bonfires and ringing of bells. The theme was deliverance: God had delivered His chosen people in their hour of need. This was, first and foremost, a great religious event, offering indisputable proof that God was Protestant. Medals were struck in England and the rebel provinces of the Netherlands, showing the ships of the Armada being dispersed by the 'Protestant' wind, along with appropriate inscriptions – 'He blew and they were scattered.' The Armada proclaimed the triumph, through divine intervention, of the international Protestant cause over the Antichrist in Rome and his wicked instrument, the King of Spain.

As it happens, the events of the next few years were to show that, at least in the short run, the victory over the Spaniards was not quite as conclusive as it must have seemed in that exhilarating autumn of 1588. Within two or three years, the Spain of Philip II was looking at least as formidable as when the Armada first set sail, and its naval recovery was sufficiently rapid for Philip to be able to order the despatch of fresh expeditions against the British Isles in 1596 and 1597, only to see them dispersed again by storms. The threat of successful invasion had now effectively passed, and with hindsight it can be seen that the Protestant cause was safe, but well into the 17th century the continent still lived under the shadow of Spain, with all the silver of America at its command.

Yet perceptions count for at least as much as realities in the shaping of national consciousness. This was true of Spain and England alike. For Spain, the defeat of the 'Enterprise of England' came as a devastating shock. When a nation thinks of itself as specially chosen for some divine purpose, failure is hard to understand. God, it seemed, had turned against it, and the best explanation for this sudden loss of divine favour seemed to be collective sinfulness. The incipient psychology of failure would be reinforced in succeeding decades by each new

reverse to Spanish arms. In England, by contrast, the defeat of the Armada was to prove a crucial element in the eventual construction of a psychology of success.

Although no special day was set aside for the annual commemoration of the great victory of 1588, celebrations of the events of that fateful year were to be subsumed after 1605 into a wider national celebration, held each November, for a second act of divine deliverance – the discovery of the Gunpowder Plot. November was also the month in which Elizabeth, of happy memory, had come to the throne. During difficult times in the 17th century, when it seemed that Protestantism and liberty were again in mortal danger from the forces of popery, the recollection of the great queen, of the defeat of the Armada and of the uncovering of the villainy of Guy Fawkes provided comforting reassurance of the mercy that could be expected for the nation if it remained faithful to its God. Then, by a supreme act of providence, just one hundred years after the defeat of the Armada, the nation was again delivered out of deadly peril when William of Orange disembarked at Torbay on 5 November 1688, and a Glorious Revolution ensured the triumph of liberty and Protestantism alike.

By the early 18th century, all the essential elements of England's national self-image were in place – a country that, against overwhelming odds, had seen off its enemies, first the

The Armada Portrait, *painted to celebrate Elizabeth's success against the Spanish*

Spaniards, then the French, and was both Protestant and free. The triumphs of the following two centuries – command of the seas, the acquisition of empire, and global dominance – only served to confirm the verdict of 1588, and reinforced the message of a divinely appointed national destiny for England and its peoples (generously embracing the Scots, the Welsh and the Irish, or at least those of Protestant descent).

Until the 19th century, the public commemoration of centenaries was unusual, and it was not until 1888 that an attempt was made to organise a centenary celebration of 1588. An appeal was launched at the Mansion House for a national memorial to be erected on Plymouth Hoe, and a rather indiscriminate exhibition of Armada mementoes was put on display at the Plymouth Guildhall. But this was essentially a West Country initiative, and at the national level the commemorations seem to have fallen rather flat. The triumph of liberty and Protestantism was now taken for granted, and Britannia ruled the waves.

Ironically, it was only in 1988, when England's global dominance had long since passed, and the national identity itself was coming to be called into question, that an exhibition was mounted which recalled the events of 1588 on an appropriately epic scale. To the expression of considerable indignation in some quarters, scrupulous care was taken at the National Maritime Museum to give the Spanish side of the story equal weight to the English. Where were the heroes of yesteryear? No longer central to the national mythology, the defeat of the Armada had disappeared from the realm of the transcendental to become one more spectacular historical event.

Arthurian Legends
John Gillingham

No British product has lasted better or longer than the Arthurian legends. They have been a source of excitement and pleasure for 1,200 years – at the very least – and their appeal shows no signs of diminishing. King Arthur is now as much at home to visitors on the internet, at sites such as Arthurnet, as he is in the landscape of Britain, at sites such as Tintagel or Edinburgh (Arthur's Seat) or in Wales at Caerleon (Arthur's Table). Children of all ages, including many great writers and artists – from the unknown ninth-century Briton who used to be known as Nennius, but who has been reduced to anonymity by sceptical modern scholars, to the late 20th-century Anglo-American team that created *Monty Python and the Holy Grail* – have been inspired by the stories of Arthur and have had enormous fun in reinterpreting them to suit their own temperaments and situations.

In his 1930 poem 'The grave of Arthur', G K Chesterton pondered the paradox of a British king who may never have lived but whose legend will never die. That too has long been part of the fascination. Did Arthur ever really exist? This is that wondrous thing, a mystery that will never be solved to everyone's satisfaction. Some argue that the name came from the Roman name Artorius, and that there must have been a real Arthur, a Romanised Briton. This is how 'Nennius' in the earliest British history locates Arthur. The scene is Britain after the legions have departed. Invading Saxons pursue a policy of ethnic cleansing, either killing the Britons or driving them out: overseas to north-western Gaul, which comes to be called Brittany, or into the poorer and hillier parts of western Britain (not just Wales, but also Cornwall and Cumberland, the land of the Cymry). The Nennian perspective still remains the favourite one for those who believe in a real Arthur. But for others his name derives from the British vernacular Artgur, meaning 'bear-man'. It can be associated with Arcturus, the bright star in the constellation of the Great Bear. This enables us to take his origins back much further in time, and see in Arthur a super-hero of Celtic myth, leader of a band of warriors who roamed the Wasteland and raided the Otherworld. He is the defender of his people not against human enemies such as Saxons, but against superhuman creatures, witches, monsters and dragons; a folklore hero who cleared the land of the giants, its original inhabitants, so that we could live there. Although clearly British, within Britain he belonged everywhere and nowhere in particular. This is why none of the early genealogies of Welsh royal and noble families ever claimed an Arthur among their ancestors – not until well after Henry VII had named his first-born son Arthur. In this interpretation, allusions not just to Arthur but also to Kay, Bedivere, Guinevere and Tristan in cryptic lines of early (but no one knows just how early) Welsh poetry, can take us back at least 2,000 years and open a window onto pre-Roman times: Iron Age Britain.

If this is so, then 'Nennius' in the ninth century was the first great reinterpreter. Writing at a time when his fellow countrymen faced increasing military pressure from the English of Mercia, 'Nennius' portrays Arthur as leader of the British resistance, crediting him with, among many other triumphs, victory at Badon – a victory that in mere history had belonged

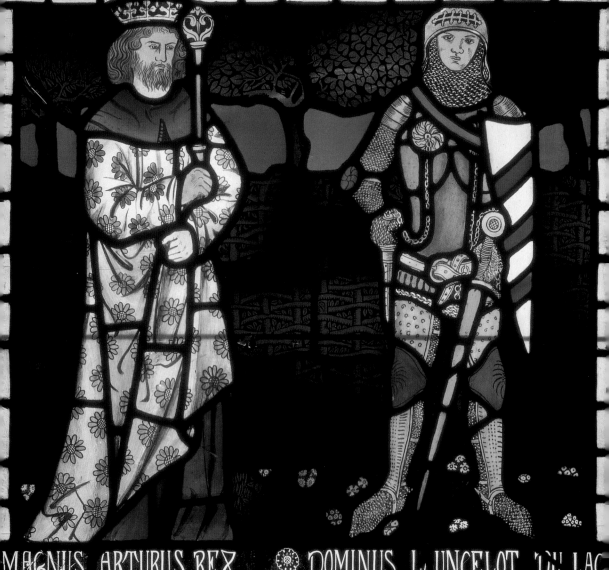

MAGNUS ARTURUS REX
POTENTISSIMUS ANGLIAE

DOMINUS L UNCELOT DU LAC
EQUES INVICTUS

to Ambrosius Aurelianus. From then on, Britons everywhere dreamed of the day when Arthur would return and restore to them their rightful dominion. The next creative reinterpretation came from a 12th-century spellbinder, Geoffrey of Monmouth. Living at a time when learned Europeans were beginning to look down on Celtic peoples as savage, primitive and immoral, Geoffrey's response was to compose, in Latin, a fantasy counter-history, the *History of the Kings of Britain*. Here Merlin is brought into the story and Arthur has become a king. Mortally wounded in battle against his nephew Mordred, he would none the less be healed at Avalon and, on the day prophesied by Merlin, he would return. He remains the British champion, but becomes much more too: a great conqueror able to take on and defeat the might of the Roman Empire, he presides over a magnificent and fashionable court. Geoffrey's book became an instant international bestseller, translated and adapted into many languages, including both English and Welsh. Translated into French, new motifs came to the fore: Camelot and the Round Table, ideas of love and courtliness. With the Arthurian romances written by Chrétien of Troyes, one of the greats of French literature, the cast of characters and themes was completed: Gawain, the love of Lancelot and Guinevere, Sir Perceval (Wagner's Parsifal) and the Grail.

Once Geoffrey and Chrétien had turned King Arthur into an ideal king for all the world, he was no longer tied down to his specific role as an anti-English Celtic hero. In any case, the convenient 'discovery' of his tomb at Glastonbury in about 1190 demonstrated that his skull had been so damaged as to rule out the possibility of his ever returning. Having been defused, Arthur could now be reconstructed yet again, this time as an English king, a process helped by the already common habit of treating Britain and England as interchangeable terms, as well as by Geoffrey of Monmouth's depiction of Arthur as conqueror of Ireland and Scotland. In time, the Welsh would find a substitute Arthur in their own local hero, the once and future Owain Glyn Dwr. Meanwhile, the first king of England to identify himself with Arthur was Richard the Lionheart, the hero who took Excalibur with him when he set off on crusade – a quest not for the Grail but for Jerusalem.

Both French and English versions of the legends were brought together in Sir Thomas Malory's *Morte d'Arthur*. Published by Caxton, King Arthur took to the new world of print as readily as he would to the internet. But in the 17th and 18th centuries, despite being the subject of an opera with words by Dryden and music by Purcell, King Arthur suffered a period of relative neglect until Tennyson's *Idylls of the King* gave Victorian Britain a mind-bending compound of chivalry, spirituality and adultery. From then on, via Mark Twain's *A Connecticut Yankee in King Arthur's Court* and T H White's *The Once and Future King*, Arthur and Merlin have enjoyed careers from which they have never looked back, on film, television, stage and now the internet – the modern virtual reality appropriate to an ancient world that could have been.

Arthur and Lancelot depicted in a stained glass window designed by William Morris

The Poetry of W H Auden
Ruth Padel

Wystan Hugh Auden (1907–1973), the most important England-born 20th-century poet, had a unique feel for the historical landscape of human suffering. Through his prodigious output and range of styles and tones (romantic, chortling, apocalyptic, lyric, bitter, didactic, tender, angry), his poems were driven by sorrow for the human condition: the whole messy package of fumbling boredom, missed buses, fun, love, ecstasy, despair. All done with a light, often satiric touch. Everyone has a 'right to frivolity' he said. 'Good poets have a weakness for bad puns.' His poetry is sorrow controlled by metre and rhyme: filigreed steel, with tears behind.

His first book came out in 1930; he spearheaded for poetry what art was learning, carnivorously, from contemporary journalism: that Thirties delight in literature as camera. How, like war photography, a poem can pan over background, showing trivia reeling on beside a tragedy, then make one detail say everything – politically, socially, emotionally. Like great painters who set martyrdoms and catastrophes in 'some untidy spot / Where the dogs go on with their doggy life and the torturer's horse / Scratches its innocent behind on a tree' ('Musée des Beaux Arts').

His work has two key features. First, the poems combine three crucial things: the memorable image, vernacular voice, and abstract thought. His big theme was the collapse of civilisation, and 'The Fall of Rome', written as Europe nose-dived into war, ends with the approaching authors of collapse, those invading Goths who brought down Rome. But the image is surreally gentle: 'Altogether elsewhere, vast / Herds of reindeer move across / Miles and miles of golden moss / Silently, and very fast.'

The voice? After Eliot's flowing line and Pound's image-fragments, Auden's voice crackled into Thirties ears as the next step after modernism: a demotic, conversational tone, generalisingly urban, socially critical, with anti-élitist fidelity to the spoken word. 'How can anyone say, "I have watched an hour"?' he said impatiently about Yeats. 'Poetry must be accurate.' He saw Yeats' mystic self-solemnity as weakness. 'You were silly like us,' he said in his elegy for him. He himself drew on English as spoken – and very variously: 'Auden ladles from every puddle,' said Joseph Brodsky, meaning he took words from everywhere: jargon, news-speak, street idiom.

And abstract thought? At a technical level, you find it in the nouns. He moves straight from bed – 'Lay your sleeping head, my love / Human on my faithless arm' – to concepts like 'Certainty, fidelity' ('Lullaby'). His poem on the war's beginning opens in a New York dive 'On Fifty-Second Street', but ends in a shower of concepts: 'May I… / Beleaguered by the same / Negation and despair / Show an affirming flame' ('September 1, 1939'). Keeping both the personal and the political constantly in play, he identifies a moral concept in every physical detail.

W H Auden as Oxford Professor of Poetry, a position he took up in 1956

These nouns reflect his need for a worked-out moral-cum-intellectual system to explain the sorry chaos of human history. In the Thirties, it was psychoanalysis and Marxism: both resonated to his hope that human beings were innately good, or healable. He lost that hope when the world – and his own life? – changed. In 1939 he moved to America, fell in love, and in a New York cinema watched Hitler's invasion of Poland. When people from the city's German quarter shouted 'Kill them!' he began to feel humanity was fallen and needed an absolute to explain and redeem it. In 1940 he became a Christian.

But his passion for order, for system, was technical too. Rhyme-schemes create inevitability: a rhyme turns an idea into something like law. His dazzling skill with verse-law was the second outstanding new feature of his work. Eliot too could be colloquial: he influenced Auden massively, especially in the way he brought jazz rhythms and syncopation into the line. But Auden combined that with strict, exquisitely worked intricacies of metre and rhyme in profuse, abstruse variety: two-beat lines, syllabics, Chinese seven-word-five-word couplets, rhyme-patterns going back to the Elizabethans. Poetry originates, he said, 'in the gut': the Freudian, subconscious 'fauna of the night' ('In Memory of Sigmund Freud'). But where poetry 'flowers' is 'the head'. 'The very nature of the form forces the mind to think.'

He was so self-critical, revising or dropping words and poems constantly, that critics barely needed to attack. But as his Thirties popularity grew, reviewers went for the kill. A poet of 29, warning you against fascism, going on about the fall of civilisation? Slap down his rhymes. '"The world is out of joint" seems to be the basis of Mr Auden's inspiration,' said de Selincourt, reviewing Auden's 1936 collection *Look Stranger!* 'He has decided things are so bad that poetry itself must change its nature.' (A derisively meant remark horribly reflected, afterwards, by Adorno's 'After Auschwitz, there can be no poetry.') Changing poetry is what innovative poets do; but to de Selincourt, Auden's ideas and rhymes were 'slapdash, restless, inconclusive'. Where Auden rhymed 'dream' with 'come' but 'dreams' with 'arms', de Selincourt derided '"new" consonantal rhymes'. 'New conventions have made such rhymes possible': 'I should prefer that the meaning, if there is one, had been conveyed in prose.'

That kind of reaction, hiddenly political, obtusely stylistic, often homophobic, plus criticism of Auden's move to America, lingered in Britain while he held the Oxford Chair (1956–61) and after his death. In 1981, *The Times* reviewed a biography under the headline 'Butterflies from the dungheap'. The butterflies were poems; the dungheap, Auden's life – this Christian who said in 1939 'we must love one another or die'; who advised a friend, 'Do not do anything that will make you feel proud'; who was humbly alert to the futility of trying to depict the world at all: 'No metaphor, remember, can express / A real historical unhappiness' ('The Truest Poetry is the Most Feigning').

Yet his own poems did, supremely, what he said poets must do: 'translate' the world, move 'from Life to Art by painful adaptation':

> Rummaging into his living, the poet fetches
> The images out that hurt and connect.
>
> ('The Composer')

The Novels of Jane Austen
Nigel Nicolson

If one were to pick a single author to define British culture, it would quite likely be Jane Austen. Shakespeare requires too much beetling of brows, and Dickens' people are sometimes apt to be caricatures. But Austen gave us the language we still use and the national character of which we still boast. The England which she depicts in her novels is the England for which many of us fought, and it is not surprising that she was the most read of our novelists in both great wars. It was not a perfect society that she described, and she never sentimentalised her heroes and heroines. But she did portray certain values that we still hold dear – tolerance, honesty, good neighbourliness and courage – and vices that we continue to deplore – snobbishness, cruelty, conceit and idleness. Her novels are sermons in the most acceptable and entertaining forms.

But her range is narrow, confined to her own experience. Unlike Fanny Burney she tells us nothing about the raffish side of life; unlike Anthony Trollope she never ventures into the worlds of politics, sport or the higher aristocracy. We never see Darcy in his role as landowner, Mr Gardiner as a man of business, or Captain Wentworth on board his ship. Indeed Jane Austen never risks leaving two of her fictional men alone together, because she did not know how they talked or what they talked about. There is little about children, because she had none, and even less about servants, for she took them for granted. Surprisingly – because for almost all her adult life England was engaged in a desperate war, and two of her brothers were officers in the Navy – she scarcely mentions in her letters or novels the elation of victory or the prospect of defeat, and only once refers, facetiously, to Napoleon.

Yet there is no doubt that she was a patriot to the core. One might even call her a xenophobe. She distrusted foreigners, and never knew one as a friend. She never travelled outside England, not even to Scotland, never saw a mountain, a large lake, a moor, a factory or a mine. She identified England with the rich farmland of the south from Dover to Exeter. Knowing no other landscape, she could imagine none more delightful. During her lifetime (1775–1817) England never looked more fair, and it is not difficult to visualise it, because much survives untarnished by road, rail or wire. Jane Austen was not much given to expressing her delight in nature, but we catch an occasional glimpse of it, as when Emma looked out over Abbey Mill Farm, and saw that 'it was a sweet view – sweet to the eye and mind. English verdure, English culture, English comfort seen under a sun bright without being offensive.' Or take the description of the sea coast around Lyme Regis in *Persuasion*, or this passage from *Mansfield Park*, when Fanny Price paces the ramparts of Portsmouth harbour:

> The day was uncommonly lovely. It was really March; but it was April
> in its mild air, brisk soft wind, and bright sun, occasionally clouded for a
> minute; and everything looked so beautiful under the influence of such

a sky, the effect of the shadows pursuing each other, on the ships at
Spithead and the island beyond.

That is the English climate caught in a single moment, and the reason why we love it.

Jane Austen was less responsive to the architecture which for many of us sums up the
taste and harmony of the late Georgian and Regency periods. She was not impressed even
by Bath, where she lived for four years, and although she was familiar with country houses
like Godmersham in Kent, which belonged to her brother, and Hackwood and The Vyne,
where she often danced, she never troubled to describe them in her letters, and there is
little detail in her novels about the fictional houses she based upon them. At a period
when nobody could make a coffee-pot without endowing it with utility and grace, she saw
no need to praise what was so familiar, and indeed she had little interest in the arts except
literature and music.

She focuses upon the people who inhabited these idyllic surroundings. We discover
exactly what she admired in human nature and what she despised. She can portray virtue
without priggishness and vice with wit. She is perpetually amazed that people can so often
give themselves away. The qualities she extols are innate: they cannot be acquired. Young
women must be energetic, fearless, sprightly, like Elizabeth Bennet, Emma, and Anne Elliot,
whose 'elegance of mind and sweetness of character' corresponded most closely to Jane
Austen's own. We must look for the ideal in Mr Knightley, a gentleman innocent of guile or
flattery; for absurdity in Mr Collins; for evil in Mrs Norris of Mansfield Park; and for passion
in Marianne Dashwood in *Sense and Sensibility*.

We know them so well that we hardly think of them as being born in the reign of
George III, and if Jane Austen was unaware of how unmistakably English they all were, it
was because she knew no others. She was excellently placed as the daughter of a clever and
sociable country vicar to observe English society upwards and downwards, humble enough to
meet villagers on terms not intimidating to them, bright enough to associate with the minor
aristocracy without awe or awkwardness. In her way, Jane Austen is to England what another
Marianne is to France – the best of the typical.

Pride and Prejudice: *Greer Garson and Laurence Olivier in the 1940 film of Austen's great novel*

The Battle of Britain
Len Deighton

By July 1940, Hitler's victorious fighting forces faced Britain all round the continental coast. Logic suggested that Britain should negotiate a surrender, but the British have never been noted for their logic. Inspired by Prime Minister Winston Churchill, virtually the whole nation was determined to continue the war.

The ensuing battle to establish air supremacy preparatory to a full-scale German invasion lasted for several weeks during the summer of 1940. After attacking coastal convoys in the English Channel, the German air force made daylight bombing raids on towns, ports, RAF airfields and other chosen targets across south-east England.

The pilots defending England against the German bomber fleets are usually remembered as young middle-class officers from public schools. It is tempting to compare them with the subalterns who served in the trenches in the First World War, their sensitivity and sacrifice recorded in the poetry and prose of that war. In fact, the world had changed. About a quarter of the 1940 fighter pilots were sergeants. Of these about two-fifths were peacetime civilians who had joined the volunteer reserve and attended local flying-schools at government expense. Other part-time flyers had spent their weekends with the fully equipped Auxiliary Air Force squadrons. Of the RAF's peacetime sergeant pilots, many had been picked from the RAF schools for young trade apprentices. No less important were the Australians, New Zealanders, Canadians and South Africans, as well as highly motivated professional pilots from the air forces of the occupied nations. A Czech pilot is usually credited with the highest number of victories during the Battle of Britain.

Commanding RAF Fighter Command was Air Chief Marshal Sir Hugh 'Stuffy' Dowding, a shy and lonely workaholic. His loyal right-hand man was Air Vice-Marshall Keith Park, an ace of the First World War, who commanded all the fighter units in south-east England, the battle area. These were men untrammelled by conventional military thinking (and who were ignominiously repaid after the victory by subjection to an enquiry and replacement by rivals; even today, despite the energetic work of the redoubtable Bill Bond and the Battle of Britain Historical Society, the men in Whitehall and Westminster resolutely oppose the creation of a proper memorial to the people who fought the battle).

Vitally important to the victory was Lord Beaverbrook, the maverick press tycoon Churchill had appointed to rectify the bureaucratic bumbling that crippled the aircraft industry. Breaking rules, and assuming powers he was never granted, the 'Beaver' was rich enough and influential enough openly to defy the civil servants, the industrialists and the bomber barons. He concentrated upon building fighter aircraft as quickly as possible and speedily repairing those that were damaged – a success for which his enemies never forgave him.

The Messerschmitt Bf109E and the Spitfire were about evenly matched in performance and effectiveness (the superiority of the Spitfire came later with the development of the Rolls Royce Merlin 60 series engines). But most of the RAF single-seat fighters were Hawker Hurricanes. Heavier, slower and less sophisticated, the Hurricanes were, whenever possible, sent to attack the bombers rather than face the Bf109s. All these aircraft had fuel enough for about one and a half hours of flying. Despite using grass airfields very near the coast, the Germans had only a brief time over England; the RAF also had to fight while watching the fuel gauge.

The RAF radar of the period was a simple device that bounced a transmitted signal off an approaching aircraft. By measuring its return, the position of the enemy could be estimated. Most of the tall radar masts along the British coast gave an approximate range and rough estimate of height and direction. To fix an enemy's position, the RAF plotters measured the ranges given by two neighbouring stations and noted the place where they intersected.

As well as having supervised the development of Britain's radar, Dowding had created Britain's unique reporting network. A 'filter room' and many 'operations rooms' processed the reports from the radar stations. The 'plotters' – young servicewomen – used croupiers' rakes to shove brightly coloured counters across the map tables. These constantly moving chips were marked to represent the enemy bombers, the enemy fighters and the RAF defenders. 'Tote boards' on the wall lit up to show local RAF fighter squadrons and the degree of their readiness (how many aircraft were in the air, how many being refuelled and rearmed, how many damaged, how many lost). Often the Germans would launch several raids at once, or a feint to draw the RAF into the air before the time of a major attack. Sitting in a glass-fronted balcony above the plot, a 'controller' watched the raids develop in his area, and decided when to 'scramble' which squadrons into the air for maximum advantage. By talking to the pilots, he could guide them to an interception. In what must remain a miracle of efficiency, the map tables were seldom more than four minutes – about 15 miles – behind events.

The world had never known an engagement like this. Height was the trump card in this sort of conflict. Here was a battlefield in three dimensions – four if the vital factor of time is included. Crowds gathered in city streets and outside village pubs to watch the fleets of bombing planes and their escorts; and the RAF climbing, climbing, climbing to intercept. And watched them tumbling down to earth.

By the middle of September, even the most optimistic of the *Luftwaffe* leaders were admitting that there was no chance of subduing the RAF fighter opposition in time for an invasion. Both sides were becoming exhausted. German flyers returned to report that there were still plenty of RAF fighters coming up to meet them. The days grew shorter, and storms and fogs and rough seas would soon come. Revisionist historians sometimes claim that the Battle of Britain decided nothing; that the Royal Navy would have protected Britain against German invasion. This idea cannot be sustained when considering the fate of warships within range of heavy bombers.

As September ended, the invasion schemes had been put back into the plans chests and the German sailors breathed a sigh of relief. Hitler turned his attention to the Soviet Union, and the *Luftwaffe* to the less challenging task of bombing London by night.

In 1940, the victories of Germany's highly professional armed forces had brought a great measure of overconfidence to all concerned. Civilian ideas, and even those of scientists, tended to be overruled in favour of traditional German military methods. Even within the *Wehrmacht*, technicians, such as intelligence officers and logistics experts, were given low ranks

and meagre resources, and found it difficult to influence the decisions of high command. In 1940, German intelligence knew very little about British defences. For example, attacks upon radar towers (tall masts impossible to conceal or camouflage) were abandoned because *Luftwaffe* planners had no idea of the vital role they played in Dowding's reporting network.

The British prevailed because their armed forces remained essentially civilian in mentality. Scientists, many of whom had already worked with the RAF to create the radar network, were welcomed into RAF meetings and messes. Everyone acknowledged that the telephone engineers, repairing lines during bombing raids, were vital participants in the battle. Lord Beaverbrook may have been the most unruly of civilians, but he became one of Dowding's closest associates.

Britain won because the British retained a healthy mistrust of uniforms and authority; and this extended even to those who wore the uniforms and had the authority. Long may it be so.

Previous pages: *Battle of Britain fighter pilots at rest, photographed by Humphrey Spender in 1940*

The BBC
Paul Fox

Arrogant. Biased. Condescending. Dumbing down. Establishment-minded. The litany continues. A haven for left-wingers. A coven of conservatives. A centre of excellence. A medium of mediocrity. The BBC has been called these and many other names in its history.

But what is the BBC for? It has to excite, innovate and stimulate. It has to be distinctive and efficient. It has to make programmes no one else will make. It is, as Jeremy Paxman once said, about ideas and allowing people to pursue them. Under its first director general, Sir John (later Lord) Reith, the British Broadcasting Corporation had shown enterprise and responsibility which gave it a unique position in the life of the country. The Second World War, and the BBC's trusted news service, enhanced its reputation at home and abroad.

What is it like to work for the BBC? On a spring day in 1950, I stood on the steps of Alexandra Palace in North London, then the home of the fledgling Television Service, to begin a fortnight's work as a holiday-relief scriptwriter on the twice-weekly *Television Newsreel*. The television I joined was in black and white, unseen north of Crewe and the junior partner to the radio bastion that was Broadcasting House. It was an adventure for the adventurous.

When the monopoly ended and ITV arrived, the BBC had to become competitive. Not everyone welcomed it. At first the BBC was trounced by the newcomer, but there were sufficient young Turks about the place to ensure that a more rational balance could be achieved. The leadership that brought this about came in the shape of Sir Hugh Greene, who took over as director general on 1 January 1960. Greene changed the BBC for the better by doing three things. He made it clear that he was editor-in-chief, exercising general control over the BBC's output of programmes; he gave priority to television over radio; and he made the BBC realise that competition could be stimulating.

This was an exciting and exhilarating time to be in the BBC. Talented peopled wanted to be part of it. Lime Grove studios became a hothouse. Here were the *Panorama* team, headed by Richard Dimbleby and including among its reporters Robin Day, Ludovic Kennedy, Michael Charlton, Jim Mossman and Robert Kee. Across the corridor were the swashbucklers from *Tonight*, led by Cliff Michelmore and including such people as Derek Hart, Alan Whicker, Kenneth Allsop, Fyfe Robertson and McDonald Hastings. One floor up was Huw Wheldon's team that made *Monitor* required viewing on a Sunday evening. Its producers included John Schlesinger, Ken Russell, David Jones, Humphrey Burton and Melvyn Bragg.

Talk of the 'golden age' of television can be hopelessly distorted by nostalgia; but the foundations were laid in those early 1960s. As always in the BBC, the wheel turned and ascendancy in the pecking order changed. Where once 'Sport' and the strangely named 'Talks' (*Panorama*, *Tonight*, *Monitor* etc) were the Grenadier Guards of the Television Service, the baton passed first to drama and then to light entertainment.

The roster of dramatists read: Dennis Potter (*Blue Remembered Hills* and *Pennies from Heaven*), Jeremy Sandford (*Cathy Come Home* and *Edna the Inebriate Woman*), David Mercer (*In Two Minds*), John Hopkins (*Talking to a Stranger* and *Horror of Darkness*), Nell Dunn (*Up the Junction* and *Poor*

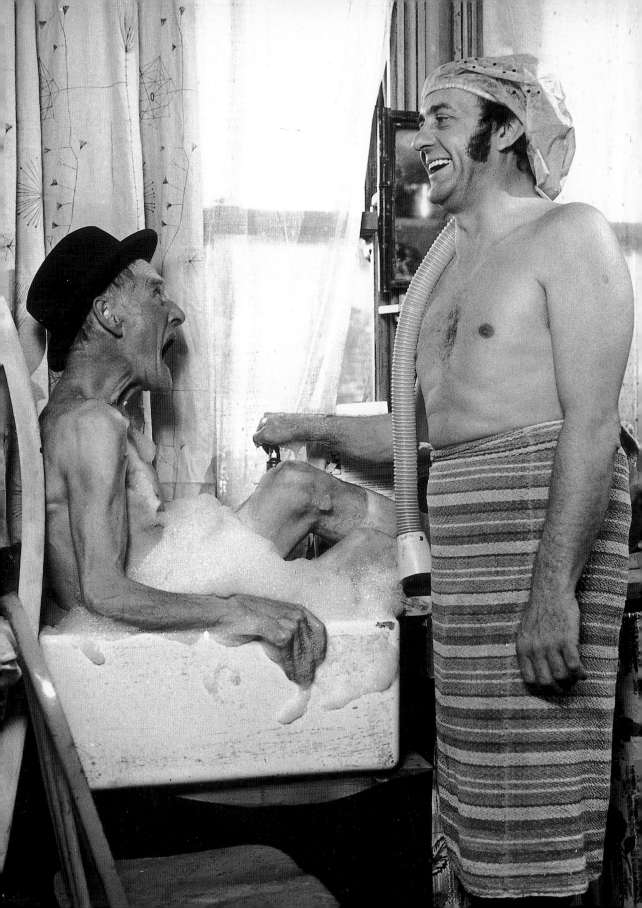

Cow), David Hare (*Licking Hitler*), and Clive Exton, G F Newton, Alan Plater, Peter Nichols and John Mortimer.

The writers also changed BBC comedy. Ray Galton and Alan Simpson reached new heights with *Steptoe and Son*, Johnny Speight created Alf Garnett for *Till Death Us Do Part*, and then came David Croft and Jimmy Perry with *Dad's Army*. Waiting in the wings were *Morecambe and Wise* and *The Two Ronnies*, *Porridge*, *The Likely Lads* and *Monty Python*. This was the time when Huw Wheldon was in charge of BBC Television. He had a simple formula for programmes: 'they should give delight and insight'.

But the BBC became complacent. Ill-prepared for the constant sniping from Mrs Thatcher's Government, it lost its confidence. What had become a cosy duopoly was changed immeasurably by the arrival of new channels and satellite television. When Marmaduke Hussey was brought out of retirement to become chairman of the BBC in 1986, his first act was to fire the director general, Alasdair Milne. He followed this up six years later by appointing, without an advertisement and without competition, John Birt as the BBC's 11th director general. Some of the changes Birt brought about were inevitable and already underway. To his credit, the licence fee is in place until 2006. So, too, is the Charter. But the heart has been torn out of the BBC; too many good and talented people departed.

Somehow, almost miraculously, the BBC still makes some wonderful programmes. Like Alan Bennett's *Talking Heads*, Andrew Davies' adaptation of *Wives and Daughters*, Stephen Poliakoff's *Shooting the Past* and, in the factual field, *The Death of Yugoslavia*, *The Nazis: a Warning from History* and *Walking with Dinosaurs*.

A new director general, Greg Dyke, is now in place. His arrival was controversial – he was not the unanimous choice of the Board – and whether he can heal the wounds it is too early to assess. But there is a great future for the BBC if it is alert, accountable, aware of its shortcomings and, above all, true to its skills in making programmes.

Funded by the licence fee, the BBC remains unique. But can this distinction remain until its centenary in 2026?

Wilfred Brambell as Steptoe and Harry H Corbett as Son in Galton and Simpson's ground-breaking series

The Beano *and the* Dandy
Joseph Connolly

A bid of three thousand pounds, anyone? Do I hear four? The fact that these are the sorts of figures that fine copies of the very first issues of either the *Beano* or the *Dandy* can now quite easily command should not really amaze us too much. There is no end to the market for British nostalgia (*i.e.* oldish and richish types eagerly buying back their childhoods before the onset of mere pre-senility – simple anecdotage – and prior to slipping seamlessly into the big and awful real thing itself). What might come as a surprise, however, in these clever-clever days of prepubescent street wisdom, label obsession and techno-omniscience, is that more than 60 years since their inception, the comics' circulations continue to prosper (the *Beano* alone each week moves about 350,000 copies, and each Christmas both annuals are always bestsellers).

How can this be? How come that these flimsy pre-war products of the famously proud and famously non-union Dundee company D C Thomson can hold up their heads in a world where any diversion that does not plug in, bleep, pass the time of day in Droog-like cyberspeak and encourage virtual and interactive mayhem is viewed by the young with deep-seated suspicion, accompanied by chasmic yawns? The answer, obliquely, is down to the loyalty and persistence of successive generations: which of us hasn't at some point during the rosy past cackled at the mischief of Dennis the Menace or Minnie the Minx, marvelled at the brazen ingenuity of Roger's dodges, or desperately wanted to be Dan (the only adult hero, here, and the sole begetter of designer stubble)? Deep down (and, yes, childishly) no one really wants to let go of any of that, and one therefore does not simply buy the *Beano* and the *Dandy* for one's children, so much as generally bequeath to them for safekeeping both the concept and the history. The built-in bonus, by the way, of such indulgence and altruism is that – supposing one is prepared properly to time the gaps between offspring and then grandchildren (any brief hiatus maybe padded out by the odd niece or godchild), it is perfectly possible never actually to miss a single issue as long as life continues.

The brilliance of D C Thomson's attitude to its comics lies in never too demonstrably rocking the boat (the *Beano*'s current editor is only the third since its founding in 1938), but subtly and constantly evolving in a way that doesn't frighten or alienate the punters, young and old (the *Daily Telegraph* is an old hand at pulling off a similar trick). Some of the gorgeous excesses of the 1950s, though, are – alas – long gone: no more will you see the monocled toff with his black silk topper, spats, spongebag pinstripes and a twinkling diamond tie-stud standing gleeful children slap-up fish suppers at the Hotel de Posh, oblivious to how many £££££ it costs him. If you are lucky you might still spot a Mont Blanc of mash with an embarrassment of bangers cantilevered proudly like the gargoyles on the Chrysler Building – maybe even a perfectly spherical Xmas pud, draped in a mantle of drippy white gooey stuff. Desperate Dan's cow pies, of course – complete with tail and horns (BSE be blowed) – remain the stuff of dreams; he will no longer fashion a pipe, however, from ripped-off guttering and a galvanised dustbin, because smoking, these days, simply cannot be allowed (so even if toffs still abounded, their Zeppelin cigars would be a no-no). Gone too are the

For children of all ages: the Dandy *'Summer Special' of 1965*

catapults (peashooters still linger), as is the predilection for bashings (old *Beano*s of the 1960s had no scruple about Minnie the Minx being set upon by a gang of boys, to be left sprawling with the full array of comic book injuries – not so much disfigurement, as a glowing still life with fruit). Nor do any of the many variations on 'Dad' (who is called 'Dad' by his wife, whom he in turn addresses as 'Mum') ritually and with grim-faced relish dole out slipperings in the closing frame. Even Bash Street's 'Teacher' (who is married to 'Mrs Teacher') has hung up his cane. Ah yes, maybe – but not his mortarboard. Now tell me: how common in Britain (let alone Dundee) is a coeducational school comprising just eight pupils and staffed by masters in subfusc gowns and mortarboards? One of the 'Kids' even wears a school cap – and all of them (save Toots, the token girl) are in shorts (as, still, is the great Dennis the Menace himself).

And what do today's *real* kids think? Well, they love it, apparently – instinctively knowing (as we did) that comics have just to be realistic *enough*: no more is required. Few children, for instance, have ever set eyes upon a pile of seeming compost liberally dotted with junk and surmounted by a sign reading 'Town Dump'; but readers of the *Beano* and the *Dandy* know that in their land such a dump will not just exist, but can always be relied upon to yield up a brass bed (on castors and with knobs) and a couple of old upholstery springs (which, when attached to one's lace-ups, will enable one to vault with grace and ease over orchard walls and snaffle apples by mouth before descending crashingly into Dad's boss' cucumber frame); there, too, will be at least one pram (wheels for 'cartie' making – in Beanoland wooden soapboxes persist) and, by way of garnish, several perfectly preserved skeletons of fish.

There have, of course, been other casualties along the way – most notably, class warfare. The mighty Lord Snooty – he of the top hat and Eton collar – hung on at Bunkerton Castle until the 1990s, when he was quietly retired (though given the state, these days, of the Upper House, where can the poor boy go?); and with him vanished the enemy oiks, the Gasworks Gang.

The innovations over the years have been various, but always pleasingly gradual. Dennis' dog Gnasher (an extremely rare Abyssinian wire-haired tripe hound) is now established as a star in his own right, as is Minnie Mark II: Ivy the Terrible. Cuddles and Dimples are big at the Dandy these days – practically babies, but what they lack in years they more than make up for in villainy and destruction. (Their 'Mum', incidentally, is unique in the canon by virtue of being a pretty young blonde in possession of extremely large and globular breasts – all other 'Mums' looking like nothing so much as 'Dads' with wigs on.)

For decades, D C Thomson resisted product endorsement of any kind; nor did the comics carry adverts. All that's changed – and every one of our deathless chums may now be seen on video, cable TV and, soon, at Beanoland in the Chessington World of Adventure. And as for the fan clubs…! The Dennis the Menace Fan Club long ago enrolled its millionth member and, very tellingly, the more recent *Beano* Fan Club offers its inaugural goodie package and T-shirt in both children's and adult versions. The free gifts still often Sellotaped to the fronts continue to be resolutely non-PC – chewy bars, tooth-crunching lollies and toys that smack of evil, such as the Menacecopter. It's great to be young. Or old. In *Beano* and *Dandy* country, it doesn't really very much matter. We *know* we're now 'Mums' and 'Dads' and 'Teachers' – of course we do; it's just that it's still not, somehow, remotely how we feel.

The British Bobby
Frances Fyfield

Fiction is not always kind to the British bobby, although he has probably featured more frequently in films and books than any other category of character and an author was crucial to his creation. Conan Doyle's Sherlock Holmes had some respect for his Scotland Yard contemporaries, but not much. By and large, the early 20th-century bobby was portrayed as a dull dog with unseasonal boots, turning his awkwardness into obstructiveness when faced with the country house set of Agatha Christie novels, and especially surly when told he could not interview the mistress because she was having a fit of the vapours. The British bobby was never really supposed to be a detective. When we think of 'bobby' we don't think 'brain', we think 'constable'. The man in uniform, plodding a lonely beat on a wet night, with his hobnails ringing on cobblestones and a woollen uniform with plenty of buttons impeding an already slow progress. Or, in rural terms, the plump fellow with a red face sweating below his blue helmet as he cycles uphill in pursuit of a car. He was not called PC Plod for nothing. He was that regular footstep in the dark, towards which a child could flee, without fear, into the arms of safety.

What makes this image persist despite huge criticism, and what makes the British bobby so special? He was a late developer, for a start. Most other countries had official police forces before England, and it might be to the advantage of ours that it was invented not by committee, but by individuals. Sir Robert Peel is credited with setting the first patrols of the Metropolitan police to work in 1829 (hence the 'bobby'), but there were earlier, amateur versions. Henry Fielding, author of *Tom Jones*, but more famous locally for his role as a Bow Street magistrate, had really created the blueprint 75 years before. It was he who set up the famous Bow Street Runners, thief-takers par excellence and particularly good with highwaymen.

The advantage of Peel's system was that it clearly separated the role of a somewhat shambolic judiciary from the role of the police and gave them independence. Peel's model for London was adopted elsewhere. These men were certainly needed. Anyone who has the idea that the English are a peace-loving lot should either consult a couple of history books or look at football supporters today. In Victorian times, one in 10 houses in London was a bawdy house, and the riots staged in previous generations make the modern ones look like Sunday school picnics. All those railings placed around houses were not there for fun. Gin was mother's ruin and, at the equivalent of 10p a pint, probably cheaper than milk. The British drink as if there was no tomorrow, a habit never lost since they got hold of the recipe, so it was hardly surprising that of Peel's newly appointed 'peelers', as they were first called, the majority were allegedly sacked within 48 hours for being drunk on duty. Maybe people were far too pleased to see them.

It is the humbleness of the role which distinguishes the bobby historically. He is not there to change the world; he was founded to keep the peace and to remind the populace of their duty to do the same. His task as first defined and still adhered to is to defuse the argument,

arrest the felon, clear the pub and leave the forensics to others. He is the foot-soldier, not the cavalry. In addition to the dangers of the job itself, the moral hazards remain the same as they were at the beginning: namely, drink, the lure of corruption and the isolating factors of cynicism and contempt. The British bobby has always been disliked as much as he has been loved, which reflects the necessities of the job. If you need a big brute to charge a crowd and save lives behind the brick-slingers and acid-throwers, it is too much to expect that he will be sweet as a lamb when he arrests you. He gets six weeks' training, not a full frontal lobotomy.

But what distinguishes him (and now her) is the fact that he is disciplined not to fight fire with fire, and that breeds a stoicism admired the world over. What inspires the admiration of the foreign visitor is the fact that PC Plod goes out without a gun, whatever he might face – and he might face anything. The constable has often been shot or otherwise murdered, by the bank robber, the fleeing arsonist, the cold-blooded Libyan terrorist shooting from a window, and the bobby's reaction has not been to demand the same firepower. Instead, he puts on more armour and changes his lead-filled truncheon for an asp (an extendable stick worn on the belt). CS gas is also used, but rarely. His chief weapon, at the end of the day, is his notebook, which is often his downfall: it is his record of what occurred at the scene, and he must not succumb to the temptation to embroider it.

The bobby's other much loved feature is his hat – a conical thing with a crest, no longer universal. The hat was to distinguish him and give protection from masonry and missiles (televisions are frequently thrown on dawn raids), but it is a cumbersome object, often abandoned, although useful in itself as a weapon. It has a use in defining him, too: not so much a warrior as a barrier.

It is said that the British bobby is not what he was. For one thing, he's shorter, since height requirements have mostly gone. But the essential character remains true. He or she is a working-class man or woman, and that is the backbone of the service. His mandate is to keep the peace, and that is where he excels. He probably earned the insulting name 'pig' by being pig in the middle.

Most people's memories of the British police are not founded on their experience of being arrested. The most common memory of the encounter with the bobby is when he brings back the dog, the car, the child, or when he finds his way into the house when the occupant has lost the key, or when he rescues the cat. Or when he is standing on the doorstep, hat in hand, to bring tidings of a death. He has a special distinction, because, in true, bungling British fashion, his role has never been comprehensively defined.

Impoliteness is a disciplinary offence for the British bobby; gentleness a habit more frequent than not. All the same, do not get in his way. He can hit where it hurts.

Previous pages: *Not so much a warrior as a barrier: British bobbies at a royal wedding in 1922*

Burns Night
David Steel

If Britain were to sink into the North Sea tomorrow, the celebrations of Scotland's national poet, Robert Burns, would not vanish with it. He is celebrated worldwide, and not only in the Scots language. So what is the secret of this 18th-century ploughman, exciseman and poet?

Burns' words speak for patriotism and for internationalism; for the lover not just of the opposite sex but of humanity. He is both satirist and romantic. I write about him automatically in the present tense because, in the words of the toast given to his memory every year around 25 January, he is indeed immortal.

However, the purpose of this essay is not an appreciation of the poet himself, but a look at that ritual that has grown up around him – the Burns Night supper. I have been an attendee of Burns suppers since my schooldays. The best of them was a supper held many years ago by the Galashiels and Hawick cycling clubs at the tiny Tibbie Shiels Inn at St Mary's Loch in the Yarrow Valley. The walls of the overcrowded dining room ran with condensation and the diners with perspiration, and there was much community as well as solo singing. I had come to propose 'The Immortal Memory'; I begged to buy a ticket as an ordinary punter the following year.

The worst was a stuffy, black-tie, overpriced event with highly paid speakers and singers in a large city hotel, where it was obvious that a great deal of Burns' radical writing would have struck few chords with the guests. They might have laughed at his humour, melted at his love-songs – but his 'Address to the Unco Guid' would probably have found few resonances.

Yet these two totally dissimilar events had the same rituals. There is the 'Selkirk Grace', allegedly penned by Burns in the Selkirk Arms in Kirkcudbright, though it has an older pedigree. It is as relevant in these days as it was in his:

> Some hae meat and canna eat,
>   And some wad eat that want it:
> But we hae meat and we can eat,
>   Sae let the Lord be thankit.

There is the entry of the haggis, while pipes are played and the company stands, the recitation of Burns' address to it, and then the ceremonial thrusting into its depths of a knife or dirk, on the cue of the lines,

> His knife see rustic-Labour dight,
> An cut you up wi' ready slight,
> Trenching your gushing entrails bright
>   Like onie ditch;
> And then, O what a glorious sight,
>   Warm-reekin, rich!

Once the corpse of the haggis has been returned to the kitchen, it is dished up with neeps (turnips) and tatties. To my mind, a plateful of this, provided the helpings are large enough, makes a perfectly adequate Burns supper, with maybe some oatcakes and cheese to follow. Haggis may be something of a joke food to those who don't know it and haven't tried it: they are sad, deprived beings. A good haggis can hold its own with simple, tasty, nutritious cooking anywhere.

But a cock-a-leekie soup or Scotch broth is usually served as well, and a variety of puddings. Posh Burns suppers tend to produce one called cranachan, which is athol brose (oatmeal, whisky, honey and cream) with fruit added; at less pretentious ones, trifle frequently makes an appearance. My wife has two favourites for Burns suppers: old fashioned curds and cream, and Selkirk bannock and butter pudding.

There are two obligatory toasts: 'The Immortal Memory', to which I have already referred, and 'The Lassies'. It is through the first of these that knowledge about Burns passes down the generations. The speaker may be a Burns expert. If not, then he or she will have to find out something about the poet that is relevant to the speech; a great deal is expected of it. The second toast has moved away from its original purpose, which was to thank the women who had prepared and served the meal. (There are still some all-male Burns suppers, including that held at the Tarbolton Bachelors' Club in Ayr, which Burns founded and whose suppers go back to his own time.) Now, alas, the speech to the lassies too often focuses on some of the more salacious aspects of Burns' love-life or can be a vehicle for sexist jokes.

To my mind, however, the best part of the evening is when the singing and the poetry start. Even at the humblest Burns suppers, the standard of performance can be remarkably high. Those who can sing or recite Burns could eat out from mid-January till the end of February, for a Burns supper is part of the social calendar of many an organisation. 'Tam o'Shanter' is possibly Burns' most famous poem: it is also probably the finest piece of dramatic narrative verse to be found in any language. It inevitably forms part of the formal programme. But there are many, many more – my own favourite, 'Holy Willie's Prayer', gets many an airing, though the eerie and funny 'Death and Doctor Hornbrook' is rarely heard. The repertoire of songs is almost inexhaustible.

I believe that the formal ritual of Burns suppers – and the linking of arms during 'Auld Lang Syne' – derives from Burns' association with the Masonic movement and its desire to honour him. It is a custom which Scots have taken worldwide – I have attended Burns suppers as far apart as Kenya and Russia. In the latter country, translations of Burns were made by the Russian poet Samuel Marsyk in the 20th century. It is strange to hear the cadences of his lines from the mouths of Russian children.

Burns is a poet for all people, all times. This was never more obvious than at the state opening of the Scottish Parliament in July 1999, when MSPs spontaneously joined in the words of the last verse of what is perhaps the greatest of all his songs:

> Then let us pray that come it may
>   (As come it will for a' that)
> That Sense and Worth o'er all the earth
>   Shall bear the gree, an a' that.

For a' that, and a' that,
　　Its coming yet for a that,
That man to man the world o'er
　　Shall brithers be for a' that.

'O what a glorious sight, / Warm-reekin, rich!': piping in the haggis in 1950

Chaucer's Canterbury Tales
Terry Jones

Imagine finding a video from 600 years ago – with the images and voices of the real people who lived then and who breathed God's air and felt the same sun on their bodies as we do today – and you'll get some idea of the excitement of picking up *The Canterbury Tales*. Forget about 'Literature' with a capital L. 'Literature' didn't exist in Chaucer's time! What you had were books. And a book was more like a scrap book. You stuck in everything you could get your hands on that you thought was worth preserving.

That's what *The Canterbury Tales* is. It's a magnificent compendium of moral fables, silly stories, sexy stories, a racist story, a parody of popular culture, a treatise on government, a treatise on religion, and so on. Don't look for a beginning, middle and end to *The Canterbury Tales*. That isn't what it's about.

Don't look for a particular literary style either. Chaucer uses lots of styles in the course of the different 'tales' because they are all told by different characters, but the key to his own writing voice is that he avoided 'Literary Style' *per se*. You hear this loudest and clearest in the General Prologue to *The Canterbury Tales*, where Chaucer describes the pilgrims who are on the road to Canterbury, each of whom is supposed to tell a story. This is where it's like having a video zoomed in on the late 14th century.

Pilgrims en route *to Canterbury: detail from a 13th-century stained glass window in Canterbury Cathedral*

Pick up almost any book from the past and you have to adapt your reading to the particular note of the period. There is usually some literary style of writing that you have to adjust to before you can hear what the writer is really talking about. Think of Shakespeare, for example, or Henry Fielding, or Alexander Pope or Charles Dickens – almost any writer you choose has the feel of their age and writes within a style that was current and is now recognisable as of that period.

But Geoffrey Chaucer doesn't. Oh, sure, you can date the poetry by the language – it's written in Middle English and the spelling is odd to our eyes and sometimes the vocabulary is unfamiliar. You have to know, for example, that 'eek' doesn't mean the writer's just had a mouse run across his foot; it simply means 'also'. But, once you get over that, I defy anyone to date the material. It's written just as people talk. It's as direct and fresh as the day the ink hit the paper. This is what is so amazing, so invigorating and unique about Chaucer's work. Chaucer writes in the simple language of everyday speech. It's like someone whispering in our ear from 600 years ago.

For example, he tells us about one character's terrible acne, and lists all the medicines he's tried with no success. Then he goes on to describe how the man gets drunk (don't forget about 'eek'):

> Well loved he garlic, onions, and eek leeks,
> And drinking good, strong wine, as red as blood;
> Then would he speak and cry as he were mad.
> And when that he well drunken had the wine,
> Then would he speak no word but in Latin.
> A few terms had he, two or three,
> That he had learned out of some old decree –
> No wonder is! He heard it all the day
> And eek you knowen well how that a jay
> Can call out 'Wat!' as well as can the Pope.

This is not the poetry of literary posturing. This is the direct racy language of someone who wants to be understood rather than 'appreciated'. It's the language of someone who reads out his own verse to an audience and who knows how to get a response.

Of course, coming to it 600 years later, we have to know a bit about the background. We have to know that this character, the Sumonour, was an officer of the Church of Rome, who wielded great power amongst ordinary folk, 'summoning' them to the ecclesiastical courts. We have to know that jays were often kept as pets for their parrot-like ability to copy human speech. We also have to know that, a few years before Chaucer wrote these lines, England witnessed one of the most cataclysmic events in its history in the shape of the so-called Peasants' Revolt, led by Wat Tyler. But there is nothing deliberately obscure about the lines. This isn't T S Eliot blinding us with a magical wand of erudition!

At the same time, Chaucer is more complex than the simple surface of his language might lead us to believe – but not for the sake of obscurity. His complexity (and difficulty) lies in his sense of humour: the fact that he very often says the opposite of what he means.

Take for example the following apparently simple lines of the Prologue (once again don't forget about that 'eek'!):

> Now have I told you truly, in a clause,
> The class, the clothes, the number and eek the cause
> Why that assembled was this company
> In Southwark at this noble hostelry
> That's called the Tabard, close to the Bell.

It seems straightforward. It's certainly geographically correct. There was an inn called the Tabard in Borough High Street in Southwark. It was there until 1884 when (in the glorious tradition of English preservation upheld in this century by the destruction of the archaeological remains of the Globe theatre) they decided to pull it down. There is now a mean little alleyway called Talbot Yard. If we look at a map for 1724 we can even see that there was – close by – another inn called the Bell. Except when we read an account of the inns of Southwark by the 16th-century antiquary, John Stow, he includes the Tabard, but not the Bell. The Bell, however, does appear elsewhere in the book – in a list of brothels! Suddenly, Chaucer's innocent remark that 'this gentil hostelrye' (this aristocratic hostelry) is close to the Bell takes on a totally different connotation.

The Canterbury Tales stands as a monument to humanity. Chaucer recorded the world as he saw it, and in doing so, he described the essential continuity of human life. His writing demonstrates that we – *homo sapiens* – were the same creatures 600 years ago as we are now. And that is an important thing to know. It means we can't afford to be complacent. It means we cannot assume that we know better than the folk who lived more than half a millennium ago. But it also means we can learn from their mistakes – in the same way that our descendants will be able to learn from ours.

There is one other reason why *The Canterbury Tales* is so special to Britain – it is one of the most important works in our language for a very particular reason. Chaucer could have written in French or Latin, which were the languages spoken respectively by the Court and the Church, but he didn't. He wrote only in English. His friend John Gower covered his bets by writing one book in Latin, one in French and one in English. But Chaucer dedicated his life to writing in his own tongue – making the storehouse of European knowledge available to the ordinary English-speaking people of his day. In doing so, he showed that the ordinary speech of ordinary people was capable of conveying everything that the classical languages could convey. He established English as a world language.

The Canterbury Tales set the scene for the world we live in today. More than any other work of literature, it is responsible for the ultimate success of a whole language – the English that you and I and so many people all round the world – are speaking now…

The Cavendish Laboratory
Brian Pippard

Experimental physics was not taught in universities until early in the 19th century, and then only in Germany. Classics, and in Cambridge mathematics, were the staple of education, but around 1860 Cambridge mathematicians noted what was beginning elsewhere and felt their talented students ought to hear something of discoveries made during the previous century. Not everyone agreed – only long-established truths were reliable as fodder for the young, and in any case there was no money to build a laboratory and pay a professor. The University Chancellor, the Duke of Devonshire, disposed of objections by providing the money himself, and in 1871 James Clerk Maxwell was appointed the first Cavendish professor of experimental physics (Cavendish was the family name of the Devonshires, and Henry Cavendish, a rather distant relation, had been a distinguished man of science). The Cavendish Laboratory was completed in 1874, but 10 years later Maxwell was dead and his successor Lord Rayleigh had retired back to his private laboratory at Terling, in Essex.

It was remarkable courage that led the electors to choose as their successor Joseph John Thomson ('JJ' to all, even his family). He was just 28, with but small experience of practical physics, and notably ham-fisted. Yet in his 35 years as professor he created a world-famous laboratory, attracted gifted research students from near and far, set them to work on important problems, and revealed a genius for suggesting how they might circumvent the obduracy of their equipment while they, at the same time, prayed that he might not lend a fatal hand to their manipulations. The arrangements for undergraduate teaching that Rayleigh had made stood JJ in good stead, and when in 1919 he became Master of Trinity College, he left the Cavendish a leader in teaching and research. The only serious rival was Manchester, where Ernest Rutherford was professor until he reluctantly left to succeed JJ. Willie (later Sir Lawrence) Bragg took over from Rutherford at Manchester and, on Rutherford's death, at Cambridge. Just as Rutherford had to pick up the pieces after the First World War, so did Bragg after the Second, and he had a severer challenge to face. The Rutherford era, when Cambridge led the world in nuclear physics, was ended and the United States began a programme of university and science development on a scale beyond anything that war-impoverished Europe could manage. Nuclear physics grew into Big Science (a term not yet invented), and particle accelerators were built that dwarfed the pre-war Cavendish machines. It seemed to many that the great days of the Cavendish were over, but Bragg's policy of diversity in research proved them wrong. In the event, it is arguable that the best was still to come.

To return to JJ, his first major discovery was the electron, in 1897. As soon as he found there were particles 2,000 times lighter than a hydrogen atom, he pictured atoms as composed entirely of these or similar tiny units, but his student Charles Barkla's studies of x-rays and how far they could penetrate matter showed him that most of the mass must be in another form. It was Rutherford who gave the answer. In Manchester, an observation by his undergraduate student Marsden had led Rutherford to his nuclear model – almost all of the mass of an atom is concentrated in a tiny nucleus; thus, as he believed then, nitrogen has a nucleus of 14

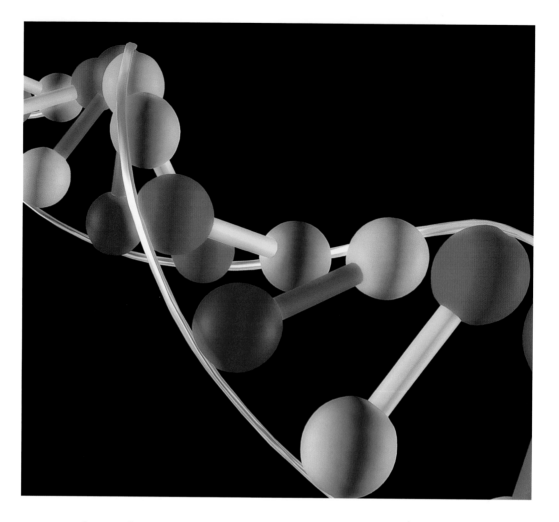

protons and seven electrons, with seven more electrons milling around it. He conjectured that each electron in the nucleus was tightly bound to a proton, forming a 'neutral doublet', but it was not until 1932, when he was back in Cambridge (where he had been JJ's research student from 1895 to 1898), that his senior member of staff, James Chadwick, found clear evidence for the neutron as a free particle. Chadwick and Maurice Goldhaber, using results from another Cavendish invention, Francis Aston's mass spectrometer, discovered soon afterwards that the neutron was slightly heavier than a proton and electron together, and therefore might disintegrate spontaneously. It does, but this was demonstrated only after nuclear reactors became available. The reactor, like the atomic bomb, depends on chain reactions set off by neutrons.

Before he left Manchester, Rutherford had knocked protons out of nitrogen nuclei by bombarding them with alpha-particles, and this was the background to his work in Cambridge. A most important new result was found when John Cockcroft and Ernest Walton built a

Life encoded: a computer representation of part of the DNA molecule

high-voltage generator to accelerate protons, which attack nuclei more readily than do alpha-particles, and in 1932 used them to split a beryllium nucleus into two alpha-particles – the first disintegration by artificially accelerated particles. This success and Chadwick's neutron can be said to mark the beginning of nuclear physics as a worldwide research topic.

Among the post-war Cavendish's non-nuclear researches, which included many into the physics of metals and other solids, two areas achieved the most far-reaching results: radio-astronomy and molecular biology.

Martin Ryle set up simple arrays of aerials to locate more precisely the few strong sources of radio waves in the cosmos, and to look for more. Eventually he found thousands and his simple aerials evolved into the aperture-synthesis system he invented. Using a few parabolic dish receivers whose spacing could be varied and very accurately determined, and relying on the earth's rotation to change their relative orientation, he obtained a huge number of items of information; combining them in cunning ways, and using sophisticated electronics and computing algorithms, he ended up with the information that would have been acquired by a dish several kilometres in diameter – accurate angular positions of the many radio sources. Their distribution and strengths gave strong support for the big-bang theory of the first moments in the universe and discounted its popular rival, the steady-state model. In the same research group, Antony Hewish built a large aerial array for other investigations, and with it his student Jocelyn Bell was rewarded with the first observation of a pulsar, the rapidly rotating and extraordinarily dense residue of a collapsed star. These researches have stimulated the transformation of cosmology from hardly more than an art-form into a rich and fascinating science.

Molecular biology was even more vigorously spurred into life by two Cavendish achievements of the 1950s. Max Perutz and John Kendrew had devoted years to mapping the arrangement of many thousands of atoms in the molecule of a protein – Perutz with haemoglobin, Kendrew with myoglobin, both carriers of oxygen in blood or tissues. The basic tool was x-ray crystallography, which the Braggs, father and son, had thought of in 1912 when Willie, the prime mover, was a new graduate (in 1915, at 25, he became the youngest ever Nobel laureate). Much ingenuity and heroic determination went into a far bigger analytical problem than had been tackled before, and Perutz and Kendrew had Bragg's full support. Their ultimate success led to what is now almost an industry of protein structure determination. Less agreeable to Bragg (who stinted no praise when it succeeded) was the maverick venture of Francis Crick and James Watson. In uneasy collaboration with Maurice Wilkins and Rosalind Franklin of King's College, London, they elucidated the double-helix structure of DNA, the very long molecule that carries genetic information and controls the building of proteins from their simple constituents.

These two seminal achievements provided the foundation for work which soon expanded beyond anything the Cavendish could hold, and will continue developing for many years, transforming nearly every aspect of biology and medicine. Probably nothing so important has come from the Cavendish – not even the electron and the neutron – and perhaps never will; but among lesser triumphs passed over in this brief story are many that have found, or will find, their way into the textbooks, and that will serve to inspire the stream of graduates who have a major part to play in the pervasive technology of modern life.

Winston Churchill's 1940 Speeches
Andrew Roberts

'Rhetorical power', wrote Winston Churchill, 'is neither wholly bestowed, nor wholly acquired, but cultivated.' He certainly worked hard to cultivate his own oratorical skills, spending hours in front of the mirror as a young man, testing out words, practicing phrases and honing his verbal flourishes. He disliked speaking impromptu, relied heavily on notes and written texts and thought nothing during the Second World War of spending 10 to 12 hours working on an important speech. He was a perfectionist rather than a born orator, and in 1940 the result was pure perfection.

The cadences of Churchill's 1940 speeches owe much to the hours when, as a young hussar subaltern stationed in India nearly half a century earlier, he studied the historical works of Gibbon and Macaulay. Churchill created his own synthesis of the grandiloquent rolling sentences of the former and the biting wit of the latter. His oratory was also informed by the late-Victorian influences of William Gladstone, the Irish-American politician Bourke Cockran and his own father, Lord Randolph Churchill.

This grand, old-style idiom did not impress everybody: some found it insincere, others pompous, yet others derided him as a cross between a ham actor and a music-hall turn. There was even one point in the devil's decade of the 1930s when the House of Commons refused to listen to him and shouted him down when he tried to defend King Edward VIII during the Abdication Crisis.

It was not really until the *annus mirabilis* of 1940 that, in that supreme test of the British people, Churchill's rhetoric at last truly matched the perils of the hour to create the sublime beauty of the best of his wartime speeches. The defeat on the Western Front, the evacuation from Dunkirk, the Fall of France, the Battle of Britain, the Blitz, the threat of invasion – all produced speeches and phrases that will live as long as does the English tongue.

The printed page is not the correct medium for them, of course. To feel the shiver down one's spine at Churchill's words, only recordings will do. They alone can convey the growls, the strange pronunciation of the letter 's', the almost comic pronunciation of 'Narzees', the sudden leonine roars, the perfectly constructed sentences, the cigar-and-brandy toned voice, the sheer defiance coming straight from the viscera, insisting upon no surrender in a war to the death.

In the summer of 1940, Churchill's speeches were just about all the British people had to sustain them. With Hitler in control of all continental Europe from Brest to Warsaw, even the Chiefs of Staff had no logical plan for victory. With neither Russia nor America in the conflict, all Britain could do was hold on, grimly praying that something might turn up. Churchill could not really appeal to the head in his protestations of the certainty of ultimate victory, so he had to appeal to the heart.

Without having very much in the way of sustenance or good news for the British people, Churchill took a political risk in deliberately choosing to emphasise the dangers instead.

'He mobilised the English language and sent it into battle': Winston Churchill in 1940

Three days after becoming Prime Minister he told the House of Commons: 'I have nothing to offer but blood, toil, tears and sweat.' He attempted no evasions about the nature of the task ahead, as his words swept away a decade of appeasement, doubt and defeatism, what he had called 'the long, drawling tides of drift and surrender'. He unhesitatingly placed the conflict in the stark context of a Manichean struggle between Good and Evil, Truth and Falsehood, Right and Wrong. It was what the British Empire longed to hear.

The effect was extraordinary. As the writer Vita Sackville-West told her husband, the Information Minister Harold Nicolson: 'One of the reasons why one is stirred by his Elizabethan phrases is that one feels the whole massive backing of power and resolve behind them, like a great fortress: they are never words for words' sake.' The mention of Elizabethan England is instructive, for Churchill enlisted the past into service to boost British morale, summoning up the ghosts of Drake and Nelson to emphasise to the people that Britain had faced such dangers before and had prevailed.

Isaiah Berlin, in his superb essay 'Mr Churchill in 1940', was at pains to point out how Churchill drew on 'an historical imagination so strong, so comprehensive as to encase the whole of the present and the whole of the future in a framework of a rich and multi-coloured past'. Churchill expected at least a working knowledge of British history from his listeners; he never talked down to them or patronised them by adapting his style to the perceived requirements of a modern mass audience. As Berlin put it: 'The archaisms of style to which Mr Churchill's wartime speeches accustomed us are indispensable ingredients of the heightened tone, the formal chronicler's attire, for which the solemnity of the occasion called.'

From the perspective of today's politics and society, much of Churchill's argument and the vocabulary in which it was couched was deeply politically incorrect. The revisionist historian Clive Ponting has complained of the way Churchill continually referred to 'our own British life, and the long continuity of our institutions and the Empire', instead of 'coming up with a view of the future designed to appeal to a modern democracy'. This was because Churchill realised that the British nation was fighting for its very identity and continued existence, rather than for any utopian ideas about decency, fraternity and democracy. He therefore appealed to a visceral, ancient, tribal belief that the British people then had in themselves, largely based on the deeds of their forefathers and pride in their imperial achievement. It is no longer an idiom politicians can turn to, but it saved us then.

There are those, such as Lord Hailsham, who consider the emergence of Winston Churchill as Prime Minister in May 1940, within hours of Hitler unleashing his Blitzkrieg upon the West, as one of the proofs of the existence of God. No theologian, I prefer to subscribe to the opinion of the American broadcaster Ed Murrow on the phenomenon of Churchill in 1940: 'He mobilised the English language, and sent it into battle.'

The City of London
David Kynaston

The City of London has arguably been the single greatest British success story of the last 20 years. It has become a truly global financial centre – far more so than either New York or Tokyo – and is the world number one in, among other things, international banking, international equity trading and foreign exchange trading. Each year the City contributes, through its 'invisible' earnings, well over £20 billion to the UK balance of payments. The City may not be universally loved, not least because of the almost unbelievable financial rewards that it generates for some of those fortunate enough to work there, but no one can deny its achievement.

Many elements have contributed to this still under-recognised state of affairs: an internationally respected legal system; low taxation; lack of government interference; the availability of a large specialist workforce; the rise and rise of English as the international language of business; and the equally happy chance of the European time zone, snugly fitting (from the point of view of global trading) between the less convenient ones of Asia and America. One more intangible factor has also been vital, going back to the days of Thomas Gresham in the 16th century: trust. 'My word is my bond', the traditional motto of the London Stock Exchange, has always meant something in the City and continues, even in today's more litigious climate, to do so.

Nothing, however, has been more important than the City's willingness – albeit, in the past, sometimes grudging – to be open to newcomers from abroad. The native financial tradition is one of solidity and reliability, but rarely creativity, and it is that crucial dimension that a series of gifted foreigners has brought to the Square Mile. During the last two centuries, three stand out: each by origin a German Jew, each the dominant City figure of his day.

Nathan Rothschild, founder of N M Rothschild & Sons (now the last surviving independent British merchant bank), was a short, heavy man with protruding lips, bulbous eyes and a quick temper. He was also, as all his contemporaries recognised from his arrival in St Swithin's Lane in about 1809 to his death in 1836, a financial genius. Bullion operations, speculative coups on the Stock Exchange, foreign exchange dealing in the Royal Exchange, organising complicated loans for foreign states – of all of these he was the nonpareil master, exploiting existing markets and in the process creating new ones. 'I wish them', Nathan said of his children not long before he died, 'to give mind, and soul, and heart, and body, and everything to business; that is the way to be happy.'

Ernest Cassel, who arrived in the City in the 1870s and rose to be King Edward VII's trusted financial adviser, was another self-made man, with little grace and less humour. Only a fool, however, doubted his judgement or his willingness to back that judgement, as in an era of supremely mobile international capital – the City's all-time golden age – he had his finger in almost every pie that mattered. Whether it was arranging loans for Morocco or China, or closer to home finding the money for London's new Underground system, Cassel was the

indispensable man. 'His perception was quick as lightning,' an associate recalled. 'He used to think of the smallest details while doing the biggest things.'

The third newcomer, Siegmund Warburg, was more responsible than anyone for the City's remarkable recovery after its long period in the doldrums between the First World War and the 1950s. Belonging to a well-known private banking family, he fled from the Nazis in the 1930s, started his own merchant bank (S G Warburg & Co) in 1946, and in the early 1960s took advantage of a temporary bout of American financial introspection to pioneer the Eurobond market – an offshore capital market, largely based in London even though dollar-denominated, and soon growing like Topsy under the deliberately benign neglect of the Bank of England. Warburg himself was a far more rounded man than either Rothschild or Cassel, but like them he had a notoriously short fuse, sometimes leading to fiery relations with the City establishment. To his younger colleagues he was an inspirational teacher, and Warburgs by the time of his death in 1982 had become the City's leading, as well as most admired, merchant bank.

Four years later, the so-called 'Big Bang' – opening up the Stock Exchange as an international marketplace – hugely accelerated the internationalisation of the City. It fired the starting gun for big foreign financial institutions, mainly American and European, to pour huge resources into their London operations, sometimes taking the form of organic growth but more often involving outright acquisition, first of securities houses and then of merchant banks. By the mid-1990s, the suggestive term 'Wimbledonisation' had been coined: the City of London, like the tennis at Wimbledon, was host to the world's greatest players, but the champions were no longer British. This concept has given rise to much agonised debate, but it is sometimes forgotten that in the old days the City's champion players seldom were British, not even in the 19th century. Ultimately what matters is where the business is done, and it is now incontrovertibly truer than ever that the more foreign talent there is in the City, the better the City does.

Has the Square Mile, through all this, managed to retain its historic intimacy and quasi-Dickensian character? Inevitably a combination of the *Luftwaffe*, post-war planning, modern office blocks and the paramount need for large trading floors has taken its toll, but with a little ingenuity it is still possible to find delightful old buildings and mysterious, twisting alleys. Moreover, it remains as true as ever it was that to stand with one's back to the Royal Exchange, and see the Bank of England to the right and Mansion House to the left, is to feel a palpable, inspiriting sense of being at the throbbing heart of one of the world's great cities. 'I have seen the West End, the parks, the fine squares, but I love the City far better,' Charlotte Brontë wrote acutely as long ago as the 1850s. 'The City seems so much more in earnest: its business, its rush, its roar, are such serious things, sights and sounds. The City is getting its living – the West End but enjoying its pleasure. At the West End you may be amused, but in the City you are deeply excited.'

City gents in the 1950s, photographed by Norman Parkinson

A Classical Education
Frederic Raphael

My father was an Oxford man. He told me, often, that a First in Greats was the best passport in the world. A rowing blue would also help, but the Greats man was universally respected (and employable) for his ability to assess the merits of any argument. Why the prolonged study of antique languages should procure such dividends in the modern world, I neither asked nor was told. Since I started life as a little American boy, I had few childhood dreams, or prospects, of proficiency in Latin and Greek.

In 1938, however, my father was translated from New York City to the City of London. When war broke out, *force majeure* despatched me to an English preparatory boarding school. Within a few weeks I was learning to love *amo, amas, amat*; *luo, lueis, luei* soon followed. *Luo* means 'I loose'; I lost (*elusa*) my Americanism. What would have been an aberrant course of study in my native land dominated my education for the next decade and more.

In 1940, when the Greeks were holding the Italians in the passes of Epirus, *Punch* published a cartoon depicting Leonidas and his long-haired Spartans – who had stopped, or at least stalled, the Persians at Thermopylae – ranged alongside our gallant (and sole) ally. The reference to 480 BC could, in those days, be presumed to be understandable to *Punch*'s middle-class readership without explanation.

Sequestered in rural Devon while the Allies suffered disasters (*clades*) and, later (*postea*), won triumphs on a global scale, my war effort was concentrated on learning what happened to the Romans at Cannae, how Fabius Cunctator turned the tables on Hannibal and how Scipio Africanus (*cf.* Montgomery of Alamein) finished him off. As our chaps hit the Normandy beaches, I was being taught that 'If only the war would end' was to be rendered by *ei monon* with the optative.

My personal victory celebration should have involved gaining a Winchester scholarship. This I almost did (*paene feci*), but – having been mysteriously deprived of what I was at first awarded – I was obliged to sit, in a hurry, for another scholarship, to Charterhouse. *Mutatis mutandis*, they did the classics everywhere. So well drilled was I that, if tearfully (*multis cum lacrimis*), I sailed through. In September 1945, I joined the Remove, the scholars' class, and resumed my ascent up the *cursus honorum* which would, if all went well, lead to Greats and perhaps (I was English now, like my father) to Whitehall or the City.

There was a strong Carthusian classical tradition; Robert Graves was the most famous living instance. *Goodbye to All That* contained a scathing attack on the school, but Graves never waved farewell to the dead languages to which he added such brilliant, idiosyncratic lustre in *I, Claudius* and his *Greek Myths*. In the classical Sixth, we had just one period a week for English; the rest of our time was devoted to the golden ages BC. Our prep was to translate passages of English poetry and prose into Latin and Greek. Hence, as if by chance, we became closely acquainted with excerpts from the great English stylists. Macaulay, Mill, Clarendon, Addison, Froude, Milton, Gibbon, Ruskin, Marvell, Dr Johnson, Dryden, Keats, Cowper, and who all else were implicit parts of a British classical education.

In the winter of 1949, half a dozen members of the Sixth went up to Cambridge to take the scholarship examination. (Light blue exams preceded those at Oxford, so providing opportunity for a 'trial run'.) When I was elected to a Major Scholarship in classics at St John's, I transferred allegiance and ambitions from Oxford to Cambridge. Instead of Greats, I embarked on the Classical Tripos. Why not? Porson, Bentley and Housman (who had failed in Greats before taking his professorial chair at Cambridge) were a trio to measure against any dark blue team. Rigorous respect for the original text, and language, was central to the tradition. 'A very pretty poem,' Bentley had said when Alexander Pope showed him his translation of *The Iliad*, 'but you must not call it Homer.'

Zeal for antique authors was, for me, soon sapped both by vulgar ambitions to be a novelist and by the rare allure of Wittgensteinian philosophy. My fellow-scholar and friend, the late J P Sullivan, the son of a Liverpool docker, had already far outstripped me in the classics. His dedication made it clear that if I had been clever enough to become a scholar, I was not scholarly enough to stay one. John, who became Dean of Lincoln College, Oxford, and eventually a professor at the University of California in Santa Barbara, was evidence incarnate of the falseness of the idea that classics were/are the preserve of toffs. As Dr Johnson and many other grammar school scholars proved, the classics often offered preferment to talent. Academic excellence sponsored social mobility (if only for clever boys; not till Jane Harrison at Cambridge, a hundred years ago, did female scholars become as they now certainly are, equally respectable). Even in the 1950s, had he not been a great Latinist, how easily would John Sullivan have transcended the circumstances in which he was born? The Jesuits beat the classics into him as no comprehensive will ever do in the egalitarian world which, oddly enough, may well leave more bright people marooned in their original class than the old 'unfair' system ever did.

There is undoubted pleasure in the exclusive freemasonry of classicists. If they rejoice, in greater or smaller measure, in arcane signals of recognition, and recondite (or puerile) jokes, they are also generous – if also, sometimes, acrimonious – with constructive criticism. One of my most valued, entirely epistolary, friendships is with a female scholar who first wrote to me, in a fury, because I misdated the battle of Leuctra (371 BC) by four whole years. Since then, with an irony she has not failed to remark, much of her scholarly effort has been directed to casting doubt on ancient chronology.

What I find most remarkable in professional scholars is their tolerance of importunity from those outside the academic world. The classics are a club with no subscription. When, after 20 years or so of ignoring the ancient world, I embarked on a translation of Catullus (preparatory to a yet-to-be-written novel), I solicited the advice, and soon the collaboration, of Kenneth McLeish, who had gone up to Oxford as a scholar from Bradford Grammar School and was then teaching at Bedales. Though Ken was always the *miglior fabbro*, we became partners, until his death, in a series of translations from Latin and Greek. We had little else in common, but the classics were quite enough to furnish our *amicitia*. The antique texts provide a basis for tiring the sun with talking on every possible topic: politics, religion, art, sex, drama, race – which of them is not accessed (as they say) from the long, dusty road of classical studies?

The cult of antiquity remains an education in accurate revision. Only plagiarism and dishonest argument, the use of doctored sources and claiming credit due to others are grounds

for ostracism. In the classics as in heaven (we have to hope), Jew and Gentile, white and black, Latin and Greek are engaged in a joint, unending conversation – literally, a turning of things over together – which offers small prospect of fame or fortune. Alas (*eheu!*), curricular philistinism and budgetary fiat are closing the file on a tradition enriched by thousands of years of accumulated wisdom. The new egalitarianism wants to replace the endurance tests of Latin and Greek with the crass facility of media studies or of computer 'literacy' (the ability to buy into easily received ideas). Opinions – each as good as its neighbour – replace knowledge; modspeak sees off grammar; the transitorily 'useful' trumps the durably useless. *Sic transit gloria mundi.*

Previous pages: *First steps on the* cursus honorum: *public schoolboys go to chapel in 1951*

The Corner Shop
Shyama Perera

According to the *Sunday Times* 'Rich List', if your surname is Patel, you're seven times more likely to be a millionaire than if your name is Smith. This suggests that the Patels as a genus must be inventors or innovators, and in one sense they are. They are reinventors and innovators. Almost single-handedly in many cities, they have rescued and resuscitated that homeliest of British cultural icons: the corner shop.

The corner shop has historically been the centre of community life. A place where you buy the staples – bread, milk, newspapers and marge. But by the late 1960s, the corner shop had outlived its shelf-life in the city and was starting to ail in rural areas. Punters were discovering there was more to life than New Zealand butter, Ceylon tea and the *Daily Herald*. The British Overseas Airways Company, a name that inspired childhood fantasies of unreachable travel destinations, telescoped to BA. The world became smaller; we talked of a global village.

The exchange of ideas, and the arrival of new immigrants literally presaged a change in tastes. A combination of urbanisation, new suppliers and an immigrant trickle struck the death-knell for the beleaguered small trader.

In my local shop, the most exciting thing on sale was a magazine called *Men Only*, which was kept in plain covers on a swivel stand between the Fruit Pastilles and the Mother's Pride. A mile down the road, however, was Queensway. Here, the Indian newsagent started selling ready-made curry from tureens on the counter: three bob for a tinfoil container of chicken madras. The Pataks, now one of the world's largest retailers of Asian spices and pickles, opened their little shop on London's Westbourne Grove. My mother and I would go there to purchase old garlic and gnarled ginger – the legacy of weeks in transit. The indigenous population experimented with Alfonso mangoes and little bundles of coriander tied with string. Demand changed.

The supermarkets were the first to notice. They immediately moved to fill the gap, offering a far greater choice and huge savings as a result of multi-selling. Even the big high-street institutions started to go under. MacFisheries, which had been the most exciting port of call as a child – they'd keep dozens of live eels wriggling in white tubs on the pavement outside – was one of the first. Woolworths, too, started closing down branches. In this climate, it appeared inevitable that the small retailers would die with them. Then, thanks to the mad excesses of Idi Amin in Uganda, the Patel posse arrived in town. And they came off the planes with all guns blazing.

The richer or more ambitious Patels headed into big-time retail and soon made their millions. The smaller families bought up the ailing corner shops and pulled on the Asian tradition of collective effort for the greater good. As soon as the kids came home from school, they were stuck behind the counter. Even old grannies who didn't speak the lingo sat by the till in white saris, glumly keeping an eye out for shoplifters. It wasn't the most auspicious of starts.

Much was said about how the whole ethos of the corner shop had been lost. We didn't like the way these newcomers installed an extra row of shelves down the middle of a space that had previously been used for gossiping. Or the way sacks of basmati rice were propped up behind the counter. Waiting to buy the *Sun*, you'd be aware that the place smelt spicy. It was a time of readjustment, both for the customers, whose senses were being challenged, and for the owners, who had not yet learned the finer points of British expectations and sensibilities – like honouring use-by dates and installing bright lights.

What none of us saw at the time, because it was unrecognisable during the transition years, was that the Patels were breathing life back into a long-standing British cultural tradition. It led to a favourite joke:

Q: Why are there no Asian footballers?
A: Because every time one gets a corner, he opens a shop.

The corner shop was back: bigger and better and far more interesting than it had ever been before. More importantly, because it was family-run and had a large staff, it became truly convenient in a way that we couldn't have imagined: the corner shop extended its opening hours – initially until 8.00 p.m., then 10.00 p.m. People started using it in a quite different way. The knock-on effect was that instead of there being one corner shop to service an area, there were often several – because a new urban constituency had been liberated by their flexibility. By the 1980s, there were corner shops staying open around the clock. In London's Edgware Road, an Arab enclave, the cafés followed suit. Instead of dying as a result of urbanisation, the corner shop had led the charge of cultural change.

Today, it is no longer a city phenomenon. Shopkeepers in even the most isolated of villages took a leaf from the Patel book, revamping and revitalising what was on offer. Small supermarket chains like Mace and Bestway started opening shopping hybrids in commuter and tourist belts – a corner shop with a supermarket feel, selling everything from ready-cooked chickens and samosas to skimmed milk and *Woman's Journal*.

What we have seen, then, is not only the rebirth (an appropriate term for a Hindu-led phenomenon) of the British corner shop, but its shaky first steps, its turbulent adolescence and, now, its focused adulthood. The concept, steeped in white British history, is now a marker of our multi-ethnic future.

The homeliest of British cultural icons: the corner shop, photographed by Henri Cartier-Bresson

The English Country House and Garden
John Harris

The Great House broods over its parkland. It is the successor of one built in the 13th century, and has been described as 'a pile'. The Plantagenet lions of England glint yellow in the ducal flag that tops all. Reminders of family longevity on this site are to be found in the paper documents in the Muniment Room, professionally housed from 1750 in one Palladian pavilion. The house is framed in gardens that have been fashioned by generations of gardeners, from London and Wise to Russell Page and recent duchesses. The Georgian church, a veritable museum of English funeral sculpture, huddles up against the back court. Knurled oaks planted in the 1690s are skeletal reminders of the criss-crossing avenues that marched across a thousand acres. A triumphal lodge shimmers in the light three and a half miles away at the end of the Great Avenue. Among the trees graze herds of deer. Adjacent are the stables with their rows of stalls, and beyond them can be found the estate yard and the estate office. Further afield, the hounds bark and snuffle in the kennels and play in one of the three huge walled kitchen gardens. The chosen yellow ochre of estate paint is an identifying colour in the surrounding villages. These are all evidences of continuity of possession.

Just turn the pages of any book on the 'Great Houses of England'. One by Hugh Montgomery-Massingberd illustrates 25 treasure houses, each containing some of the greatest works of art and furnishings in the world. All are veritable museums. Syon has an Anti-Room of Imperial Roman splendour, Powis Castle a museum of Clive's Indian collections. Haddon has its magical long gallery, Knole its Jacobean furniture. Woburn has its walls of Canalettos, Wilton its Double Cube Room with Van Dyck's *Pembroke Family*; Waddesden its French treasures that make the French drool in envy, Chatsworth its gallery of 18th- and 19th-century sculpture; Petworth, Holkham and Woburn their galleries of ancient Roman marbles. And as for libraries, at Chatsworth, Longleat, Petworth, Tatton or Shirburn Castle are the stuff of bibliophiles' dreams. The National Trust, with 250 houses, is custodian of artistic possessions equivalent to those of a Metropolitan Museum of Art.

Gardens surround these houses in every style: Powis Castle with Italianate terraces, Melbourne Hall with formal avenues, Castle Howard with templescapes, Blenheim Palace with Capability Brown's landscapes, Osborne House with Victorian formal parterres, or Goddards with Gertrude Jekyll's herbaceous borders.

Despite the fact that country house auctions continue to be commonplace, England must still possess 200 of these treasure houses, and it is all the more extraordinary when we take into account the fact that in the aftermath of two world wars more than 1,600 houses of moderate to large size have been demolished and their contents spewed out across the markets of the world.

This survival is primarily due to primogeniture. Britons never succumbed to the curse of the Napoleonic division of property at death, which has led to the emptying of the French chateaux. The French have a wealth tax, the Swedes a penal one. This induces a phobia of publicity and photography or access to family archives. But primogeniture is not the sole

reason why a guide such as Hudson's *Historic Houses and Gardens in England, Scotland and Wales* can list more than 1,380 properties open to the public. Our tradition for country house and garden touring is an ancient one. Even in the 18th century, country house owners could complain of lack of privacy due to nosy visitors staring through windows. Topographical and antiquarian enquiry, not least by incumbents of churches, has been a pastime since the early 17th century. What other country has a magazine such as *Country Life*, publishing articles on country houses since 1893? In recent years, populist visiting has been boosted by television programmes such as *Upstairs Downstairs* or productions of Georgian novels.

This focus upon all aspects of the history of the country house and its environment has been accompanied by a depth of scholarly study of architecture, interior decoration, furnishing, family genealogy, social and political history, and garden history, without parallel in any other country. The envied Attingham Summer School is a by-product of this study. Surprisingly, these researches have been encouraged by the phenomenon of our County Record Offices, which since the 1930s have been legally required to preserve and calendar the paper history of the county. Yet there are other consequences too, of greater influence here than in Europe: namely, the popular strength of the preservation movement that led to the founding of the Society for the Preservation of Ancient Buildings, the Georgian Group, the Victorian Society, the Twentieth Century Society, the Folly Fellowship, the Mausoleum Trust, the Garden History Society, SAVE Britain's Heritage, and a vast network of local history societies.

When the Victoria and Albert Museum hosted the *Destruction of the British Country House* exhibition in 1974, left-wing radicals were violent in their condemnation of any attempt to introduce legislation to stem the carnage (typified by the black year of 1955, when one decent country house was demolished every two and a half days). It would be foolish to suggest that there might not be a dormant virus in the patient. But we are the envy of the rest of the world in the solutions we have found for the preservation of our country houses, and in the recognition that as entities they represent one of our greatest contributions to European civilisation.

A mid-18th-century view of Chatsworth, Derbyshire, from the south-west, by Thomas Smith of Derby

The Works of Charles Dickens
Peter Ackroyd

The novels of Charles Dickens may be said to embody the tidal reaches of the English imagination. From the very beginning of his career, he was widely applauded as a representative writer who had somehow managed both to understand and to project the spirit of the nation in its celebratory and its lachrymose modes. In his earlier works, it was the middle and lower classes which grew beneath his pen, in particular the Cockneys of the 1830s and 1840s, who found in Dickens their first sympathetic chronicler. It would not be going too far to suggest, in fact, that the author created a whole new strand of urban society. Just as the city grew into prominence as the single most advanced emblem of the 19th century, so Dickens attended to the lives and miseries of city dwellers.

Even as he touched upon the essential spirit of the people, the public itself responded with enthusiasm to his fictions. Within a very few months of his first appearance as a novelist with the serialisation of *The Pickwick Papers*, he became the most popular author of the age. But despite his fluency and success, he was by no means a facile or unserious writer, and almost from the beginning he espoused conscious artistic aims. From him sprang the phrase 'streaky bacon', by which he designated the effect of joining together comedy and pathos, farce and horror; when these forms were effortlessly intermingled, a quite particular brightness and interest spread across his pages. The grotesque comedy of Fanny Squeers is mitigated by the hapless fate of poor Smike, while the happy ending of *Oliver Twist* is shadowed by the horrifying destiny of Nancy. This spirit of contrast, or of heterogeneity, in fact deeply imbues the English genius; the more sober critics castigated Shakespeare for precisely the same fault, but that delight in variation has been evident since the days of the medieval mystery plays.

This in turn helps to explain the confluence of Dickens' imagination with the native spirit, since his was an innately theatrical genius. He dressed in very loud clothes; he loved the company of actors, and all his life engaged in theatrical performances. Like Fielding and Smollett, he was a playwright as well as a novelist, and his fictions are striated with the gas lamp and the red curtain. There were elements of melodrama and of farce, of Gothic grotesquerie and harlequinade, within his most ostensibly 'serious' novels; there is no doubt that stage-fire was the defining light of his work.

Nevertheless, Dickens took his novels very seriously indeed, and in many of them he addressed what was known as the 'condition of England' question. Whether it was the nature of the judiciary in *Bleak House*, or the state of private schools in *Nicholas Nickleby*, he believed that part of his purpose – and part of his power – lay in exposing the weaknesses and hypocrisies of the nation. He was by nature a conservative reformer, one of those mid-Victorian radicals who adopted a strict and somewhat paternalistic attitude to the complaints of the poor and oppressed.

And this again was an intrinsic aspect of his English genius. He considered the nation to be a kind of enlarged family, in which domestic values were more significant than economic

theories or political programmes. That is, after all, the theme of one of his most popular works, *A Christmas Carol*, where Ebenezer Scrooge undergoes such a beneficent transformation. In the process, the reformed miser joins that parade of Dickensian characters who seem to comprise their own distinct world – even if it is also a distinctively British one. From Miss Havisham in her frozen state to Quilp in perpetual motion, from Mr Dick to Fagin, from Mr Pecksniff to Mrs Gamp, from Uriah Heep to Little Nell, Dickens created a host of 'particulars' which is unsurpassed in the literature of any nation.

Indeed, with his great fund of sympathy and humour, extravagance and theatricality, Dickens can essentially be seen as representative of the 19th century. It has been said that a genius is one who stands in symbolic relationship to his age; in his gift for entertainment and his capacity for polemic, in his energy and animation, he has some claim to being the quintessential Victorian.

A host of 'particulars' unsurpassed in literature: Dickens' Dream *by Robert William Buss*

The Ealing Comedies
Alexander Walker

'Cry God for Ealing, Balcon and St George.' That's how it might have gone. Sir Michael (Mick) Balcon, the head of Ealing Studios for almost 30 years, wasn't a man for war cries, however. His love of England resounded in his heart, not in his eardrums: the crack of bat hitting ball was the only sound of battle he enjoyed. His last words to me, spoken as I left his country house after Sunday afternoon tea one day in 1959, when Ealing Studios had shut down, were ones of sorrow that he wouldn't live to see the fine willow row he'd planted a few years earlier grow into cricket bats.

Like the man himself, his films spoke for Middle England, or rather (among the 30 films he produced from 1938 on) the half-dozen did that we call 'Ealing comedies'. Appositely, the year Ealing ceased production, 1958, was also the year R F Delderfield (best known for his West End hit *Worm's Eye View*) published his novel *The Dreaming Suburb*. Ealing films, I've often thought, were the dreams those suburbs dreamed: they were the fantasies that the middle classes let loose in the hours when their respectability was off guard.

Yet the Ealing comedies were rooted in the shabby-heroic realities of post-war Britain: a land of bombed sites, spivs, rationing, men and women demobbed from war work or the front line, politically radical but patriotically conservative, and Whitehall bureaucrats still reluctant to surrender their power over the people. Ealing had made its wartime name as a realist cinema with docudramas like *Ships with Wings*, *San Demetrio London* and *For Those in Peril*. Peace provided the opportunity to continue the war by other, gentler means.

Passport to Pimlico defied the Men from the Ministry (Basil Radford and Naunton Wayne, of course) by a unilateral declaration of independence (long before devolution) and setting up an independent dukedom in SW1, where Stanley Holloway was Prime Minister (for a day and a night anyhow). *Whisky Galore*, with its islanders outwitting their (English) Home Guard commander (Radford again) to plunder the wrecked ship of its cargo of spirits, enlisted the sneaking British sympathy for a certain class of law-breaking that was victimless. Similarly, *The Lavender Hill Mob* gave those who dared – the commuting classes – a vision of quick riches that would have to wait another 50 years for the National Lottery to make it a weekly reality, and then wouldn't be half so exciting as a police chase up and down the Eiffel Tower. Even where victims existed, they were eccentric ones. Dennis Price in *Kind Hearts and Coronets* worked his way through all eight of the d'Ascoyne line of toffs, one by one, all of them looking like Alec Guinness even in drag, as if he were coolly pulling together some loose threads on a modern Bayeux Tapestry of mass carnage. And *The Man in the White Suit* released other passions about 'them' and 'us', particularly the Luddite mistrust of Big Business.

Again and again, Ealing's comedies celebrated the British love for all things old: old puffers (*The Titfield Thunderbolt*), old tubs (*The Maggie*), old piers (*Barnacle Bill*), old crocks (*Genevieve*, which, though made at Rank's Pinewood Studios, was originally an Ealing project). Ealing Studios were based on Ealing Green, North London, and that leafy and herbivorous address suggested – if only in the mind's eye – the seductive perspective of an England that Mick

Balcon and his team of writers and directors treasured like a bit of the National Trust. They oversaw a land much like a large village common, where everyone knew his place and getting above yourself in such a community, even if you'd invented a white suit that never wore out, never needed cleaning, carried risks of upsetting the liberal paternalism of settled life.

Upset it had to be, of course, usually by some quixotic individual (Margaret Rutherford in *Passport to Pimlico*, Alastair Sim as the cartoonist whose fantasies become gangster reality in *Hue and Cry*); but the harmony of consensus politics was always restored. It was a storm in a teacup, never a typhoon. The 'little man' ruled – in the last reel anyhow – as modestly heroic as he'd looked in Straub's famous pocket cartoons in the still rationed newsprint. Small was beautiful. *Whisky Galore* was retitled *Tight Little Island* for US audiences; for once, the sea change was apt. Ealing's outlook was insular, little and uptight where the more dangerous passions were concerned.

Like sex and violence. In such things, Balcon shared Middle England's reticence. Yes, *The Ladykillers* postulated social disorder, even serial murder, but it was the innocent and sweet old lady (Katie Johnson) who finished up acquiring the loot (and tipping a pound note to the street artist who'd crayoned Winston Churchill's portrait on the flagstones), while the mutual immolation of her would-be murderers was 'just the ticket', a guilt-free placebo in a land that still hanged its murderers.

Sex, though, was the great untreatable on screen, just as it was still the great unspeakable in public. Story conferences at Ealing – self-deprecatingly advertising itself on billboards, in a perfect English understatement, as simply 'The Home of Good Pictures' – preferred to speak of the 'love interest', and not much of that, either: romance from the neck up, not below the waist. Kenneth Tynan dismissively spoke of Ealing heroes as 'men who communicate with their women mainly by post-cards'. But Balcon saw nothing reprehensible in that; and Britain agreed with him, or at least the male kingdom did.

Now we look back and perhaps the word 'quaint' comes to our lips. If so, it would be as unjust as it is unkind. Ealing Studios might have produced comfort food for Middle England that sat well with the national stomach in a nation that, possibly for the last time in its modern history, saw itself as a unitary community. One may blame the films for their conservatism, for their punishment of individual pushiness, their love of communal cosiness, veneration of consensus politics and toleration of subversiveness only so long as it was benign, comic and ultimately hurt no one. Ealing was only a brief moment in cultural history which ended as a new, thrusting and liberated generation came of age in the late 1950s. But, for that moment, studio and nation were at ease with each other. The plaque put on the wall at Ealing Green when the studios were sold to the BBC says it all: 'Here during a quarter of a century were made many films projecting Britain and the British character.' The claim could scarcely have been more modestly assembled, or more truthfully made.

Overleaf: *Alec Guinness and Stanley Holloway in* The Ladykillers, *1951*

The Edinburgh Festival
Ian Rankin

The Edinburgh Festival doesn't exist. It's an umbrella term beneath which shelter several concurrent festivals, all taking place in August so that, hopefully, no festival-goers need resort to any real-life umbrellas.

Originally, there was just the Edinburgh International Festival, conceived as a restorative to Britain's post-Second World War blues. Then the upstart Fringe Festival appeared and soon began to swamp the 'official' festival in terms of the sheer number of artists and activities on offer. Now there's a Book Festival, too, and a Film Festival, a TV Festival… not forgetting the nightly spectacle of the Edinburgh Tattoo. Edinburgh's goal, it sometimes seems to the wary resident, is to be an all-round festival city. At different times of year can be found a children's festival, science festival, beer festival, folk festival, blues… One year there was even an attempt at a punk festival. It is as though the words 'Edinburgh' and 'festival' have become synonymous.

Yet for much of the year, the city remains bridled, hidden, douce. It was once called a place of 'public probity and private vice'. The Edinbourgeosie would loosen their moral and spiritual stays, but only when privacy was assured. It has never been a great city for outward show. Every Friday night without fail, in some pub somewhere in Edinburgh, some drinker will sigh and say 'Aye, but we're all Jock Tamson's bairns', meaning that we're all similar, and shouldn't get above ourselves.

The August revels provided by the Festival are therefore greeted ambivalently by the locals. Some of them cynically rent out their flats and houses for exorbitant sums, fleeing to the foreign beaches for the month on the proceeds. Others stay at home and grumble about the increased traffic and squalor, the foreign intruders, the sense of violation. But the majority, though they may have their gripes, will be queuing for tickets along with everyone else, thrilled by the chance to experience so much culture in so little time and at such little cost.

The programmes themselves have become daunting challenges, because first of all you must know what's on and who's coming. The Fringe programme is like a weekly listings magazine, and there'll be everything in it from well-known TV faces to half a dozen different sixth-form productions of *Waiting for Godot*. With so much on offer, reviews become a crucial way of sorting out the wheat from the chaff – after which comes the surge in ticket sales… or an ever-dwindling audience. As August arrives, so Edinburgh's population is said to double, and it's easy to believe from a walk down the Royal Mile. Actually, at the height of the season this is less of a walk and more of an assault course. Students keen for punters thrust handbills at anyone within striking distance. Jugglers, buskers and mime artists vie for space. Actors in fancy-dress yell with the conviction of town-criers, exhorting all and sundry to come see their show. There's always one 'controversy', one show or stunt which gets the lifeblood of publicity. Tory councillors are hounded for their opinions of the

Dr Faustus performed at the Fringe, 1999

graphic sex and violence in the latest interpretation of *Love's Labour's Lost*. Sex sells: and it shows at the Fringe.

Such is the pressure upon space in the city that touring companies can find themselves in living-rooms turned into dorms, half a dozen sleeping-bags lined up on the carpet. The participants, fuelled by adrenaline, can be slow to spot that the chosen venue for their radical new production of Joe Orton's *Loot* is not ideal: even the most hardy Fringe-goer can be deterred by the prospect of a witching-hour three-mile hike to a disused church. Character-building it may be, but the result is often a near-empty auditorium and an early departure from Edinburgh for the company concerned.

Back in my student days, I was a reviewer for a local radio station. It was brutal stuff. There were shows at eight in the morning, and shows which started past midnight. They took place in Morningside basements, New Town churches, and scout halls in Newhaven. The enthusiasm of the cast was often the only positive note. But then that's what the Fringe is about. It's about pick 'n' mix and experimentation, it's about trying your best. And the talent-scouts are out there somewhere, seeking the next Paul Merton or *League of Gentlemen*, the next *Young Ones* or Robert Carlyle.

The International Festival can seem a more sedate affair. It sells itself by the quality of the goods on display. The year I went to the Usher Hall to see Vladimir Ashkenazy, I didn't notice him outside before the show handing out flyers. This is where the 'other' Edinburgh, the genteel, refined city, gets its kicks: good opera and classical music, quality drama companies, enterprising exhibitions. It seems to me (mind you, I'm biased) that the best of both worlds is contained within the Book Festival, where the erudite and the philosophical rub shoulders with Postman Pat and Barney the Dinosaur. You can tuck into a breakfast of coffee and croissants while listening to Allan Massie or Michael Dibdin, and end the day with an event combining rave music and the words of Irvine Welsh.

While not as riotous as the Fringe, I still have the sense that it's at the International Festival that Edinburgh really comes out to play. Edinburgh is a small city (around 500,000 people) with large ambitions. For many years, it seemed insular and inward-looking, saddened by opportunities squandered and a parliament lost to London. In recent years, however, it has begun to feel a new confidence, a new and more vibrant sense of itself. At last, Edinburgh feels that it deserves the Festival. The word 'international' has seldom rung so sweetly in the city's ears.

The Music of Edward Elgar
Michael Kennedy

Elgar is regarded as the musical quintessence of Englishness. When we hear the Woodland Interlude from *Caractacus*, Falstaff dreaming of his youth in the symphonic study *Falstaff*, the 'Welsh tune' in the *Introduction and Allegro*, the autumnal glow in the slow movement of the Cello Concerto, we also see in our mind's eye the Malvern Hills, the Wye Valley, the Sussex woods. Yet today this music seems alien to many foreign listeners and musicians, who cannot understand why we rank it so highly. They ought to respond to it, because this 'English' music does not draw on folksong, as that of Ralph Vaughan Williams does, but is a compound of the influences of Brahms, Wagner, Strauss, Bizet, Saint-Saëns and Dvořák. Nothing in Elgar is drawn, as it is in Vaughan Williams, Britten, Tippett and some others, from the music of Tallis, Byrd and Purcell. The nearest he comes to them is Handel, and after that perhaps Mendelssohn – Germans who became English composers *honoris causa*. In the years up to the First World War, Elgar was cherished and admired by the great foreign musicians of the day. They – and a handful of English musicians and critics – first recognised his genius.

Elgar famously said: 'Music is in the air all around you. You just take as much of it as you want.' He took his from the English air and, whatever he absorbed from the music across the Channel, somehow English air got into it and transformed it. As a boy, he sat on gravestones in Worcestershire churchyards studying Beethoven symphonies and lay among the reeds on the banks of the River Severn 'trying to fix the sounds and longing for something very great'. Years later, when his Symphony No 1 in A flat was being rehearsed for its first performance, the Austro-Hungarian conductor Hans Richter described the slow movement as 'a *real* Adagio, such as Beethoven would have written'. But Elgar, when he rehearsed orchestras in the second movement of the symphony, told them to play it 'like something you hear down by the river'. Beethoven and the Severn reeds – the Edwardian wind in the willows – found their apotheosis in what has been called the first great symphony by an Englishman.

This Englishness, musically inexplicable as it may be, is extremely potent. Writing of that self-same *Adagio*, Vaughan Williams said that 'it has that peculiar kind of beauty which gives us, his fellow-countrymen, a sense of something familiar – the intimate and personal beauty of our fields and lanes'. A music critic, writing at a Three Choirs Festival in the 1920s when Elgar was conducting his own music, declared that 'the very walls [of Worcester] cry out to us from the same romantic past that has bred his music'. There he put his finger on it, for the appeal of Elgar's music to his fellow countrymen is that he was always at heart a romantic spirit, inspired by a nostalgic yearning for an ideal England that he felt was now out of reach but probably had never existed. One moment his music makes the breast swell with pride, the next it makes the eyes smart with tears. When Elgar wrote his first major orchestral work for the 1890 Worcester Festival, he called it *Froissart*, after the French chronicler of chivalry, and headed the score with a Keats quotation: 'When chivalry lifted up her lance on high'. The 33-year-old composer was lifting up his lance on high, too, ready to charge the ranks of the English musical establishment with works of a richness and colour and emotional uninhibitedness (rather un-English – his critics called him vulgar) that none of his contemporaries could rival.

But at first the charge swept little before it. It was not until 1897, the year of Queen Victoria's Diamond Jubilee, for which he wrote the *Imperial March* and *The Banner of St George*, that London audiences recognised a musical laureate who captured the spirit of the time – imperialism, jingoism, patriotism. He wrote to a friend: 'I hope some day to do a great work – a sort of national thing that my fellow Englishmen might take to themselves and love.' He did just that in 1899, with his portraits of his Malvern friends in the *Enigma Variations*, and in 1900 with his choral masterpiece *The Dream of Gerontius*, a setting of part of Cardinal Newman's poem and an avowal of Elgar's own Roman Catholicism – 'this is the best of me,' he wrote on its score. But although these, the symphonies, the concertos, *Falstaff*, the *Introduction and Allegro*, and *Cockaigne* (his portrait of Diamond Jubilee London) have been taken into the hearts of his fellow countrymen – never more so than today – it was the first of his five *Pomp and Circumstance* marches in 1901 that made him a household name, especially in the following (Coronation) year when words were put to the wonderful tune of the trio section and 'Land of Hope and Glory' became a second national anthem. 'A damned fine popular tune' was Elgar's own verdict, but to some ears it branded him as a musical vulgarian and populist.

Like Tennyson, Elgar could appeal to many sides of the national character, as patriot, poet and peasant. He wrote exquisite little gems like *Salut d'Amour* and *Chanson de Nuit*, as well as the oratorios *The Apostles* and *The Kingdom*. He could reflect a national mood of sorrow, although both 'Nimrod' and the funeral-march-like slow movement of the Second Symphony were composed as tributes to personal friends, not as expressions of national mourning. 'Stately sorrow', 'heroic melancholy' – these phrases have been coined to describe his music, and they are accurate. When the First World War came, he was quick to realise its enormity and as it was ending he wrote the Cello Concerto, in which the old exuberance is muted, the wistfulness intensified to regret. 'Never glad confident morning again!'

The Englishness of Elgar's music resides in his complex personality. The music reflects the man. He was poet and dreamer, but was fascinated by science and inventions. He was at one moment the joker, life and soul of the party, kite-flier, bicyclist; at the next depressed, insecure, self-pitying, rude. He walked with kings and became an OM, GCVO, baronet and Master of the King's Musick; but was embittered to the end by the knowledge that he was a shopkeeper's son, a common touch he tried all his life to lose. He wrote one of the greatest of all religious works, but was in turn devout, agnostic and unbeliever. He cherished friendship; but when war was declared in 1914 he wrote: 'The only thing that wrings my heart & soul is the thought of the horses – the men and women can go to hell.' In his declining years, he said he preferred the company of dogs to humans. Yet the sheer humanity of this strange man's work transcends mere music for thousands of his fellow countrymen. It enters the bloodstream. Its poignancy can seem unbearable, yet it becomes a solace, a renewing stream. When in 1997 Anthony Payne miraculously breathed life into the sketches of the Third Symphony, left like pieces of a jigsaw when Elgar died in 1934, is it any wonder that audiences responded with joy and felt that the composer's spirit had returned to rebuke with his music a Britain he would have found distressingly alien?

'Music is in the air all around you': Sir Edward Elgar

The British Empire
Brian Moynahan

Melbourne is one of the most agreeable of old colonial cities, a quality it shares with the Victorian prime minister for whom it is named. 'Nobody ever did anything very foolish,' he once said, 'except from some strong principle.' In that, he caught the genius of the British Empire, its resolve to avoid resolution. It was, without question, the grandest the world has seen, five times larger than the Roman; its artefacts – the botanical garden, naval dockyard, Anglican cathedral, cockatoo-topped governor – gave it an unmistakable aura; its many offspring, trivial and profound, include the current global language and superpower, the Boy Scout, the button-down collar, and the games of snooker and bridge.

Yet it is difficult to identify why the Empire happened, what it was for, or indeed quite what it was. (Or is, since it retains a motley of islands, on the walls of one of which the legend 'Brits out' still appears.) Its only constant was that, by necessity, the enterprise was entirely sea-born, and thus suited to what Daniel Defoe called 'an ill-born amphibious mob' with a brilliance for doing business in great waters.

Its prize possession was once Aquitaine, and then Calais, surrounded, like Dublin, by the 'English Pale', a six-foot bank and ditch; when that was lost in 1558, its centre of gravity shifted to the American colonies. It stamped them indelibly in institutions, language and frame of mind; with hindsight, this was perhaps the most significant phase of all. It did not seem so then, and, unabashed by their loss in 1776, the Empire went elsewhere.

So many places were then acquired, and often in so bizarre a manner – Heligoland, for example, was taken from the Danes in 1807 to provide a base for British smugglers during the Napoleonic wars, and swapped with the Germans for Zanzibar 80 years later – that it was hard to keep track. The men who drew up the Colonial Office List in the 1890s did not bother to tabulate them all, wearily ending the list: 'And countless other smaller possessions and nearly all the rocks and isolated islands of the ocean.' British Somaliland was indisputably a colony, for the flag flew, but its owners cheerfully admitted that, 'since our authority has never remotely approached that necessary for census-taking', the number of Somalis could only be guessed at. The estimate was, of course, imperially precise; 344,323 natives and 26 British.

The Empire had no emperor, at least until Victoria became Empress of India; and when she did, Gladstone mocked the 'fictitious and tawdry lustre' of a title that was used nowhere else. It was formless, a lash-up of dominions, colonies, paramountcies, mandates, leases, condominiums and protectorates. A Royal Navy captain governed Ascension Island, since it was considered a ship for administrative purposes; Tristan da Cunha was run by a chaplain of the Society for the Propagation of the Gospel. In Egypt, the khedive had his own flag, government and army, but for 30 years the power in the land was the British consul, Evelyn Baring, at whose approach the khedive would nervously say: 'Listen, I hear the runner in front of Baring's carriage. I wonder what he will tell me today?'

It was sometimes unclear whether it was a public or private enterprise. Robert Clive, from Eccles, won the battle of Plessey and became master of Bengal on behalf of the East

India Company. The shareholders of the Hudson's Bay Company owned huge tracts of Canada, as the British South Africa Company was the beneficial owner of Rhodesia. Stamford Raffles founded Singapore as a settlement in a purely private initiative against London's wishes. The Cocos Islands in the Indian Ocean were owned and ruled by the family of a Scottish seaman, John Clunies-Ross, for 150 years; the explorer and pirate-hunter James Brooke became Rajah of Sarawak, founding a dynasty that lasted for a century.

The morality of Empire was as flexible. The grand Georgian terraces of Liverpool were built with the profits of the 'attractive African meteor', the coy name for the slave trade; when the moral U-turn was made, the Royal Navy hunted down slave ships, whilst escorting the convict ships that continued to transport men and women to people Australia. The missionary John Williams evangelised the Solomon Islands for the salvation of his fellow men until, as he knew was likely, he was clubbed to death and eaten in 1838; the following year, gunboats battered the Chinese into opening their ports for the opium trade. The *Pax Britannica* was brought to large parts of Africa, so that an officer's wife in northern Nigeria, seeing a group free of fear of slavers and tribal raiders, said that ever after 'I would think of those women who, because of England, could walk safely through the bush, singing'; Africa was also given the Boer War.

Foreigners, and more recently the British themselves, took this for hypocrisy. *Perfide Albion.* It looked so. How could the same people hero-worship the saintly Dr Livingstone and the fierce Cecil Rhodes? How could they run, at least for a time, what were essentially two empires, where one had the vote, and the other did not? The white dominions, partly populated by people for whom the British had no further use at home – Scottish crofters, Irish rebels, Cornish miners, slum orphans – were largely self-governing. The rest was not; at the time Uganda joined the Empire, the new British rulers were outnumbered by 4,400 to one, a fact that made 'natural authority' and a reputation for fair play a necessity, not a luxury.

But the Empire had a quality more subtle and impelling than hypocrisy. It was run by ambivalence – the best of British traits, because it allowed free rein to all the others. (The American philosopher George Santayana listed these as 'individuality, heresy, anomalies, hobbies, and humours', which is a fair stab, though he might have added the imperial virtues of bellicosity, curiosity and rapacity.) Strong principle, as Melbourne suggested, was dangerous. The influence of the Empire is a portmanteau into which any number of items can be stuffed, including survival in two world wars (remember the Anzacs, Canadians, Indians, Gurkhas, Vimy Ridge, the Western Desert, Burma); ambivalence prevented it from doing anything very foolish on the way.

Overleaf: *The Empress of India, Queen Victoria, attended by one of her subjects, 1893*

The Voyage of the Endurance
Stephen Venables

In the annals of polar exploration, the British have displayed a particular genius for heroic failure. The pathos of Captain Scott's eloquent last words, scribbled in his journal as he lay dying of scurvy and starvation on his way back from the South Pole in 1912, is etched into the national consciousness. However, while Scott's poignant death still produces a lump in the throat, it is to Scott's great rival, Sir Ernest Shackleton, that we turn for perhaps the most stirring, improbable survival tale of all time.

Shackleton never actually reached the South Pole. He attained the most southern point on Scott's first expedition in 1903. On his own 1909 attempt, he turned back tantalisingly close, just 100 miles short of the Pole, writing to his wife: 'I thought you would rather have a live donkey than a dead lion.' That determination not to take senseless risks, but to bring himself and his companions safely home, is the real heroism, which reached its apotheosis six years later when he failed even to set foot on Antarctica and his ship, the *Endurance*, was crushed, leaving 28 men marooned on the floating ice of the Weddell Sea.

The *Endurance* set sail from Britain in August 1914, as hostilities broke out in Europe and Shackleton's offer of assistance to the war effort was declined with a laconic 'Proceed' from the Admiralty. Unlike Captain Scott RN, Shackleton was a merchant sailor. English snobbery had no place on his team, with its unusually large contingent of Irishmen, Scots and colonials. Divisions between officers and lower ranks were blurred. Even the scientists had to get down on hands and knees alongside working-class trawlermen to scrub the decks, and Shackleton himself was very much one of the boys, known to all as 'the Boss', with all the affection and respect that that conveys.

Despite unusually heavy pack ice, the expedition almost achieved its aim of attempting the first crossing of the continent; but in January 1915, with land in sight, the ice finally won. Gripped in its implacable vice, the ship drifted back north, away from Antarctica. As failure turned gradually into a battle for survival, Shackleton's gift for leadership shone ever more brightly. If there was anything particularly British about the way he and his team coped, perhaps it was their dogged optimism, their humour and their backs-to-the-wall determination to get themselves out of a tight fix. Also peculiarly British was their anguish at having eventually to shoot the dogs which were to have towed their sledges across Antarctica. And there was something rather British, too, about their inspired improvisation, making do with what they had salvaged from the *Endurance* before she sank beneath the ice in November 1915.

Shackleton hoped to be able to march across the sea-ice to the *terra firma* of the Antarctic Peninsula, but as his floating camp drifted north, he and his 27 companions were eventually forced, as the ice broke up around them in April 1916, to take to their three tiny lifeboats. It seems fitting that this diverse band, drawn from the world's greatest maritime empire, were saved ultimately by masterly seamanship. The initial escape to the desolate, uninhabited shore of Elephant Island was a miracle of survival. Even more miraculous was the subsequent voyage of the 22-foot *James Caird*, with its improvised canvas deck and makeshift rig, 850 miles across the Southern Ocean, at the onset of winter, to South Georgia – the nearest habitation, where lay the only hope of a rescue. Shackleton's ghost-written account of what he and his five companions endured is the most famous, but the more moving version is by his navigator, the *Endurance*'s captain, Frank Worsley.

Worsley's more florid passages, which convey the terrifying immensity of the giant southern rollers dwarfing the tiny boat, are tempered by moments of classic understatement. He describes hanging up clothes to dry during a brief lull between storms, 'to alter their condition from wet to damp – a pleasant change'. Throughout, the stoicism is sustained by humour, and he recalls with affection the stalwart Irishman Tim McCarthy: 'When I relieved him at the helm, boat iced over and seas pouring down our necks, one came right over us and I felt like swearing, but just kept it back, and he informed me with a cheerful grin "It's a foine day, sorr."'

Despite getting only two chances in 14 days to take sights of the sun, and having to rely mainly on dead reckoning, Worsley navigated with pinpoint accuracy, to make a successful landfall on South Georgia. Then the worst gale hit, rising to hurricane force. The men came within a whisker of shipwreck before they could finally get ashore on the 16th day. Neither men nor boat were fit to make any further headway round the north-west tip of the island to the whaling stations on the far coast, so Shackleton, Worsley and Tom Crean embarked on the final improbable stage of an already miraculous journey – crossing the unknown, unmapped interior mountain ranges of South Georgia, with ship's screws for boot nails and the carpenter's adze for an ice axe.

No fictional *Boy's Own* tale could upstage the implausibility of that final mountain crossing. The three men were incredibly fortunate that the gales held off for the 36 hours it took to reach help. Shackleton and Worsley both acknowledge the part played by 'Providence', but, in Worsley's account especially, you feel that if anyone ever deserved luck, it was these men. The British have sometimes had a reputation for avarice and small-mindedness, but Worsley's description of himself and his companions, as they near the end of their epic odyssey, is pervaded by humour, tolerance and a heart-warming generosity of spirit.

When the three men walked into Stromness whaling station, 17 months after they had set off in *Endurance* for the Weddell Sea, now carrying nothing but a compass, the ship's log and the tattered, blackened clothes they stood in, the manager and his colleagues were flabbergasted. Shackleton's terse account underplays the Norwegians' incredulity at what he had achieved, but Worsley quotes the old salts' praises in full, as if to put the record straight. He and his five companions – and the 22 marooned men who will now be rescued from Elephant Island – know, like Henry V's men on the feast of St Crispin, that they are a part of something unique and that their story will be told and retold, 'from this day to the ending of the world'.

Overleaf: *Stuck fast, January 1915: the* Endurance *in ice, photographed by Frank Hurley*

The English Language
Melvyn Bragg

My spoken English began in dialect – like that of linguistic kindred in Jamaica, Texas, Toronto, Bangalore, Adelaide and Capetown. For most people over the last millennium and into the 21st century, a dialect was and is their first point of entry. Culture, class and mobility of several kinds might propel them into a more standardised pronunciation of the language. But even as it branches into more and more corners of the world – places which would have amazed the monks in Winchester whose writings in Old English give us an invaluable early staging-post in the great journey of our most extraordinary tongue – the dialects of English are still its lush and essential roots.

As a boy in the small town of Wigton in Cumbria in the far north of England, I would employ Old English words in an accent as thickly coated as any over the last millennium. Earth, stone, sheep, cow, brother, sister, father: all these Old English words were and still are intact, but their sound in the 1940s – or my sound – was far nearer Chaucer than the BBC. Cow was *ku*; stone was *stee-ane*; brother was *bruuther*. I would also – without knowing it, of course – be using Celtic remnants when going to anywhere beginning Pen, Tor or Blen, and my part of northern Cumbria is full of such place names. Anglian words were there – like fluke (meaning a flat-fish), gavelock (a crowbar), and those terrible twins owt and nowt. There was also a massive inheritance, in the Lake district, from the Norsemen who occupied the central massif of the place near-uninterruptedly for over a thousand years; and beck (stream), yem (home), yek (oak), yet (gate), forelders (ancestors) – literally thousands of my childhood words – came from Scandinavia via Ireland. Further richness arrived with the Romany gypsies who used to trade and camp around the town. A girl was a mort, a man was, and still is in Wigton, a gadji, a dog was a dukal, clothes were togs, barry was good. And of course, again without my knowing it – like the man in the Molière play who had been speaking prose all his life without knowing it – there was, increasingly as I went through school, an admixture from Greek, Latin and French.

Winchester is a useful staging-post because of the 11th-century Benedictine monk Aelfric, whose colloquies – almost mini-playlets, produced to teach boys Latin – offered the tremendous bonus of a translation into Old English above the Latin text. This has enabled scholars to grip the language and chart its journey. The beginnings of Old English go back to the seventh century, but Aelfric's many works, which became vastly popular and spread over the land, were the first embodiment of standard English.

It is fascinating that just when English was taking hold it met its first and far and away its greatest challenge – from France. The Battle of Hastings not only destroyed almost all the English aristocracy and in one fell coup gave Normans the leadership of Church, state and administration, and ownership of over 90 per cent of the land; it also threatened the most basic and cohesive cultural force of all – the language of the people. The first six Norman

---

From dialect to standard English: Audrey Hepburn and Rex Harrison in My Fair Lady, *1964*

kings spent less than half their time in this country and there is meagre evidence that any of them spoke the language. To get on you had to learn French, the language of the Court, the language of patronage. Moreover, about 10,000 northern French words planted themselves on English soil, never to be washed away – key words such as peace, battle, arms, siege, enemy, armour, religion, saint, miracle, chase, scent, design, beauty, music, romance, dress. Sometimes words paired together, like French archer and English bowman, or French liberty and English freedom. Sometimes they came in triples: kingly (Anglo-Saxon), royal (French) and regal (Latin). The melting-pot was already steaming. Class came into it, of course. The Englishman lived in a home, the Frenchman lived in a manor. The peasant tended oxen and sheep or pigs (English words), the French rulers ate beef, mutton and pork. And as the centuries went on, the French invasion continued – one of its most successful lines of attack can be seen on the menu of any restaurant (both French): plaice, cream, onion, salad…

Yet remarkably, English survived. The spoken language would not be razed, and when in the 1390s Chaucer wrote his *Canterbury Tales*, they were not in Latin, which some of the pilgrims in Canterbury would have spoken, nor were they in French, which was still the language of the Court. He wrote in what we today can enjoy as English. We may need some help here and there, but Chaucer clearly points us towards Shakespeare, from whom so many English blessings flow.

English not only inherited more foreign words, it also coined words of its own. It has been estimated that over 100,000 new words were coined (*i.e.* invented) in the 20th century alone: words often jammed together – cameramen, hatchbacks, loudspeakers – or invented for new things – radiator, torpedo, parachute, Rolls Royce – and used all over the shop – motels (motor-hotels), heliports (helicopter ports), Oxbridge (Oxford and Cambridge). New words can be formed by shortening existing words – grid from gridiron, porn from pornography, fridge from refrigerator. Science has bred words like rabbits, often using Latin or Greek roots: abdomen, corolla, cortex, equilibrium, genus, quantum, stamen, cathode, zoology, Palaeolithic, Silurian – words often deliberately classical to confer status.

It would be possible to fill this book with further examples of the richness of English. In one way, of course, this book is already necessarily full of such examples, which help show the apparently unstoppable diversity of a language which, from that dark and cloud-laden island off the edge of Europe, now has independent branches in the Americas, in Asia, Africa, Australasia; while over the rest of the planet it is cultivated as the language of international business and diplomacy, and increasingly of entertainment. The roots of English may be obscure and elusive. Its routes have made highways through the cultures and the centuries.

The Decoding of Enigma
Hugh Sebag-Montefiore

If the Battle of Waterloo was won on the playing fields of Eton, then the battle for the Enigma code during the Second World War was won in the common rooms at Cambridge. Many of the codebreakers who helped break the code, and particularly the all-important naval Enigma, were still students or fellows at Cambridge University when war was declared.

The code they were asked to decipher had been produced on the Enigma cipher machine which was being used by Nazi Germany's armed forces. The Enigma machine looked like a typewriter, but it had scrambling elements inside, and different enciphering procedures were adopted for different sections of Germany's armed forces. The Enigma code used by the German Navy was the most difficult to break, but it was also the most important strategically. There is general agreement amongst historians that when the Bletchley Park team broke it they shortened the war by one to two years.

Most of the codebreakers were selected after their names were submitted by tutors or colleagues who were asked to put forward their brightest young men and women. Once a name was submitted, there was nothing other than an informal interview to stop the person in question being hired to work in one of the codebreaking huts at Bletchley Park. Security checks were only a minor barrier to entry.

For example, one young woman, 18-year-old Mavis Lever, befriended a couple of German spies before she was interviewed. Yet even after they were caught, she was not only allowed to work at Bletchley Park, but was asked to work on the Enigma cipher used by the German intelligence service, the *Abwehr*, for transmitting its spies' reports. Fortunately, she turned out to be the perfect recruit, and went on to break the *Abwehr*'s Enigma code without anyone outside Bletchley Park being any the wiser. Alan Turing, a young don attached to King's College, Cambridge, before the war, did more than anyone else to break the naval Enigma code. Yet he was a practising homosexual at a time when such inclinations were mostly kept in the closet, a state of affairs which made him easily blackmailable. He also managed to keep the British Enigma secret, both during and after the war.

Mavis Lever was a linguist. However, the majority of those picked out were mathematicians with first class degrees. The way one of them was approached was typical. David Rees (later an eminent professor of mathematics) was visited in his rooms at Sidney Sussex College, Cambridge, during 1939 by Gordon Welchman, one of his mathematics tutors, and another Cambridge don. They told him they had a job for him connected with the war, but they would not tell him what it was or where he was to work. Eventually, the bemused Rees blurted out: 'How will I know where to report to if you won't tell me where to go?' Only then did Welchman and his companion tell him to make his way to Bletchley railway station, where he would be met and briefed. He was duly picked up at Bletchley and informed there and then that he was to work on the German Enigma.

Thanks to this informal selection procedure, which allowed academic professors rather than civil servants to take the lead role, Bletchley Park was full of brilliant mavericks far

removed from the straight-laced bureaucrats one expects to find in the civil service. Alan Ross (later a professor of linguistics and the inventor of the concept of non-U speech made famous by Nancy Mitford's *Noblesse Oblige*) was notorious within Bletchley Park for sedating his son with laudanum and laying him out on the luggage-rack whenever they were travelling together on the train. Bentley Bridgewater, the future Secretary of the British Museum, became a legend after he chased Angus Wilson, his homosexual lover, into the lake in front of the Bletchley Park mansion after a quarrel. Angus Wilson, who was to become a well-known novelist in later life, himself suffered from uncontrollable tantrums. One was so severe that it only subsided after he had kicked in his landlady's front door. Such behaviour overshadowed even Turing's eccentricities: he chained his coffee mug to the radiator and bicycled around the countryside wearing a gas mask in order to ward off the pollen.

The codebreakers had an indomitable spirit, which they shared with most of the British population during the dark days of 1940. This was sometimes the result of having triumphed over adversity: for example Harry Hinsley, a grammar school boy who won a scholarship to study at St John's College, Cambridge, was the son of an impoverished out-of-work labourer. He played an important role in breaking the naval Enigma. Other codebreakers acquired their stiff upper lips thanks to surviving the rigours of the British public school system. As a result, difficulties encountered at Bletchley Park – the codebreakers dealing with the Enigma were not given enough equipment or personnel – led not to resigned apathy, but to rebellion. Four of the codebreakers wrote a letter of complaint about their lack of resources to Churchill, who immediately instructed that they be given what they needed.

Having so many independent-minded workers could make Bletchley hard to run. In one classic exchange with Alistair Denniston, the acting head of Bletchley Park, Dilly Knox, the classics scholar and star codebreaker, stated that he was used to seeing his work through from start to finish, 'from the raw material to the final text'. He did not take kindly to its being presented to the intelligence huts by someone else, and accused Denniston of having the mentality of a grocer for expecting him to agree to the arrangement. Denniston would not back down, and wrote back: 'If you do design a Rolls Royce that is no reason why you should yourself drive the thing up to the house of a possible buyer.' However, on other occasions Denniston supported the absent-minded professor codebreakers against the Bletchley Park managers, reining in his robust deputy, Edward Travis, with the words, 'One does not expect to find the rigid discipline of a battleship among the collection of somewhat unusual civilians who form GC & CS [as Bletchley Park was known]. To endeavour to impose it would be a mistake and would not assist our war effort.'

Paradoxically, this group of non-team players created one of the most effective and creative teams ever put together – so effective, indeed, that it should be presented as a model case study to all managers, whether of scientists, business executives or football players, who instinctively shy away from individualist 'troublemakers' in the mistaken belief that only by encouraging conformity will they achieve their finest hour.

The Enigma encoding machine in action on board a German train, 1940

Fish and Chips
Rick Stein

Let me describe the restaurant to you. It's called Wacker's and it's in Scarborough. It's big: there are over 200 seats, most of them banquette seating, high-backed, polyurethane-covered foam rubber. This is all in turquoise, and there's an orange and brown carpet with a pattern of swirls, and matching turquoise tables and chairs at the front with brown tops. The waitresses wear brown and white and have little brown headscarves.

It's not licensed and there's no takeaway. You get tea, bread and butter, cod or haddock and chips. It's packed, but everybody's cheerful. The staff are plain Yorkshire and nice to you. It's a happy and successful place – and the fish and chips almost bring tears to your eyes, they're so good. The cod is thick milky curds, the batter is deep brown, crisp and fragrant, and the chips are as thick as your thumb, with a sandy texture on the outside and a soft dry whiteness inside. Above all, the taste – delicate and not at all overpowering – is the taste of the frying medium: dripping. Not any old animal fat either, but the dripping from British beef. You walk into this restaurant, or the Magpie café up the coast in Whitby, or the Liverton Mines Fisheries outside Middlesbrough, and it smells as if Sunday roast is in the oven. You feel at home, welcome and pleased with everything.

Those fish and chip maestros in Yorkshire really know how it's done. So do their counterparts on the east coast of Scotland. There they favour haddock and, though dripping is popular, they often use pure lard instead. Whatever the fat, it has to be changed often and kept scrupulously clean by pumped filtering. The place must smell inviting. For me, the first impression of a fish and chip shop is always supplied by the nose: the acrid, dark smell of old oil is mean and depressing, and you know it will permeate your clothes like the smell of beer, stale cigarettes and damp in run-down pubs (which also normally carries overtones of foetid frying oil).

It would be hard to think of a more uncomplicated dish than fish and chips, but it's so easy to get it wrong. The fish, of course, has to be absolutely fresh. The best fish and chips are made with recently caught large fish in good condition, but since so much fresh fish is not like that, it would be wrong to assume that frozen fish is always inferior. For example, frozen Icelandic cod can be excellent, because the fish from the cold waters off Iceland are bigger, and big cod has more flavour. They look after their stocks successfully in Iceland, whereas in the North Sea the cod and haddock are getting ever smaller. The trick with buying frozen fish is to know when it was caught and frozen. It is normal for the best Icelandic cod to be frozen within three hours of being caught, and as long as the frozen stock is then used quickly, which means within a couple of months, the fish will be excellent – much better than a small fresh codling fillet, which will often come out soft and mushy.

Chips require minute attention to detail, too. They should be made with just a few types of potato with a low sugar content – Maris Piper and a couple of others, Crown and Cara.

Cod and chips twice: the perfect street food

Potatoes are just as delicate to store as grapes. They must be kept above freezing and must never be jostled or dropped, otherwise the starch in them turns to sugar and they go black and greasy when deep-fried. A good fish and chip fryer will test each new batch of potatoes with a diabetes testing kit called Diastix, which is designed to test the sugar content of urine. Low sugar content means dry, light brown chips.

Finally, the batter. So many shops talk about secret recipes and ingredients, which normally means one thing to me: monosodium glutamate, that palate-stimulating seasoning which promises much, but leaves an insistent flavour in the mouth for a long time afterwards. The best places, though, will tell you there's nothing to batter – just flour, water, salt and bicarbonate of soda. The secret is to make it and throw it away if it's not used within an hour or so, just like tempura batter, the light, crisp Japanese coating for deep-fried morsels of fish and vegetables.

Fish and chips are perfect street food, a crisp parcel easy to pick up and eat with the fingers, a good economic balance of lots of carbohydrate with a little protein. It's Britain's most distinctive contribution to the world's menu of cheap and satisfying everyday food – samosas, tacos, poh boys, empanadas, hamburgers, pizzas – and like them, it's something we crave for the comfort it gives us, but feel slightly guilty about, because somehow it's not considered good for you, like salads and raw vegetables and chargrilled fish.

I ate fish and chips recently in Ullapool on the west coast of Scotland. I didn't order the mushy peas, just cod and chips. They came in a shallow cardboard box with a lift-up lid. I leant against a wall overlooking the harbour and fishing docks. I bunged a chip at a seagull, who flew up, judged the arc of the chip perfectly and swallowed it with one neat extension of its smooth white neck. I only threw one because they were so good. So was the cod and the batter. It was a beautiful placid evening, the small red and white and blue and white boats motionless on the almost mirror-like water, and golden sunlight picking out the mountains all around.

I thoroughly enjoyed the sheer ordinariness of it. It's not a big event, eating fish and chips. You don't need to feel awed by it. You just lean on the harbour wall and lob the occasional chip at a seagull.

The Forth Bridge
Kevin McCloud

Nine miles upstream from Edinburgh, at Queensferry, sit the Forth Bridges, one rail, one road, at a point where the estuary narrows to a width of a mile or so. Each bridge speaks wholly of the century it was built in. The road crossing is an elegant, minimal structure, a version of the 20th-century standard design for a twin-tower suspension bridge, that steps across the water in two elegant tiptoes. The rail bridge is its 19th-century forebear, a powerful structure, all flexed muscle that seems to spring out of the water. I don't know if all bridges, like ships, are female, but this one, despite its machismo, is strangely feminine. If it were a ship, it would be the *Ark Royal* at full steam; it is a battleship-cruiser among bridges, a great elderly iron maiden. To some it is even a formidable Victorian Scottish maiden aunt. Perhaps it's those big sweeping curves.

Over the last century and a quarter, the bridge has accreted something of an iconic status. It has become emblematic of Scotland and is now part of the Scottish tourist trail, together with Edinburgh Castle and the Loch Ness Monster. Its picture sits on postcards and shortbread tin lids. But it is not uniquely Scottish. It was commissioned by a consortium of mainly English companies that ran the east coast rail lines in the 1880s, and who were in desperate competition with the west coast companies in a bid to connect Scotland with the south of England. They were building a British network. And it was not designed by a Scot, but by a London firm of engineers, Messrs Harrison, Barlow, Fowler and Baker, who had been responsible for (among many other fantastic feats of engineering) the Aswan Dam and the London Underground. These men considered nothing beyond their reach.

But they were not the first. There had been other designs, most of them unbuilt. But in 1878, work had actually started on a design by a Scottish engineer, Thomas Bouch. He was the most eminent and prolific railway engineer north of the border. His revolutionary design was for a twin-tower suspension bridge, bizarrely similar to the modern road crossing and, remarkably, even higher. (I've seen his huge drawing, which was recently discovered in a government file by an enterprising historian, Ian Archibald.)

Bouch's concept was daring and futuristic but it was never to be realised. On 28 December 1879, Bouch's great bridge over the River Tay collapsed in a storm, killing all 75 passengers who were crossing on a train. A public enquiry was held and Bouch found culpable, partly because he had made no provision for wind-damage in his design. He retired from public life, disgraced, and died four months later. Work was immediately halted on his design and the project handed to Baker and Fowler.

But in a way we have Bouch to thank for the continuing survival of the bridge. In 1882, Baker received a parliamentary stipulation that his design should 'gain the confidence of the public and enjoy the reputation of being not only the biggest and strongest but also the stiffest bridge in the world'. So he deliberately over-designed it.

Overleaf: *An old brontosaurus? The Forth Bridge under construction*

It is super-strong, relying on principles that Baker had developed, using tubular arms to take compression and open zigzag trusses to take tension. He also took advantage of new steel production methods, allowing for the manufacture of steel of consistent engineering quality. This allowed him to create the two massive spans, each 1,700 feet wide, three and a half times wider than anything previously built.

It is extraordinary facts like these that define the bridge as one of the great engineering wonders of Britain. And these facts roll on and on. This is a unique design, using giant repeated cantilevers (long arms held out beyond the supporting frame) never seen before. It is over a mile and a half long, was the biggest bridge in the world, contains 39,000 tons of steel, and yet took only three years of fabrication to build. It moves, and is a metre longer in summer than in midwinter. It contains some 4,200 tons of rivets. Joseph Arrol, who built it, was a British genius of construction. His firm pioneered the use of caissons (hollow tubular dams) to build the piers that support the cantilever frames. He also invented for this job the forerunner of the pneumatic drill (in order to break up the compacted clay of the estuary bed), as well as the hydraulic riveting machine and a specially adapted cage-riveter.

But these are not just a list of facts and statistics: they represent a defining moment in the history of our built world, an event and a period that showered the world with new ideas. The building of this giant structure was the equivalent of America's space race 70 years later, its ambition such that a whole raft of new technologies, principles and inventions found a place in its genesis, or were specifically designed to help realise it. As a NASA engineer might say, it pushed the envelope a whole lot. Baker himself said: 'If I were to pretend that designing and building the Forth Bridge was not a source of present and future anxiety to all concerned, no engineer would believe me. Where no precedent exists, the successful engineer is he who makes fewest mistakes.'

What a statement. What a risk. It could only have been taken in the engineering culture of the times; in a period of fevered construction, of invention and patents, when engineers could meet in clubs, when they were fêted by society, when they could live, breathe, sleep and most importantly dream engineering. Not a single architect seems to have been involved on this project.

And the bridge doesn't have a single decorative element (except perhaps for the stone piers that support the approach ways: they have an elegant and slightly decorated tapering shape, reminiscent of Egyptian pylons). The overall outline of the structure, its stretched, arching spans, its height, mass, details, presence in the landscape, even its colour, are all there because they need to be. The Forth Bridge is testament to the heretic idea that good design and even good style do not require aesthetic involvement; that they can spring solely out of engineering need. It was certainly a heretic idea then: John Ruskin, when he saw it, wished he had been born blind; William Morris thought it the 'supremest specimen of all ugliness'. Nowadays, we can see in it something we call 'functional beauty'. It is a sign of its pre-eminence that it embodied the modern movement maxim 'form follows function' 30 years before the phrase was invented.

And although it is over a century old, it still amazes, it still excites. And it is still useful, still the main rail link on the east coast. It still carries 200 trains a day. It is still being repainted.

I spent a week on the bridge in 1999, in its 110th year. I climbed all over it, felt and saw it flex and move as great expresses passed over and through it. That was an extraordinary sensation. I also saw from the top how the long strained cantilever arms whip and shudder up their length as they take the weight of a train. In those moments, when it creaked and wobbled, it resembled some great creature stirring, shaking off the rust – and all that history with it. It became what John Betjeman saw it as, an old brontosaurus.

And yet, of course, it is not extinct. It is a living thing, a breathing being of steel sinew and movement. It is as vital as it ever was.

A demonstration of the physics of the Forth Bridge

British Humour
Howard Jacobson

I have a distant but vivid memory of sitting cross-legged on a soggy beach in Blackpool (itself an instance of the grotesquerie of our national humour) watching Mr Punch, unrepentant wife-beater and child-murderer, getting the hangman to help him with the noose. If he is to hang for his crimes, he will hang dextrously. How does this work? Where is it I put my head? Obligingly, the hangman shows him, slipping the rope around his own neck, like so. Whereupon Mr Punch tightens the noose and hangs the hangman. That's the way to do it!

I loved it. We all loved it. We chewed our fingers when we thought Mr Punch was going to get his comeuppance, then we cheered and roared when he cheated justice, in the process chalking up yet another murder. It wasn't that we were lawless little ruffians ourselves; we simply understood intuitively how drama worked – we suspended our disapproval in appreciation of the protagonist's vitality. And if we felt a little queasy even as we roared – well, that was part of the drama too. The grotesque is meant to kick the ground from under you and send your heart into your mouth.

The British didn't invent Mr Punch out of thin air. There are many early Italian scenarios in which Mr Punch's forerunner, Pulcinella, brings the law down on himself, then tricks the hangman into being his own executioner. And behind Pulcinella there are the demoniac hero-villains of the ancient world. But in Punch and Judy the British evolved a form of comic knockabout which for violence and extremity far outstripped its antecedents.

More than anything else, it is that violence which distinguishes our national sense of humour. Watching English pantomime for the first time, the French poet Baudelaire was astonished by the Pierrot figure, who in France had lost his hump and grown effete, but on our stage made his entrance 'like a hurricane and tumbled like a buffoon'. What exhilarated Baudelaire wasn't only the extravagant physicality and gluttonousness of the actor, but also the wildness of the audience's appreciation of him. 'The whole action of this extraordinary piece was played on a sustained note of fury. The atmosphere was one of dizzy and bewildering exaggeration.'

If we are sometimes accused of unsubtlety in our comedy, of lacking light and shade, here is the reason – we prefer exaggeration, and look for truth in vehemence. Whether we have in mind Ben Jonson's *Volpone* and *The Alchemist*, the satires of Pope, the caricatures of Rowlandson, the novels of Dickens, *Fawlty Towers*, the plays of Steven Berkoff, or even the chants we would sometimes rather not hear on our football terraces, it is evident that our culture is characterised by 'a sustained note of fury'. Who we might happen to be furious with at any time is not the issue. Nor does it matter why. We value fury, simply, as an aesthetic good in itself.

When Pope wonders where the virtue lies in 'breaking a butterfly on a wheel', he is being disingenuous. The virtue lies in the sheer joy of doing it. Myself, I found a similar disingenuousness in Johnny Speight's often-voiced dismay that television viewers had mistaken his intentions in *Till Death Us Do Part*, and that Alf Garnett was not meant to be sympathetic.

As though a character capable of such grand tirades of irrational rage, of such grotesqueries of ill-informedness and intolerance, of such spiralling spite and satire, wasn't always going to find his way into the hearts of the British people! The further Alf Garnett departed from moderation and fairness, the more we loved and understood him.

It wouldn't be fanciful, remembering Mr Punch, to ascribe this love we feel for figures of such invincible irascibility as Alf Garnett – Victor Meldrew is another – to a desire to see death cheated. One foot in the grave, but not yet awhile. Till death us do part, but you'll have to catch us first. To cheat death one must be indomitable, and to be indomitable, we British have come to understand, it is necessary to be permanently furious – not so much a person as a caricature of a person, not fashioned out of ordinary materials, but reconfigured to be grotesque.

No one understood this better than Dickens, which is perhaps why no writer has ever seemed more quintessentially British. Yes, he gave us English Christmases and plum puddings and tankards of foaming ale and Little Nell to touch our stout hearts, but that was just tickling our peripheries; where he really found us was in his comedy of deformed vitality – call it caricature, if you will, call it the truest depiction of our souls. Remember that twisted, dwarfish life-force, Quilp, a sort of Mr Punch incarnate, whose idea of a good time is to breakfast with his mother-in-law, eating eggs with their shells still on while chewing tobacco and watercress and biting his cutlery until it bends? For Quilp, being an affront to life is life itself.

'What displeases us in Dickens', wrote the American critic Santayana, 'is that he does not spare us; he mimics things to the full… he wallows.' By 'us', Santayana means only a part of us. 'Cultivated English feeling winces at this brutality, although the common people love it in clowns and in puppet shows…' In this, as in so much else, cultivated English feeling, so often aspiring to be French or something else not native, entirely misses what's best about us.

Long may we remain uncultivated.

Overleaf: *'A sustained note of fury'*: A Hitt at Backgammon *by Thomas Rowlandson (1756–1827)*

A HITT AT B

GAMMON.

Rowlandson Del. 42

The Industrial Revolution
Sally Dugan

In *1066 and All That*, W C Sellar and R J Yeatman provide the ultimate in cynical definitions of the Industrial Revolution in Britain. It was a time, as they describe it, when 'many very remarkable discoveries and inventions were made. Most memorable among these was the discovery (made by all the rich men in England at once) that women and children could work for twenty-five hours a day in factories without many of them dying or becoming excessively deformed. This was known as the Industrial Revelation and completely changed the faces of the North of England.'

At the turn of the 19th century, the smoking chimneys of Manchester – 'Cottonopolis' – and the glowing forges of Ironbridge became staging-posts in a dark version of the Grand Tour. Visitors from Europe and beyond came to marvel at this vision of hell on earth – then went home to copy it. For however satanic the mills may have been, they certainly made money for their owners.

The big puzzle which continues to exercise historians is: why did the Industrial Revolution happen when and where it did? What was it about this scraggy little island which made the conditions right for industrialisation? Traditionally, the history of this era has been taught as a list of names – Hargreaves, Arkwright, Watt, and all the rest. But no one country ever has a monopoly of inventive talent, so this can hardly be the full explanation. If it were, China would now be the most industrialised nation on earth, as many of the inventions that made the Industrial Revolution possible originated there.

To some extent, the story of the Industrial Revolution is the story of the inspired amateur. James Hargreaves was a humble weaver and carpenter from Blackburn, who invented his spinning jenny after watching his wife working at her wheel. Richard Arkwright, originally a barber and wigmaker, got the idea for his water frame while travelling around collecting human hair for wigs. Edmund Cartwright, an Oxford don and clergyman, had the inspiration for his power loom while having dinner with a group of industrialists.

Then there is the tradition of individualism, the cross-fertilisation of ideas and kindly tolerance of harmless – but possibly constructive – eccentricity fostered by gentlemen's clubs and organisations such as the Lunar (nicknamed Lunatic) Society. This very British organisation was founded by Darwin's grandfather, Erasmus Darwin, and used to meet once a month on the full moon for six hours. Its members included some of the greatest inventors and industrialists of the 18th century, and it was groups such as this which helped people with ideas find people with money.

Spotting a need and finding a niche in the market was the secret of entrepreneurs like Josiah Wedgwood. He capitalised on the British fondness for tea by providing elegant cups for the middle classes to drink it from – and providing them on a massive scale. This was made possible by the scientific efficiency of his production lines in Staffordshire – but

Satanic mills: The Canal Bridge *(1949), by L S Lowry*

the elegant ladies who twirled their parasols around his fashionable London showroom saw no sign of this. They were flattered by invitations to ticket-only private views by the 'Potter to Her Majesty'. It was an early example of the creation of a designer label, and a marketing triumph.

Marketing of a particularly ruthless kind was behind the success of Sir Richard Arkwright, who insisted on selling his water frames only in units of 1,000, effectively forcing others into operating on a factory scale. Portraits of Arkwright show him as the archetypal well-fed capitalist – a typical example of the kind of larger than life figure (in more ways than one) who dominates the era. When he was made Lord Lieutenant of Derby, he revelled in the dressing-up opportunities the position offered, swaggering around on horseback accompanied by trumpeters dressed in rich liveries of scarlet and gold.

However, telling the story of the Industrial Revolution as a story of personalities can be misleading. Most inventors stand on the shoulders of those who have gone before. James Watt, for example, is widely credited with inventing the steam engine – perhaps largely because of the romantic schoolboy picture of him sitting in the kitchen watching his mother's kettle boil. In fact, steam engines had been pumping water out of Cornish tin mines long before Watt came along, and his improvements in their design might not have got anywhere had it not been for the business skills of his partner, Matthew Boulton.

The People in History approach also leaves out other completely unrelated factors. A revolution built on coal, iron and steam would clearly not have been possible in a desert – and, added to our natural resources, there is Britain's status as an island. Not just any old island, but a particularly cold, damp and drizzly one. This has fostered an enthusiasm for exploring other, less drizzly places, and produced technical expertise in making ships and cannons. It has also helped to produce a strong work ethic, since there is little opportunity to lie around having siestas in the sun.

Tourists today flock to heritage attractions to stare with a kind of horrified fascination at the grim working conditions endured by those who helped to make their employers rich. Charles Dickens, in *Hard Times*, produced a spectacularly unappealing portrait of the heartless industrialist in the bombastic Josiah Bounderby of Coketown, the man convinced that every Hand was out to eat turtle soup with a gold spoon, when in fact all they wanted was bread on the table.

Of course, the Industrial Revolution had its villains. But for every Bounderby, there were other more philanthropic factory owners. They thought they offered a fair bargain: houses, gardens and schools in return for hard and dangerous work. By the standards of the time they were enlightened employers. Now they stare out from their gold-framed oil portraits, their unblinking confidence undimmed by the passage of centuries. They were people of imagination and vision, and an enviable lack of self-doubt.

James Bond
Joseph Connolly

Tuesday 15 January 1952 – that was the day. 8.30 a.m., local time. Ian Fleming – *Sunday*
Times journalist – was seated at his desk in Goldeneye, the house on Jamaica he had bought
just one year earlier for £5,000, a tortoiseshell cigarette-holder clamped hard between his
teeth. The 43-year-old's eyes had adjusted to the pale bright morning light – and now his
hands reached out to the Imperial portable typewriter before him; he had no notes – a
vague idea, a few thoughts, maybe, but nothing like a game-plan. His fingers hit the keys:

> The scent and smoke and sweat of a casino are nauseating at
> three in the morning. Then the soul-erosion produced by high
> gambling – a compost of greed and fear and nervous tension –
> becomes unbearable and the senses awake and revolt from it.
> James Bond suddenly knew that he was tired.

And thus, in the opening lines of the very fine novel *Casino Royale* (complete in eight
weeks), was secret agent 007, arguably the most famous fictional hero of all time, tentatively
introduced to the British reading public. And despite Bond's much touted literary antecedents
– Sapper's Bulldog Drummond, Haggard's Allan Quatermain and even Buchan's Hannay
(Sax Rohmer maybe holding some sway over the villains) – no one had ever before
encountered a man, or a thriller, like this one. Because the 'real' James Bond – as opposed
to his later various movie incarnations – was truly hard and cold and mean and brutal, and
this pleased, I'm afraid, both men and women. There were no easy laughs in the novels –
no fatuous quips nor excruciating punning. This man was a loner in peril, who lived by his
wits – an undercover agent with a licence to kill, for God's sake: there was nothing remotely
funny about it.

All of which may come as a shock to the post-1960s generation of filmgoers, who may
even be surprised to learn that there are such things as Bond novels at all. But long before
Sean Connery's triumphant debut in *Dr No* in 1962 (in which he was, for the larger part,
hard and cold and mean and brutal), Fleming's novels had proved a multinational – if not yet
international – hit. The Pan paperbacks were flagged as bursting with 'Terror and Torture!
Romance and Murder!' – though for every critic who cited Fleming as 'the best new English
thriller-writer since Ambler', or much lauded contemporary such as Raymond Chandler, who
hailed Fleming as 'probably the most forceful and daring writer of thrillers in England', there
were many who simply loathed each and every annual offering – cocktails, as a both shaken
and stirred Paul Johnson famously fumed, of 'sex, snobbery and sadism'. Which probably
moved a good few copies.

One can see quite clearly, though, why – despite the carpers – James Bond quickly became
so huge a success in the generally style-starved 1950s. For the vast majority of (mainly male)
readers, such exotic locations as Istanbul, Zagreb, Kingston or Miami were no more than

dots on the map; while the average worker was less likely to take to the office a 7.65mm Walther PPK automatic or a flat throwing knife than a clutch of luncheon vouchers and a tightly rolled umbrella. And as for the gorgeous women… Bond simply used them as they arrived (and, being Bond, arrive they did); plus he was a 60- or 70-a-day man (Morlands cigarettes, not women: there are limits) and, despite all the subsequent vodka-martini hoo-ha – a very occasional drink for Bond – he put away a lot of Bourbon on the rocks. Fast and powerful (British) cars were also a thing (a four-and-a-half-litre convertible Bentley in the books – Amherst-Villiers supercharged and in battleship grey: matt, not gloss). Something similar was briefly glimpsed close to the beginning of the film *From Russia with Love*, but otherwise the famous and wonderful Aston Martin DB5 was the undisputed star of the movies, before things went downmarket (and then German).

Vicarious (but safe) sex, pain and danger, then, were much on the menu here (as Fleming said: 'the target of my books lies somewhere between the solar plexus and the upper thigh'), and all Bond's idiosyncrasies went a long way in establishing him as a real live (if bloody singular) man and agent. Odd, then, that his creator saw him as little more than a blank canvas – one upon which the male identifier could daub his own looks and mannerisms (Bond was meant to be about 38 years old, but to this day there are few would-be 007s between the ages of 15 and 80 who would dream of letting a little thing like that come between them and their innermost fantasy).

The films, of course – courtesy of producers Cubby Broccoli and Harry Saltzman – were the turning-point. The first (and best) three – *Dr No*, *From Russia with Love* and *Goldfinger* – marked the globalisation of Bond, and so it came to pass that Thomas Connery (later Sean) did – as women will tell you – make the word flesh. Roger Moore was also in the frame for the debut outing (due to the success of TV's *The Saint*), as was Patrick McGoohan (due to the success of TV's *Danger Man* – isn't showbusiness wonderful?), along with many others. Fleming's rather eccentric first choice (given that he saw Bond as a 'hero without any characteristics, simply a blunt instrument in the hands of the government') was David Niven – who did go on to star in the dire spoof *Casino Royale* in 1967 (three years after Fleming's death, mercifully for him). And, incidentally, Fleming wanted no less a name than Alfred Hitchcock to direct, but as it turned out was very well served by Terence Young, with the aid of the great Ken Adam's unforgettable sets.

There remain very many questions about Bond the character: how, we might feel entitled to enquire, could an incorruptible on Civil Service pay afford to own a Regency house in a square off King's Road, Chelsea, and be cared for by a housekeeper? Or run that Bentley? Or indulge his taste for Sea Island cotton or heavy silk shirts and hand-made cigarettes (not to say Beluga and Dom Perignon)? Poetic licence, naturally – pure and simple: we are talking fiction, after all. More engaging is the mystery of the longevity of Bond the phenomenon. The films were the height of cool in the 1960s, of course, but when Connery finally (well – not finally, as it turned out: never say never) elected to hang up his toupée, that, surely, should have been that. But Roger Moore effortlessly conquered his own generation – 007-dom even survived George Lazenby. Timothy Dalton was greeted with a degree of respect – while

Hard, cold, mean and brutal? The first Bond film: Sean Connery and Ursula Andress in Dr No, *1962*

Pierce Brosnan seems to have (Amherst-Villiers) supercharged the entire multibillion-dollar cavalcade and single-handedly propelled it into the 21st century.

High-tech disaster and tough guy films come and go, and appear not to make the tiniest dent in the world of Bond; even the hugely successful string of Indiana Jones movies – surely the ultimate sort of jaunty, quirky, tongue-in-cheek and pell-mell action that the Bond films became – failed to quell anticipation for the Big One: the next Bond movie (or even – in the light of Brosnan's rumoured retirement – the next movie Bond). This is simply because – like diamonds – Bond is forever; the message has been clear for a long time – James Bond Will Be Back. Not, of course, that he ever went away.

Postscript: According to Ian Fleming, the name for his hero came to him when he registered on his bookcase at Goldeneye the spine of a much-loved work called *The Birds of the West Indies*, by James Bond. And 007? During Fleming's days at the Admiralty, he recalled, all top secret signals were prefixed with a double-0, and the memory lingered. But did you know that in a story by Agatha Christie, 'The Rajah's Emerald' (one of 12 in the *Listerdale Mystery*, 1934) the hero is called James Bond? Or that in Kipling's *The Day's Work* of 1898 there is a story entitled simply '.007'? Neither, apparently, did Fleming.

Trial by Jury
Clive Anderson

Trial by jury deserves its place in any collection of British greats. Certainly, it developed in a quintessentially British way. Jury trial was not the product of a logical codification of the law, nor did it leap, fully formed, from the mind of an inspired legislator. Rather, it started life as something completely different, took hundreds of years to evolve and is, in many respects, rather barmy. But that is how we like things in Britain.

It has to be said, too, that trial by jury flourishes rather more vigorously in America these days, though, in a way, even that underlines just how British the whole thing is; after all, so many great British ideas go on to greatness overseas.

But let us begin with the barmy. Under the jury system, important legal decisions are made by people specifically recruited because of their ignorance of the law. And having made a decision, they are neither required nor allowed to explain how they reached it. It is as though the treatment for a disease were to be decided not by the patient's doctors, but by a panel of people lacking any medical training and thereafter absolved of all responsibility for the treatment they prescribe. The reason why this seems such a good system is that, however mad or bad a jury may appear to be, at least it is better than leaving it to the judges.

The origins of the jury system in England can be traced back over a thousand years. It is not just that Magna Carta in 1215 famously maintained a freeman's right to be tried by his peers. In Anglo-Saxon times, 12 men could be sworn in to initiate criminal proceedings – a precursor of the Grand Jury, which performed a similar function in England until the early 20th century and which is still going strong in the USA to this day.

The Norman kings developed the swearing of oaths to tell the truth as a way of enforcing their rule, a procedure which in the 12th century Henry II adapted to a variety of judicial purposes. Local worthies who were expected to know something of the background of the case were brought in to resolve legal disputes. Once a litigant could get the magic number of 12 of these good men to swear in his favour, he was declared the winner. This was a jury system, but not yet quite as we know it.

Criminal cases in those days were actually decided by trial by ordeal – seeing if you could hold a red-hot bar without developing blisters and the like. Or there was trial by battle – having a fight until you or your opponent cried 'craven' and lost the case. Then in 1215 trial by ordeal was outlawed by the Pope. And trial by battle also fell into disuse. Something was needed to replace these outmoded if entertaining systems, and the tradition of swearing honourable men to resolve court cases was pressed into service. The jury trial was beginning to emerge.

In Scotland, which has a quite separate legal system from England, the jury was also developed to replace trial by ordeal. Scottish juries did not and do not have to be unanimous, as was the case until recently in England, and Scottish juries are made up of 15 people to allow for majority voting. The Scottish verdict of 'Not proven' allows the jury to return a rather cruel verdict which is not 'Guilty', but not quite 'Not guilty' either.

It is, however, the English form of the system which has formed the basis of jury trial in the English-speaking world. In 1968 in America, jury trial in criminal cases was held to be a constitutional right, and juries there are extensively used in civil cases. There is no such security of tenure for juries in Britain. With the exception of defamation, juries are no longer used in civil cases at all. And although with legal aid the number of criminal jury trials has expanded dramatically since the Second World War, that has in turn led to restrictions on the type of offence for which jury trial can be claimed by a defendant. There will be more to come if the government gets its way. In Northern Ireland, the troubles of the last few decades led to the suspension of jury trials because jurors could not be protected from intimidation.

The great merit of jury trial is that it gives the ordinary person a say in the system of justice. In 1670, Bushell's case established the jury's right to return the verdict it wanted, even if it contradicted the views of the judge. Thus, jurors can acquit if they think the law is unfair or they otherwise have sympathy for the accused. This they do not do perfectly. For all the acquittals returned by juries suspicious of the authorities, there have been many miscarriages of justice, notably in high-profile terrorist cases, which have not been detected by 12 good men and true.

But a jury trial is the setting for a courtroom drama like no other. Perhaps it is this aspect of real-life theatricality that has captured the imagination of the public over the years and will ensure its survival as an institution, however inconvenient or expensive it is to the authorities. At any rate, trial by jury is not as bad as burning your hand on a hot iron bar, or being tried by a bored magistrate.

To sum up: trial by jury may be said to be the least worst system on offer. It may be more accurately described as English or Scottish or American. But in the submission of the defence it is still entitled to be called one of Britain's greats. I rest my case.

The procession of King's Counsels at the opening of the Law Courts, 1913

Kew Gardens
Jane Fearnley-Whittingstall

Go down to Kew in lilac-time, in lilac-time, in lilac-time;
Go down to Kew in lilac-time (it isn't far from London!)
And you shall wander hand in hand with love in summer's wonderland;
Go down to Kew in lilac-time (it isn't far from London!).

(Alfred Noyes)

Kew (not far from London) was once a fashionable village beside the River Thames. Today it is a fashionable suburb easily reached from the city centre by train, bus, bicycle or boat. Considering its nearness to the centre, it is profligate of space. Even outside the walls of the Royal Botanic Gardens there is an open green large enough to play cricket on. The high stone and brick walls hide and protect 121 hectares of lawns, flower beds, shrubberies and woodland.

The British think they are the best gardeners in the world, and here is the proof they are right. Kew's unrivalled collection of useful and ornamental plants has been developed over nearly 250 years, a timescale which gives the landscape an air of mature tranquillity. Even at midsummer weekends, the wide green spaces and secluded glades of the gardens are never too crowded. Formal walks and avenues are broad enough to accommodate numerous families with toddlers and babies in buggies, and extensive, informal lawns allow groups to picnic without encroaching on each other. Branching off from the more frequented routes, serpentine paths leading from glade to glade allow you to lose yourself among stately trees.

The gardens cast their spell at all seasons. In winter, when they are deserted, you can indulge a taste for solitude and study the tactile bark and skeletal shapes of leafless trees. A sudden shower or gust of frosty wind may provide an excuse for retreating to the warmth of one of Kew's glass palaces: the Palm House, the Temperate House, or the Australian House. In the Princess of Wales Conservatory you will find the famous *Victoria amazonica*, the giant waterlily from Guyana, with surreal leaves two metres in diameter. Going from one glasshouse to another, you can visit a rainforest, a desert or an Alp.

Kew's glasshouses and other buildings add greatly to the gardens' charm. Kew Palace, a more intimate building than its name suggests, is a fine example of 17th-century domestic architecture. Its garden is planned to reflect the period of the house, with pleached *allées*, a nosegay garden, parterre, bee garden and box mound.

The multistoried Chinese Pagoda is a landmark visible from inside and outside the gardens, designed by William Chambers. He was commissioned to landscape the grounds in 1757 for Princess Augusta, widow of Frederick Prince of Wales and mother of George III.

A handsome Orangery (1761), now housing a restaurant and shop, was also designed by Chambers. Another convenient bolt-hole in bad weather is the Marianne North Gallery. It is a well-kept secret, invariably empty of visitors. Built in 1882, the mundane brick exterior conceals

---

The delights of the garden: poster for the cactus house at Kew Gardens

a multicoloured jewel box. Miss North was an interesting example of a type generally considered to be a typically British eccentric: a single woman, travelling in remote parts of the world with no regard for her personal safety and very little regard for her comfort. Her plant portraits were painted in jungles and on tropical islands. They positively vibrate with exotic colour.

Marianne North's paintings are just a tiny part of Kew's archive. The library houses over 750,000 botanical drawings, paintings and publications. The herbarium contains six million botanical specimens, and there are more than 30,000 types of plant growing in the gardens: resources which contribute to the Royal Botanical Gardens' international importance as a centre of scientific research.

From their beginning, the gardens were developed with a serious purpose. In 1759, Princess Augusta, with Lord Bute as her botanical adviser and William Aiton from Chelsea Physic Garden as head gardener, designated 3.5 hectares of her Kew estate to start a botanical garden. Thirty years later, Aiton was able to list 5,500 plants in his book *Hortus Kewensis*. When Princess Augusta died in 1772, her son George III combined the Kew estate with the neighbouring royal estate of Richmond, and appointed Sir Joseph Banks to oversee the enlarged garden. Banks was a man of immense energy and entrepreneurial skills, and under his direction the botanical garden progressed in leaps and bounds. He indulged a very British passion for collecting, by subsidising plant-hunters and organising expeditions all over the world, amassing a magnificent collection of plants of economic, scientific or horticultural interest.

Today, the declared mission of the gardens is 'to ensure better management of the Earth's environment by increasing our knowledge and understanding of the plant kingdom: the basis of life on Earth'. Kew is still sending explorers and researchers into the field, and in Kew's Jodrell Laboratory, scientific work continues in an atmosphere of growing urgency. The threat of global warming, the destruction of rainforests and industrial pollution have provided fresh incentives to discover and record endangered plant species, to test plants for medicinal qualities and to assess others as food crops. An important part of the work of Kew's researchers is the sharing and exchanging of information with other botanical centres throughout the world.

For Kew's living plant collections to thrive, a skilled team of gardeners is essential, and places on Kew's horticultural training schemes are much sought after; 'Kew-trained' on a young gardener's CV is practically a guarantee of a job almost anywhere in the world. For amateur gardeners, part of the fascination of a visit to Kew is to watch the team at work and, for some, to pester them with questions. Recently, the managers at Kew have responded to visitors' curiosity about horticultural methods used in the gardens by opening their compost-making operation to the public. A viewing platform overlooks the stable yard, where a classic recycling operation takes place. Every week, some 100 tonnes of plant waste from the gardens is augmented with 20 tonnes of horse manure from the stables of the Household Cavalry and the Metropolitan Police. The mixture is watered and turned daily and after just 12 weeks it forms compost that, after mechanical sieving, is ready for use in the gardens as a soil additive or mulch.

After two and a half centuries, the legacy of Kew's founders is still very much alive. Under Kew's patronage today, the great British tradition of plant collecting thrives in a world where there is still plenty to discover, and Kew's 21st-century scientists confidently focus far beyond the British Isles, looking at botany and horticulture with a worldwide perspective, just as their predecessors endeavoured to do.

Keynesian Economics
Will Hutton

Why are some countries, cities and towns richer than others? Why is there inflation and unemployment? Why do some companies prosper and others do not? Why does money matter? Are there rules and principles that underpin economic phenonema?

Economists have been struggling to explain economics for more than 200 years. The core or classical position is that we should understand economic forces as essentially natural. In the same way we respect nature to find its own answers and evolve through the survival of the fittest, so we should respect the capacity of the market economy to evolve and produce its own answers through a Darwinian process of economic selection. The market has natural laws; prices communicate all that any economic actor needs to know; all is for the best in this best of all possible worlds.

It is a pitiless message, and one with depressing implications for the human spirit. We cannot act on the economic world in any other way but as profit-maximising individuals and companies operating in capitalist markets; to do otherwise is to offend economic law. Governments, trade unions and any other non-market organisations get in the way of efficiency, harmony and growth.

It was the British economist John Maynard Keynes who put the humanity and spirit back into economics, and as such is the founding father of an alternative economic tradition which stresses the dynamics of economic behaviour and accepts an important role for government. He set out to demonstrate that market economies do not operate on a kind of economic auto-pilot; rather they can oscillate between boom and bust. That natural selection in economics means little more than the emergence of private monopoly. And that there was nothing inexorable about economic events. People, in the form of their governments, can shape the world if they choose.

His radical insight was that human beings operate in conditions of uncertainty. We find it hard enough to work out our own feelings and emotions in the here and now – but how we might react to events in the future and what those events might be is beyond our calculus. We are fundamentally at risk. The information we need to make good judgements cannot be in our possession, and the idea that it could be contained in nothing more than a price of a good or service is risible. Of course prices cannot tell us whether it is right to buy or sell now given what prices might be in the future or what our desires might be. We are reduced to acting on a hunch; to make bets; to find ways of laying off the risk. The notion that there are economic laws that can describe a route to some economic harmony or point of balance is silly.

Economics is rather a description of a process of permanent experimentation in which economic actors try to come to terms with risks and their own changing preferences. Moreover, because we buy and sell goods with money, and because when we abstain from buying necessarily we save, the financial system is the locus of all these instabilities; where we build up too much cash or borrow too much credit as we grow bearish or bullish about risk. The interest rate, the price of money, is helpless 'naturally' to co-ordinate all our decisions and feelings about risk. This is why the state has to stand by ready to soak up idle cash and spend it in recessions, or to cut its own spending when the market gets carried away and offers too much credit or carries stock market values too high in booms. Markets are much to be preferred to any other form of economic organisation, agreed Keynes, but to make them work well they need watching, monitoring and managing by a kindly and disinterested godfather – the state.

This is the heart of Keynesian economics. It may sound little more than common sense, but its policy implications are profound. What it meant in the 1930s, when Keynes published his most famous book, the *General Theory of Employment, Interest and Money*, was that the government should act as a spender and borrower of last resort. Instead of trying to balance the books in the recessionary circumstances of those times, it should borrow idle money and spend – preferably on schools, hospitals, roads and railways, but if necessary just on paying men to dig holes and then fill them up again. What you could not expect is that idle money would price itself into use; if people felt too bearish to borrow, then the money would remain idle, and so would factories and workers. The government had to act where the market would not.

Keynes was a lifelong liberal. His mission was to save capitalism from its worst excesses and proclivities through the wise intervention of the state. He was an important figure in Britain's economic management of the Second World War, and afterwards applied his insights to how the international trade and financial system should best be organised. Although he had to compromise his ambition to establish an international financial system which would allow countries time to get their international accounts in order if either in surplus or in deficit – essential, he thought, to avoid the inter-war plague of protectionism – the 'Bretton Woods' system of adjustable exchange rates established after the war was essential to post-war prosperity.

In short, Keynes reshaped not just economics and how governments set about managing the economy, but the international economic system. In doing so, he gave economic teeth to the liberal left everywhere, and authored a political as much as an economic philosophy – Keynesian social democracy. Although the Conservatives made a massive effort to discredit his ideas in the 1970s and 1980s, his world-view remains as valid as ever – if necessarily updated for our times. Very few economists anywhere have made such a notable impact; he and his ideas are an all-time British great.

Campaigning for the right to work: a badge from the Jarrow Hunger March, 1936

JARROW
PROTEST
MARCH
TO
LONDON.

The London Taxi
Stephen Bayley

The black cab is an example of that extraordinary British talent for doing unlikely things very well – only it has been much, much more successful than the hovercraft.

Since Checker Motors Corporation of Kalamazoo, Michigan, abandoned production of its own mighty Model A8 cab in 1982, only the British – alone among the inhabitants of planet earth – have had a purpose-built taxi. Even the French, normally ingenious in matters of vehicle design, make do with ordinary cars: a Paris taxi is a family Peugeot, Citroën or Mercedes-Benz in working clothes. New Yorkers now get by with wallowing Ford Crown Victorias or Chevrolet Caprices, whose only concessions to passenger comfort are slick vinyl seat-covers and whose only concessions to convenience are yellowing bullet-proof plexiglass partitions to isolate the monosyllabic Armenian or Nigerian from the passenger space.

In comparison, the British taxi seems immeasurably more civilised. You might even say that the black cab is a miniature of British values, the sensible shoes of the global transport system: ubiquitous (except when it rains), reliable, decent, practical, distinctive, but unostentatious.

At the same time, to trace the DNA of the black cab is to explore the eccentric pathways of British social and industrial history. The cab's unique architectural space – quite unlike any other motor vehicle ever made – was laid down by the original Hackney Carriage legislation of 1834, which required that there was space by the driver for a bale of hay, and assumed that passengers would be wearing headgear requiring ample vertical accommodation. Never mind that nowadays the hay space tends to be reserved for used tabloid newspapers, old mineral water bottles and trainers: it's a touching reminder of horsedrawn days. As, indeed, is the name: 'hackney' has nothing to do with the London borough, but comes from the Old French *haquenée*, which means a horse for hire (from which we derive, even more incidentally, the derisive term 'hack'). With a nice poetry appropriate to so efficient a vehicle, a 'hack' was usually a cross between a racehorse and carthorse.

France has had a further influence in this history, or at least in this etymology. 'Cab' is from cabriolet, an open tourer. Again, we get the term 'taxi' itself from the taximeters which measured the fares on the old dobbin-powered fiacres (the sort mentioned in the old Baedeker guides, the ones that take you from Central Station to Grand Hotel for a few *sous* or *centimes*). Again, the modern black cab can be traced directly back to a French import of 1902, when a firm called Mann & Overton brought a Unic taxi into London, to join a handful of spluttering Fiats and Panhards.

The next event in this evolution was the founding, in 1919 in Coventry, of a firm called Carbodies, a specialist coach-builder supplying Jaguar and Rolls-Royce. (The same company, perhaps rather less grandly, up to 1964 supplied Ford with the bodies for Consul, Zephyr and Zodiac convertibles.) It was a collaboration between taxi specialists Mann & Overton and Carbodies immediately after the last war that produced the 1948 Austin FX3. Relatively short-lived, the FX3 was replaced 10 years later by the FX4. Following takeovers

by Manganese Bronze in 1973 and 1984, Carbodies and Mann & Overton were merged to form London Taxis International.

Definitive is a sometimes carelessly used term, but the 1958 Austin FX4 was the definitive black cab against which all its predecessors, competitors and successors have to be judged. And the judgement was that here is an astonishing success of intuitive design. Charles Eames, the legendary American furniture designer, said the FX4 was 'the best piece of industrial design in the world'. In terms of vehicle technology it was primitive even by the standards of its day, with its heavy ladder-frame chassis, its atrociously cumbersome steering, noisily underpowered flatulent diesel and forward visibility like that from the turret of a tank, from which the cab also derived many of its handling characteristics.

The sensible shoes of the global transport system: the black cab in action

Great designs can be measured by two things. The first is whether they can be improved by having anything taken away or having much added. The FX4 passes this test. The second is longevity, and in terms of design life the FX4's only rivals have been the Land Rover (*b*.1948), the Mini (*b*.1959) and the Porsche 911 (*b*.1963). But unlike these cars, the old black cab was never a masterpiece of technology. Instead, its supreme achievement was passenger ergonomics: a superb mobile controlled environment offering a perfect combination of protection and seclusion with accessibility and visibility, cosseting and convenient, even with crude rubber mats and plastic upholstery. I have myself slept and written articles in the back of black cabs. I have held conversations and given interviews. I have had lunch, read, wept, laughed, made 'phone calls – although, since my period of using cabs has not coincided with my Romeo phase, my catalogue of cab-borne achievements cannot rival that of Alan Brien, who claimed in 1972: 'I have done almost every human activity inside a taxi that does not require main drainage.'

Eighty-eight thousand FX4s were manufactured over 38 years. From birth in 1958 to its death on 7 October 1997, many inherent technological shortcomings were smoothed by evolutionary development, and the final version – known as the Fairway – included refinements undreamt of in 1958, including wheelchair access and an advanced (Japanese) engine. Nevertheless, as a remaining token of British heritage, the FX4 retained its flat windscreen, headlights borrowed from a Mini and rear lights cannibalised from the Mark II Austin 1100.

There is something peculiarly British in the fact that the person responsible for this last version of the FX4 had wanted to be a policeman, not a taxi-designer. Jevon Thorpe was also responsible for the TXI, the new black cab that London Taxis International introduced in late 1997. Just as Volkswagen cleverly reinterpreted the original Beetle, so Thorpe, with great finesse, reinterpreted the black cab. The TXI accepts all the civilised assumptions of its classic predecessor, but provides a far higher level of vehicle dynamics and quality, as well as far superior driver and passenger comforts. It is the modern black cab: what it offers is just like that first sip of gin and tonic – a tangible sense of relief.

Society women used to whisper 'NSIT' to their daughters. The 'not safe in taxis' imprecation warned the girls against the gropings of companions taking advantage of the capacious privacy of a black cab's passenger cell. Lust apart, there are few safer places to be than a British taxi: while the Metropolitan Police has no control over what goes on in the back of the cab, it is fastidious about what goes on in the front. Taxi drivers not only have The Knowledge, they must also have The Integrity. The greatest danger facing a black cab passenger is an opinionated rant about the *issues du jour* or the recent performance of Arsenal.

The black cab is a unique design that has created a unique culture. When I am somewhere wretched abroad and I want to be reminded of home, there is no more certain method than to imagine lying in bed in London on a rainy night and then hearing the distinctive clatter of the black cab diesel and the signature door-slam as a neighbour leaves the security of the taxi for the less certain wet and windy street. Immediately, it summons up a particular vision of Britain: eccentric, decent, convenient, safe, comforting. The best of Britain on wheels.

The Longbows of Agincourt
Robert Hardy

'Be it thy cause to busy giddy minds with foreign quarrels,' says Shakespeare's Henry IV to his son Hal, who was to become Henry V, the victor of Agincourt – the best-known and best-documented battle of the Hundred Years War. As so often, Shakespeare has his finger on the pulse of history, and in his *Henry V* the new young King says:

> I will keep my state,
> Be like a king and show my sail of greatness
> When I do rouse me in my throne of France!

Claiming that throne, as his great-grandfather Edward III had done, Henry Plantagenet invaded France just two years after his coronation, laying siege to Harfleur on 18 August 1415. With him were 2,000 knights and men-at-arms, 8,000 longbowmen and 65 gunners. There were priests and cooks, sappers and pioneers, farriers, painters, armourers, tentmakers, bowyers and fletchers, masons, cordwainers, carters, turners and carpenters. There were dukes at a daily rate of 13 shillings and fourpence; earls at six and eightpence; barons at four shillings; knights, esquires and men-at-arms at two shillings, one-and-sixpence, and a shilling respectively. The thousands of longbowmen were paid a new rate of sixpence a day.

The siege lasted well into September, and by the time the town surrendered, war, heat, desertion and disease had taken a rough toll of Henry's army. His war council advised him to call it a day, go home, raise more money and troops and continue the campaign in the spring, but an almost mystical belief in his destiny determined him to overrule them and march to English-held Calais, some 150 miles to the north, through hostile territory. Such was his faith in himself and his archers – his 'yew hedge' he called them – that the depleted army marched out of the north gate of Harfleur on 8 October.

We can be pretty sure of the numbers that accompanied Henry: his chaplain counted 900 knights and men-at-arms and 5,000 archers, marching through Normandy in unseasonably bad weather to a very uncertain future, but held in the hand of an inspired leader. Their hope of crossing the Somme by the ford that Edward III had fought his way through before Crécy was lost when they found it blocked and heavily guarded, and for the next week the drenched and tattered army moved eastwards, feeling for a crossing, which they eventually found on the 19th. There followed another week of marching north-west in appalling weather, dogged by the French, whose massive and ominous tracks they came upon in the mud, crossing their line of march.

On the 24th, they reached a little river, the Ternoise at Blangy, and pushed up the steep incline beyond it. A scout came spurring back, and as each contingent reached the top they saw the vast army of the French moving slowly up the open valley to their right. Henry drew up his army for battle, but in the fading October light the French moved on behind the woods until they reappeared ahead, right across the road to Calais through the flat country between the villages of Maisoncelles, Tramecourt and Azincourt: three great masses of men and horses, gleaming with armour and lances, forested with bright heraldic banners – 'in multitudes compared with us,' said the chaplain, 'an innumerable host of locusts'. Henry heard Sir Walter Hungerford say he wished they had 'ten thousand more good English archers, who would gladly have been there'. Henry replied: 'You speak as a fool... I would not have one more even if I could... The God of Heaven... can bring down the pride of these Frenchmen, who so boast of their numbers and their strength.'

On the morning of 25 October, St Crispin's Day, the two armies drew up for battle, the giant and the dwarf, the disproportion estimated at anything between three to one and 10 to one. The three masses of the French were crowded one behind the other; the English had 6,000 men on a front of approximately 1,000 yards, the 900 lances in three small battalions – 'battles' – four men deep, the much greater force of archers on their flanks. The movement of either army was limited by the woods of Tramecourt to the east and Azincourt to the west.

Argument continues as to the exact formation of the archers: two contemporaries who were there speak of them being 'in two wings' and 'at the two sides of the men-at-arms'; while the chaplain, sitting on his horse to the rear, says they were 'in blocks (or wedges) intermixed with each battalion'. What is certain is that they must, however placed, have occupied much more ground than the men-at-arms, and that they would have been positioned so as to have their whole front, and the enemy's, within their shooting range – about 300–350 yards.

No doubt they were a raggedy mob to look at, those 5,000 archers, but they represented a broad cross-section of the tough rural population of England and Wales. They were men used to living by physical labour and the strength of their bodies – a strength developed from their early years, through practice enforced by statute, into great skill with the longbow. At Agincourt that strength and ability were goaded into supreme action by despair. They were up against fearful odds, yet somehow their extraordinary leader kept them together and summoned their spirit for them. Henry had also told them the French would cut off the drawing fingers of every archer captured. They meant to die hard. They were sure of their familiar weapons, heavy yew longbows which could shoot mail- and plate-piercing war arrows at a minimum rate of 10 arrows a minute. (Five thousand men shooting – do the sums!) If the weapons found in the Tudor *Mary Rose* were typical of those used 130 years earlier, these longbows would have had a draw-weight ranging from 100–170 pounds, which the archer would have had to hold briefly at an average full draw of some 30 inches – and this after a march of 260 miles in 17 days with only one day's rest.

Since crossing the Somme, each archer had carried a pointed stake, which on this morning of battle he drove into the soft ground before him, angled breast-high towards the enemy. Onto those pointed stakes the French flank cavalry lumbered through the mud and the huzzing arrow storm until, maddened with pain, the survivors plunged back into the front line which was advancing on foot behind them, funnelling into the narrowing space between the woods where Henry had established his final line. When the armies crashed together and the archers could no longer shoot, they abandoned bows and quivers and went in with sword and maul, dagger and war-hammer, mounting on the growing piles of French dead to strike at those below who came on into the shambles, pressed by the thousands still

behind them. As one French writer put it: 'the superiority of the English archers rested in their ability to transform themselves in an instant into men-at-arms… French archers could do nothing beyond drawing their bows.'

After the battle, the exhausted, triumphant army slept where they had the night before. In the morning, they marched through the heaps of stripped dead (between 6,000 and 10,000 of them), and as they passed the files of French prisoners it is said that they mockingly held up the first two fingers of their right hands – their drawing fingers – thus, if the story is true, giving birth to the V-sign. St Crispin's had been a monstrous day, but at the end of it it was to the ordinary men of England, the yeomen of the shires and their many Welsh colleagues, with their simple longbow and their giant spirit, that the victory of Agincourt belonged.

Henry V's 'yew hedge': the longbows at Agincourt in Laurence Olivier's 1944 film

Longitude
Robin Knox-Johnston

Imagine setting off in your car towards a known destination with no speedometer to tell you how many miles you have gone, a hand-drawn and inaccurate map, and consequently no real idea of the direction and distance you need to travel. Furthermore, there are no signposts. Well, that was how navigators had to work their way across oceans right up to the 18th century. Whilst (thanks to the Portuguese tabling the sun's movements in 1485) they could work out their latitude – their distance from the equator – using the sun at its highest elevation at noon, they had no accurate means of establishing their longitude, namely how far east or west they were.

Instruments existed to measure the altitude of heavenly bodies, such as the astrolabe and later the cross-staff; and around 1596, John Davis, the greatest of the English Elizabethan navigators, produced an even better instrument, the back-staff, which could produce an accurate latitude to within a few miles. But latitude is only half the answer to finding a position. To complete the 'fix', you need to know the longitude as well. It was known how to calculate longitude from the altitude of the sun taken with one of these instruments, and even if a misreading of a minute of arc could mean a mile's discrepancy in position, that was still a huge improvement on what was available before. But the calculation to produce this result depended upon accurate timekeeping – accurate to within seconds – and no timepiece of such accuracy had ever been created.

Without longitude, navigation was a bit of a hit-or-miss operation as the European nations developed trading routes in the 16th and 17th centuries. By observing how long a piece of wood took to drift past the ship they could work out their speed through the water; and their compasses would show them the course they had taken. But if the water was moving, as it does in the ocean currents of the world, or if their ship was experiencing leeway – drifting due to the effect of the wind – they had no means of establishing the quantity of this drift. On a long voyage this could amount to a considerable mileage, and land could be found late or, far more dangerous, early.

The cost in lost ships and lives was enormous. Millions of pounds and thousands of lives were lost by the Portuguese alone on the South African coast, as ship after ship was wrecked on the voyage back from India. Not until longitude could be calculated was it realised that in places the coast was up to 60 miles east of where it was shown on the existing charts.

Although it was an Englishman, Francis Drake, who completed the second successful circumnavigation of the world, and English sailors were voyaging across the Atlantic, England remained a small player in maritime trade right through the 16th century. However, the defeat of the Spanish Armada in 1588 gave England new confidence at sea, and by the end of Elizabeth I's reign, English seamen were challenging the Spanish and making their first tentative forays into international trade. Perhaps more importantly, they were beginning to study and understand the science of navigation, as demonstrated by John Davis' back-staff.

Britain's overseas trade grew rapidly during the 17th century, with the establishment of colonies in North America and the expansion of the East India Company. This commercial activity brought the need to maintain a strong fleet to fend off any further Armadas and to check the challenge from the Dutch, who had developed their East Indies trade more quickly and were jealous of competition. The expansion in shipping created an economic and naval pressure to find a means of calculating longitude. Under Charles II, the Revd John Flamsteed was created 'Astronomical Observator' with the task of 'correcting the tables of all heavenly bodies for the use of seamen', and in 1675 the Observatory was constructed at Greenwich for the advancement of navigation and nautical astronomy. As no accurate mechanical timepiece yet existed, this Observatory was trying to establish whether the passage of the planets past the stars could be predicted with accuracy and if it could provide an alternative means of astronomical timekeeping to help the navigator.

If the British Government needed any reminder of the importance of the problem, it came in 1707 when HMS *Association*, the 90-gun flagship of Sir Clowdisley Shovell, was wrecked on the Scilly Islands, many miles from where she thought she was. To provide some impetus to the search for a solution, a Board of Longitude was established in 1714. Recognising that the solution lay in accurate timepieces, the Board offered a reward of £20,000 to anyone who could produce a chronometer that would provide accuracy to within 30 miles on a six-week voyage to the West Indies. The sum was an absolute fortune in those days – more than sufficient to buy a major warship – which gives an indication of the desperation to find a solution. The story of John Harrison, the Yorkshire carpenter who produced four chronometers over 25 years to win the prize, is now well known. (All four of these magnificent instruments are on display at the National Maritime Museum at Greenwich.) Sadly, Harrison spent the last years of his life trying to obtain the second half of the proffered reward, which was not granted to him until 1773, three years before he died. But to him, as much as anyone, goes the credit for the establishment of Greenwich Mean Time.

The astounding success of Harrison's chronometer in service with Captain James Cook on his second voyage demonstrated that the problem of calculating longitude had finally been resolved. Only a few years earlier, in 1731, another Englishman, John Hadley, had produced his quadrant, in reality an octant, from which the sextant was shortly afterwards developed. This could give far more precise altitudes of heavenly bodies than Davis' backstaff, and as a result accurate position-keeping at sea at last became possible, provided the sun, moon, stars or planets were visible. Cook had an error of less than eight miles in longitude on his return from his second voyage around the world – a phenomenal result for those times which would be creditable even today.

Cook's voyage marks the end of the era of guessing a vessel's position and of 100 years of development by English astronomers, instrument-makers and navigators of systems and instruments which at last gave seamen the means to work out where they were on the earth's surface. Cook's charts are amazingly accurate, in part due to his own abilities as a navigator, but also because he had the means to calculate positions with previously unheard-of precision. Ships continued to be wrecked, since a position derived from astronomical observations is dependent on the heavenly bodies being visible, and cloud, rain or fog often prevent this. But at least when a known heavenly body could be seen, the navigator could find out where he was, even if he might have to fall back on his log and compass when the sky was obscured.

Recently, man-made satellites using radio waves have enabled navigators to pinpoint their position day or night regardless of the weather. But for 200 years, until the 1970s, it was on the same basic equipment that Captain Cook used – equipment invented and developed by Englishmen – that they relied to establish their whereabouts as they travelled the oceans of the world.

Navigator, explorer and inventor John Davis' back-staff

Wordsworth and Coleridge's Lyrical Ballads
Neil Wenborn

Lyrical Ballads is a book rooted in the English countryside. It was conceived on a West Country walking tour. Its subjects are drawn for the most part from rural life. And its language is designedly that of everyday working folk in the fields and villages of late 18th-century Britain.

The book was the fruit of the most fertile year of perhaps the most fertile partnership in the history of English poetry. Deeply troubled though their relationship was later to be, in 1797–98 William Wordsworth and Samuel Taylor Coleridge were living as near neighbours amid the rolling scenery of the Quantocks in Somerset, where they spent almost every day in each other's company, talking endlessly about poetry, philosophy and politics, and making grand plans for the projects they would develop together.

It was on a winter walking tour to the romantic wildness of the Valley of Stones near Lynmouth that the two young men, accompanied by Wordsworth's devoted sister Dorothy, sowed the seed of a new work that was destined to change the course of English literature. They decided to collaborate on a poem and sell it to pay for the trip. The idea gathered pace like a rolling snowball, and by the spring of 1798 the projected collaboration had expanded into a book. The publication itself, a collection of two dozen anonymous poems, most of them by Wordsworth, appeared a few months later, in September 1798.

The title – *Lyrical Ballads with a few other poems* – hints at the 'work-in-progress' character of the project. It is also rather misleading. Few of the poems are ballads in the traditional sense, and conventional lyricism is deliberately avoided. Most therefore belong to the 'few other' category. Nor at first sight do they seem to have a lot in common, despite the claims of Wordsworth's prefatory 'Advertisement'. Take, for example, the two long poems which serve as a sort of frame for the collection – Coleridge's famous 'Rime of the Ancyent Marinere', with its deliberately archaic diction and nightmare gothic imagery, and Wordsworth's measured philosophical meditation 'Lines written a few miles above Tintern Abbey'. They hardly seem to belong to the same century, let alone the same book.

So why did this slim volume come to establish itself as one of the defining texts of English Romanticism, and why has it continued to exert its power over generations of readers?

Today, some of the poems are so familiar that it is hard to recapture the force of their novelty in 1798. Now everybody knows (if many misquote) the Ancient Mariner's 'Water, water, every where / Ne any drop to drink', or the concluding lines of the same poem: 'A sadder and a wiser man / He rose the morrow morn.' But this familiarity obscures the fact that *Lyrical Ballads* was a self-consciously *avant garde* enterprise. Wordsworth himself described the poems as 'experiments'. The language was deliberately non-literary, almost conversational, the subject-matter mainly based on incidents in 'low and rustic life'. There had of course been a pastoral tradition in English poetry as least as far back as Spenser's *Shepheardes Calender* in the 16th century. But the situations Wordsworth in particular chose for his contributions to the book were largely uncharted territory – the ramblings of a deranged mother, the untrammelled perceptions of young children, the tribulations of a female tramp.

Other poems, such as 'The Thorn', the ballad of 'Goody Blake and Harry Gill', and most famously the 'Ancient Mariner' itself, are based on tales of the supernatural. What unites them all, however, is their attempt, as Coleridge later put it, at 'awakening the mind's attention to the lethargy of custom, and directing it to the loveliness and the wonders of the world before us'.

Wordsworth expected the book's first readers to be confused and disorientated, to look for poetry and find only 'strangeness and awkwardness'. Indeed, that was exactly what he and Coleridge wanted. *Lyrical Ballads* was meant to unsettle the preconceptions of the poetry-reading audience of its time, brought up on what Wordsworth dismisses as 'the gaudiness and inane phraseology of many modern writers'. This was a new kind of poetry, and one which required a new kind of language and a new kind of response. Above all, it required the stripping down of poetic diction to its bare essentials. On occasion, this results in lines of notorious bathos, as when the garrulous narrator of 'The Thorn' says of a mysterious pond: 'I've measured it from side to side: / 'Tis three feet long, and two feet wide.' At its best, it creates a medium of extraordinary transparency, perfectly adapted both to that 'spontaneous overflow of powerful feelings' which Wordsworth saw as the essence of great poetry, and to the direct communion between man and nature which lies at the heart of the *Lyrical Ballads*.

> Come forth into the light of things,
> Let nature be your teacher

Wordsworth writes in one of the finest of the poems, 'The Tables Turned', and goes on to set out the profoundly moral, almost religious, dimension of that tutelage:

> One impulse from a vernal wood
> May teach you more of man,
> Of moral evil and of good
> Than all the sages can.
>
> Sweet is the lore which nature brings;
> Our meddling intellect
> Misshapes the beauteous forms of things;
> – We murder to dissect.
>
> Enough of science and of art;
> Close up these barren leaves;
> Come forth, and bring with you a heart
> That watches and receives.

This is the Romantic world-view in a nutshell. And for a key to its enduring appeal one need look no further than Wordsworth's own Preface to the much expanded second edition, in which he spoke of 'the encreasing [sic] accumulation of men in cities, where the uniformity of their occupations produces a craving for extraordinary incident which

the rapid communication of intelligence hourly gratifies'. If on the threshold of the 19th century the *Lyrical Ballads* were conceived, in part, as an antidote to the pressures of British urban living in an age of information explosion, how much more relevant are they to us at the beginning of the 21st.

'A sadder and a wiser man': the Ancient Mariner blesses the watersnakes in the moonlight (Gustave Doré, 1875)

Magna Carta
Asa Briggs

Runnymede, by the Thames, a great meadow between Staines and Windsor, is a very English place. It was there on Monday 15 June 1215 that King John, in what Winston Churchill called 'a quiet short scene', sealed the hastily drafted parchment document that came to be known as the Great Charter – Magna Carta.

It was called 'great' – 'magna' – not for the same reasons that 'the Great War' or 'the Great Reform Act' were called great, but simply because it was long. It had a total of 63 clauses, most of them highly practical in intent, some now very difficult to understand. No fewer than 24 of the 63 clauses, on a strict interpretation, dealt specifically with taxation – always a political topic of importance in any generation, though 13th-century taxation was as different from 20th-century taxation as 13th-century technology or politics. The fact that John sealed the document rather than signed it is almost as big a difference, but it did not stop 19th-century painters from depicting him vividly with a pen in his hand.

The document must be related in the first instance to a dramatic sequence of events during the 17 years of the reign of King John, from 1199 to 1216. In his play about him Shakespeare did not once mention Magna Carta or Runnymede. There was plenty to write about without doing so. Clever, restless, agile, cruel and ruthless, John had quarrelled bitterly not only with his barons, but with merchants and with the Church. There was more than one crisis. In 1204 he lost the whole of Normandy. In 1209 he was excommunicated by Pope Innocent III. In 1213, faced with the threat of foreign invasion, he yielded to the Pope, making England a fief of the Papacy. He was forced to accept the English-born papal nominee for the Archbishop of Canterbury, Stephen Langton, made a Cardinal by Innocent in 1206, who exacted from him an oath 'to restore the good laws of his predecessors… and to do justice to all men according to the judgements of his court'.

Langton played an important part in the creation of the coalition of John's opponents, who made their way to Runnymede after John had failed in an attempt to restore his military fortunes in France, an attempt which involved exceptionally repressive taxation. The barons drafted a list of demands which John did not accept, and went on to present him with the text of Magna Carta, a feudal document which looked both forwards and backwards and to which he attached his seal.

There was a precedent in a coronation charter of promises made by Henry I when he came to the throne. There were many sequels too, for the Charter in revised form was to be reissued many times, and at the end of the 13th century was the first document to be recorded in a new statute-roll. Its language was subsequently to be incorporated in many non-feudal documents, produced in very different circumstances, like the Petition of Right presented to a very different king, Charles I, in 1628, the Habeas Corpus Act of 1679, and the 14th Amendment to the Constitution of the United States, passed in 1868 after the American Civil War.

'The historic rights of Englishmen': the Magna Carta manuscript

John's own reign did not end until 1216, and the immediate effect of the Charter's sealing was royal repudiation and baronial insurrection. Almost at once, the king abjured what he had solemnly sealed, winning the support of about half the country's barons and of the Pope whose vassal he now was. The remaining barons, however, invoked Clause 61 of the Charter and declared a feudal rebellion (*diffidatio*) against the King. John died before the contest was resolved, although after it began, with the help of mercenaries, castle after castle fell to his armies, and the insurrectionaries called in Prince Louis, heir to the King of France, to assist them. John's death radically changed the situation, for the regents of his successor, his nine-year-old son the young King Henry III, now reissued a shorter version of Magna Carta – and Louis was persuaded by various means to return to France.

When royal powers were restored in 1225, a still shorter version was produced, cut down by a third from its original size to 42 clauses instead of 63, and this is the version usually referred to during the centuries that followed. Enshrined in the constitution, it pledged all kings to uphold 'the law of the land', by which was meant the common law. For one outstanding 20th-century Englishman, the lawyer Lord Denning, among his other duties for 20 years Chairman of the Commission on Historical Manuscripts, the common law, along with the English language, was at the very heart of the national heritage.

None the less, the language of Magna Carta was riddled with what would now be called 'jargon', feudal jargon; and it was not common law, but feudal law that was set out in it. 'Liberties' meant baronial privileges. The concordat between king and subjects was based on feudal contract. The great 17th-century lawyer, Sir Edward Coke, Lord Chief Justice, who made use of Magna Carta in the constitutional conflicts of his period, did not interpret it in this way, but rather in terms of 'fundamental law', picking out in particular clauses like 'No free man shall be arrested, or detained in prison, or deprived of his freehold unless by lawful judgement of his peers and by the law of the land.'

It is the presence in Magna Carta of such clauses, which include 'To none shall we sell, refuse or delay, right and justice', which have converted it from a feudal English document of its time into a universal timeless declaration. It has become a precious symbol rather than a piece of parchment, with originals kept in Lincoln Cathedral, from which it paid a brief visit to Australia, and the British Museum. It has even been compared with the Ten Commandments and with the Twelve Tablets of ancient Rome. In its national context, it seems to enshrine 'the historic rights of Englishmen' – not abstract rights, but rights rooted in the distant past.

Welsh Male Voice Choirs
Neil Kinnock

Picture the Thracian Orpheus on board the Argo *with a lyre in his arms, singing so sweetly that he c
ould charm beasts and even rocks. See him in the Underworld, pursuing his beloved Eurydice, killed
by snakebite and allowed to return to life as long as her tormented tenor did not turn to gaze at her.
Adoration overcame caution. He looked longingly. She expired permanently. But his sadness did not subdue
him even then. When he met his death – and suffered dismemberment by the Thracian women – his
severed head was still singing as it washed up on the shores of Lesbos. A dedicated musical man is truly
hard to silence…*

Three millennia later, economic refugees from the rural areas flocked to the coalfields of
South and North Wales in their scores of thousands. To the shanty villages, and then the
stone-built towns, they brought traditions of non-conformist chapel singing, the memories of
folk songs, and the habits of unrehearsed musical exuberance on *nosonau llawen* (happy nights).

They also brought great thirst. Alcohol was the only intoxicant that compared with religion
in driving the ache out of muscles, inducing amnesia about the danger and insecurity of
work, and lightening the drabness of homes and streets. Prayer and pints numbed adversity.
And in chapel and pub, misery was suppressed by song. For the men at least.

In every village and town, battle was then joined between booze and Bible. The brewers
multiplied and prospered. And the Temperance movement developed some cunning tactics
in its holy war on the Drink and its devastating effects. Sunday Schools and the Band of
Hope offered children extra education, messages of divine love, down-to-earth discipline,
jolly hymns, cakes, 'pop' and trips to the seaside. Bible classes and mothers' circles gave
respite and respectability to women. And for the men, organised singing in choirs – with
piano, organ or accordion accompaniment and a real conductor – came to combat the
temptations of the tap room and to celebrate fellowship and the joy of making true music.

Orpheus was their chosen patron. And Orpheus Male Voice Choirs spread like migrant
starlings across the Welsh coalfields. By the 1880s they were an organic part of every
community, growing alongside the brass and silver bands that had arrived from Germany *via*
England and the British and Salvation Armies. Philanthropic (and enterprising) employers
sponsored them. Posh people patronised them. And, in full imperial splendour, Queen
Victoria heard them at Windsor Castle. History does not record whether she was 'amused'.
But the Choristers were. National recognition of their prowess – and two days off work with
'All Found' – guaranteed that.

The repertoire of the choirs started with hymns already beloved at the *Cymanfau Ganu*
(religious singing festivals) in the gigantic thousand-seater chapels being built in the mining
valleys. It quickly spread to oratorio selections and special arrangements of religious anthems.
The sweet, strong and savage choruses of Verdi and Wagner ensured that *Nabucco, Tannhäuser,
Il Trovatore* and every other snatch of grand opera that could be sung in four parts was added
to the concert list.

Lachrymose late Victorian ballads, military marches, bouncy bits from operettas, Coleridge Taylor thrillers, spirituals and special settings of psalms were adapted for 80 or 100 voices. Glee Parties of 12 or 20 sprouted like multiple offspring. And the blessing of tonic *sol fa* meant that everyone able to sing a scale could make music and harmonise without formal tuition.

The century rolled on through wars and strikes and slump. In most of South Wales the Male Voice Choirs endured through the 1950s and 1960s, staggering a little as unprecedented affluence provided other social diversions, shrinking in some places as coal mines closed, the steel industry receded and communities aged. But by the 1970s national and international tours, modernised repertoires, and the simple desire for company and creativity were all providing new strength – and that has been sustained.

To sing in a good Orpheus Choir is to be uplifted. Collective control and individual self-expression come together. Parts practiced solo in bathrooms and rehearsed on week nights by the full choir (overtime and shifts permitting) meld in harmony. Rousing blasts of music, crescendos, alleluias and amens inject power straight to the veins. In full confident voice a hundred men can bend windows and crack paint. To stand among them singing your soul out is to know that Joshua's choristers really could have brought down Jericho's walls. Then – *diminuendo, pianissimo* – soothing, sobbing whispers of reverence or sadness or choking passion stroke the heart. To share in passages so softly sung that the breathing is louder is to be part of a miracle of soughing, disciplined moderation.

The rules of engagement are simple but stern: know the piece, know your part, never sing so loudly that you can't hear the man next to you, remember that shouting is a sin, and never – but never – take your eyes off the baton. Conductors plead: 'Look at me. Look at me even when you *think* you know the piece better than your own secrets.' They order: 'Let me *hear* the words clearly. The words *are* the music.' They rebuke: 'You can't sing straight if you don't stand straight. Heels on the floor, heads up. Now – let's do it *right* this time.'

Then the concert comes. Performances as favours for old age pensioner gatherings, festival events in Ottawa or Pretoria, Prague or Pittsburgh, the lethal gladiatorial competition in the *Eisteddfodau Genedlaethol* (national Eisteddfods), thousand-voice epics at the Royal Albert Hall, TV appearances to provide backing for Shirley Bassey, Tom Jones, Denis O'Neill or Bryn Terfel – all get the same commitment. Only the clothes change – smart blazers, matching ties and knife-sharp trouser creases for the day and early evening events, tuxedos and bow ties for the night performances. And, after the show, the singing spills into musical merriment of every kind. When the hosts have laid on refreshments at the concert venues, or pubs are invaded, or as the choir bus heads homeward, the songs go on. But then the repertoire changes radically. Beatles and Beachboys, Max Bygraves and Max Boyce, Rice and Lloyd Webber, Country & Western and – inevitably – hymns and love songs from every generation and many countries bubble from solos, duets, quartets and *le tout ensemble*, generally with wives ('the lady supporters of the Choir to whom we owe so much') joining in. Harmonising, naturally.

Orpheus is alive and well and – when not globetrotting – living in Wales. I hope that some of his sons will come to sing at my funeral. If I don't join in, I'll definitely be dead.

A principal tenor at the end of his shift at the Abercynon Colliery, 1951

Mallory and Irvine's Bid to Climb Everest
Stephen Venables

In the whole history of mountain exploration, nothing haunts the imagination so vividly as the account by the geologist, Noel Odell, of his last sight of George Mallory and Sandy Irvine disappearing from view, close to the inviolate summit of Mount Everest at 12.50 a.m. on 8 June 1924. 'Another black spot became apparent and moved up the snow to join the other on the crest. The first then approached the great rock-step and shortly emerged at the top; the second did likewise. Then the whole fascinating vision vanished, enveloped in cloud once more.' The discovery of Mallory's body 75 years later may have answered a few questions, but we still do not know whether he and Irvine reached the summit on that fateful day. The mystery remains satisfyingly unsolved, the poignancy of it all reinforced by the sight of that injured body, resting high on the North Face, in its bleached layers of wool and tweed.

Of all the relics brought down by the 1999 search expedition before they buried Mallory where he lay, perhaps the most poignant of all was the unpaid bill, found in one of his pockets, for two pairs of fives gloves. What a touchingly incongruous memorial to find on those desolate wind-scoured scree slopes high above the Tibetan plateau, 5,000 miles from the Surrey public school where, as a master, he must have played that esoteric, quintessentially British game! And yet, thank God, he rose above the prevailing heartiness evoked so depressingly by one of his pupils, Robert Graves, in *Goodbye to All That*. He loved literature and was a darling of the Bloomsbury set. He moved in intellectual circles and his mountaineering was informed by a strong aesthetic sense.

Mallory has often been depicted as a fanatic, dangerously obsessed with Everest. In fact, as his housemaster at Winchester, R L C Irving, pointed out, Mallory only drifted accidentally into mountaineering during a school visit to the Alps when he was already 18. A natural athlete, with a fine sense of balance and daring, he proved an elegant mountaineer, prompting Irving to write that 'climbing with him was inseparable from artistry'. Seventeen years later, in 1921, when the first British reconnaissance expedition set out for Everest, Mallory, one of the few younger climbers to have survived the trenches, was an obvious choice, recruited, in the time-honoured British fashion, through the old boy network. Of all the Everest expeditions, that reconnaissance was the most gloriously exciting. Mallory's letters to his wife Ruth overflow with the romantic thrill of discovery, but when he returned in 1922 for the first full attempt at the summit – and then again in 1924 – some of the thrill was diluted by moments of doubt and boredom with the long, dusty march across Tibet.

Far from being a fanatic, Mallory displayed a healthy ambivalence. Both he and many of his colleagues on those first Everest expeditions questioned the whole laborious bandobast – reminiscent of Colonel Younghusband's 1904 military mission to Lhasa – with which they had somehow got involved. And yet they felt, probably, that if Everest were to be climbed, it should be by a British team. No other foreign nation had access to the forbidden kingdom of Tibet; so until the 1950s, when Nepal opened up the south side to the general public, Everest expeditions were an exclusively British game. It was also an extraordinarily haphazard, apparently amateurish, game. There was a typically British mistrust of science and technology, with the result that few of the climbers put any serious effort into developing oxygen equipment.

Many of those early British mountaineers, in comparison to their Alpine contemporaries, were, on the face of it, woefully inexperienced. And yet now, when modern-equipped expeditions struggle to retrace their steps, clipped into the safety lines their predecessors never bothered with, we marvel at what they achieved in the 1920s on those precarious tilted slabs approaching 28,000 feet, where the air pressure is only a third of that at sea level. Amidst our self-indulgent hype, it is refreshing to recall their understated nonchalance. When Colonel 'Teddy' Norton was returning from his legendary struggle to within 900 feet of the summit in 1924, his companion, the talented medical missionary, artist and musician, Howard Somervell, lingered behind him. Norton carried on, assuming blithely that Somervell had probably stopped to do some sketching. Sketching! Having just climbed higher than any human had ever been! Establishing an altitude record for oxygenless climbing which would remain unsurpassed for 54 years! In fact, Somervell had been coughing up most of the mucous lining of his larynx, nearly choking to death in the process.

Four days later, Mallory and Irvine disappeared on the second, and final, attempt. A few months before setting out on the expedition, Mallory had earned his place in the *Oxford Dictionary of Quotations* with his famous 'Because it's there'. One can imagine the scene: Mallory on an American lecture tour, besieged by journalists demanding fatuously to know 'why' he wanted to climb Everest, tired of trying to explain the unfathomable, fobs them off with a one-liner that manages to be supercilious, yet hints at the magic and mystery of that supremely useless goal. Of course he wanted to reach the summit. Who wouldn't? But equally, one can empathise with his inner turmoil, struggling with the opposing forces of ambition and anxiety, excitement and homesickness, as he set off on what he had determined would be his last attempt.

That determination to finish the job once and for all prompted Mallory, against his sporting and aesthetic instincts, to give oxygen a try. That was how he justified choosing the virtual novice, 22-year-old Irvine, as his companion, instead of the older, more experienced Odell, who was the obvious choice. Irvine, a compulsive mechanic, was the one person who could get the faulty, cumbersome apparatus to work properly. But perhaps the real reason was that Mallory just liked him. At 38, Mallory still had the good looks which had sent Lytton Strachey into palpitations, and – even if there was nothing overtly sexual about it here – he responded to young Irvine's own good looks. They made a handsome pair for this great chivalric quest.

At some point after Odell saw them on the afternoon of 8 June 1924, the two men fell down the treacherous sloping terraces of the North Face, breaking the rope that joined them. They were probably on their way back to the top camp when the accident happened. The likelihood is that they had turned round without having reached the top of the world. However, it is possible that they died having stood on the summit. It is even conceivable that they fell on 9 June, having survived a night in the open close to the summit, just as Dougal Haston and Doug Scott – the first Britons known to have climbed Everest – were to do in 1975. Possible, but unlikely. One day we may discover the full story, but most of us, I suspect, would prefer not to lose that achingly sad, mysterious image of two brave Englishmen disappearing into the clouds.

Overleaf: *Irvine (top left) and Mallory (next to Irvine) at the start of the 1924 expedition*

The Mini Minor
Stirling Moss

The marvellous thing about it was how classless it was: the Mini really cut across the whole spectrum like nothing else ever had before, and not merely because it was so cheap. It also looked like nothing ever had before. Suddenly everybody seemed to be buying them, and even if they were just intended as second cars, many people eventually started to leave their 'proper' car behind in the garage and take their Mini everywhere instead. Of course, they were all a bit basic to begin with, in 1959, but we could all see that they had huge competition potential from a very early stage, and once people like John Cooper and Don Moore got their hands on the engines they were just extraordinary…

I liked the Mini for a number of reasons. The engineering package was very clever, and just like the Morris Minor, which Alec Issigonis had already designed, it was all incredibly well thought out. With some vehicles you cannot be exactly sure what the designer is looking for, but it was very clear from the outset that Issigonis was trying to redefine the small car in terms of which component could rely on another one, and so build it more economically with less weight, make it affordable, and – most importantly – make it handle well.

No one had thought of the engine and gearbox sharing the same oil before, for example, which made the whole layout very compact and allowed for four real seats; and even if the early ones were uncomfortable – really dreadful, in fact – you could always change them for something more supportive. It was front-wheel drive, of course, so there was a flat floor, and with the engine being transverse, and the gearbox in unit with it, you got a car which used its small length to amazing effect. You could park it anywhere. All the things you could do to a Mini to make it nicer, to personalise it – whether it was tuning it, painting it, trimming it or whatever – almost gave rise to a whole new industry; so many firms got involved that quite soon you could virtually design your own. With a decent engine and brakes, a proper seat, a radio, a heater (originally an extra) and so forth, you could go anywhere in it.

Of course, it wasn't long before people started to race them. It was actually my sister Pat who gave the Mini its first serious competition win: the Tulip Rally in 1960. And Paddy Hopkirk winning the Monte Carlo Rally in one didn't do any harm either. Quite soon you had people like John Rhodes and John Whitmore doing the most fantastic tricks with them. People simply couldn't believe it, watching these tiny little things bouncing round corners almost on their door handles; no one had seen anything like it before. I think more people started racing at club level with Minis than with any other type of car. From my point of view, that makes it even more important as a milestone, because it allowed beginners to learn the business of motor racing quite cheaply – and, believe me, that was just as important then as it is now. So British motor sport as a whole really owes it a lot.

The Mini handled beautifully as well. The driving position took a little getting used to – a bit like a miniature bus – but after a while it was actually everything else which started to

Minis being put through their paces in The Italian Job, *1969*

PARAMOUNT PICTURES Presents
AN OAKHURST PRODUCTION
MICHAEL CAINE and NOEL COWARD
in
"THE ITALIAN JOB"
Color · Panavision® · A Paramount Picture

69/290

feel odd by comparison. The Mini really changed the way people felt about cars, because this was one which would do almost everything you asked of it. And although motorways were always going to be a bit of a struggle in a standard one, the rate of progress on ordinary roads was fantastic compared to even a more powerful conventional car. What it lacked in top speed (it was never exactly aerodynamic) it made up for in manoeuvrability. It was a very fair swap.

I can't think of any other car which had such an impact across the board. Just imagine it: the Lotus Elite, the E-type Jaguar and the Mini, perhaps the three best-regarded cars in the world, all being designed and built in Britain at the same time. Between them, they typified the 1960s, and the fact that the Mini is still being made just as it always was, and looks just the same as it always did, more than 40 years later really shows you how Issigonis got it right first time – and that is a very difficult thing to do in car design.

I suppose the most enduring image we have of the Mini these days comes from the film *The Italian Job*: the three of them – red, white and blue of course – leaping over rooftops. But I remember the BMC rally victories just as well. After all, it was the Mini Cooper's competition success which really gave the opposition such a surprise. It caught them out so much that the French even managed to change the Monte Carlo Rally rules once to exclude them.

Almost every small car built these days owes at least something to the Mini, particularly in terms of the general architecture of the transverse engine, front-wheel drive, quick steering and four seats. But what makes it so important is that it was the first. It's rather like the business of building racing cars: once someone has made something like that, there is no going back. I don't believe the Mini could have been produced by any other nation at any other time. Innovative and bold, it reflected the whole British car industry as it was – and how different it all is now! – during its golden age of the 1950s and 1960s.

The Miniskirt
Mary Quant

'What does the mini mean?' I am always asked, and I feel in charge of some obstreperous child who ought to speak for herself. The Sixties mini was the most self-indulgent, optimistic 'Look at me. Isn't life wonderful?' fashion ever devised. It expressed the whole decade, the emancipation of women, the pill and rock 'n' roll. It was young, liberated and exuberant. It was called Youth Quake. It was the beginning of Women's Lib.

The mini 2000 says 'Isn't it wonderful to be a woman? We are bigger, better, brighter and stronger. And love being female.' It suggests 'I am in charge.' It looks like Job Done for Women's Lib. And the heyday for Big Girls – Grown-ups.

Nudity and miniskirts seem to coincide with times of huge energy renewal and financial success. But fashion anticipates social change as much as economic change. The mini 2000 suggests the complicated nature of a woman's life today. The ruffle-frilled miniskirt is worn with a short, sharp, snakeskin jacket and a schoolmarm blouse with a fat bow at the neck that means business. Miles of perfect leg are thrust into chrome, strappy mules on four-inch heels. And no doubt tiny, red, girly, gingham knickers match her red lipstick. It is perverse and schizophrenic, but it is a totally accurate look at a woman's life at the beginning of the 21st century.

Women are now hairless nymphets except for the hair on their heads, which is lushly conditioned, spiked and rumpled as though straight from bed. The flesh is polished stone, the muscles trained to athletic fitness. Make-up feeds and glosses the skin while it flatters or plays surreal colour games with the face.

Women have never looked so terrific. They are six-foot tall with muscular shoulders, fake buff-coloured skin and command training. Women organise the mortgage, plan their own pregnancy and show off the bulge. Women shop on the web and cook in the microwave. These superwomen rule the roost. To watch the Williams sisters, Lindsay Davenport and Amelie Mauresmo is to know that women will soon beat men at tennis. Martina Hingis looks like a doll, like a different species. Next stop soccer.

My early fixation with the mini hit me at dancing class when I was about seven. The girl I wanted to be did tap dancing. She wore opaque black tights and about nine inches of black pleated miniskirt – a skinny black polo-neck sweater and basin-cut bobbed hair. But the punchline was her white ankle socks worn over her black tights and black patent leather shoes with ankle straps and a button on top. This vision of chic branded itself on me.

Thanks to the fashion revolution in the Sixties and the evolution of fashion and make-up since, we now have fashion freedom. We have been taught by the fashion magazines and newspapers how to take it or leave it alone. There are so many looks and hemlines to flatter and disguise. There is no in or out of fashion – fashion is ongoing. But always just ahead of the game – desirable if you can reach, but there for everyone to use or abuse. Fashion projects the role you want to play and makes it possible to indulge your individuality.

London is at the heart of this movement. Paris now appears beautiful, nostalgic and rather broke. Tokyo looks disappointed. New York thrives. But London booms with energy and optimism. It's the place that everyone wants to be.

In the Sixties, London was crusading on its own, but now it has become the bridge or link between Europe, America and Asia. We are the multicultural, multiracial, high-tech melting-pot of design, ideas and originality. We have the best fashion and design schools. London is now a world design centre.

Design accessorises our lives. We buy the platinum nail polish and lip colour to match the car we want because the girl in the TV ad is wearing a micro-mini when she puts her polished toes hard down on the accelerator. Virtual reality is where we live. I love it. I have always tried to avoid 'real life'.

The new breed of women move like athletes, sit like men with their knees well apart. Their children take their mother's surname. These awesome, gorgeous amazons can sell their eggs and buy their sperm when needed. They are in control. Marriage is a romantic extra.

For generations the natural role for women was a permanent state of pregnancy, birth and miscarriages. County women rode hard to hounds when pregnant to see if this one stayed the course. Without the strain of permanent pregnancy, women will probably become larger than men.

Now designers can work from anywhere and anytime – in the real reality of mud, cows, grass and gumboots in watercolour Surrey. However, it's the provocative chemical colours of virtual reality for fashion or vacuum cleaners that stomp the computer screen because that's what mauve Apple Mac likes and that decides what we like.

The speed of change is now from a.m. to p.m. Mobile telephones have cured us of any shyness. Everyone can speak on the hoof as Americans have always been able to do. Soon it will be easy to make a slim, edited version of yourself on the computer screen, wearing the fashion and make-up you like, and send that to the virtual reality board meeting with virtual speech in a virtual environment. Perfect legs, perfect fashion, perfect you in a mini 2000.

Two symbols of the Sixties: Twiggy in a miniskirt

The Monarchy
John Grigg

The British record for inventiveness is undeniably good, in the arts (above all literature), in philosophy, in pure science, in engineering and technology, and in the evolution of law and government. In the last respect, one of the greatest of all British inventions is constitutional monarchy, though too often it is either disregarded or taken for granted.

Since the American and French revolutions, there has been a tendency in most of the world to regard monarchy as a thing of the past, and to assume that any free, go-ahead, modern state should be a republic. A fair number of countries have resisted this fallacious assumption, but it is still widely prevalent. Most of the world's nations – particularly those which came into existence during the last century when the European empires broke up – have republican constitutions. In practice, many of them, perhaps the majority, have despotic regimes, more or less thinly disguised.

By contrast, the monarchies that survive, or have been revived, include a disproportionate share of the world's truly stable democracies. Even if we put a question mark over Japan (whose democracy is still, perhaps, a bit problematical) and Belgium (because of the instability caused by the Flemish-Walloon divide), we are left with Britain, Canada, Australia, New Zealand, Norway, Sweden, Denmark, the Netherlands and now Spain, to mention only countries of significant size. Among republics, which can match these in combining freedom with stability? The United States, France, Germany and most of the other EU republics, Switzerland, India (fingers crossed) and South Africa (even more so). For the rest, the picture is surely bleak. To argue that people are manifestly better off living in republics is to ignore the evidence.

Those monarchies which are free and stable are based on the British constitutional model. This emerged from the 17th-century conflict between king and parliament, and has since adapted itself to democracy as the franchise has been progressively extended. Four centuries ago, the British monarchy had absolute power within a small but dynamic island. Today, it has no political power, only influence, but its prestige is worldwide. No other monarchy, apart from the Papacy (a rather different sort), has universal status and appeal.

By another strange twist, the British monarchy now commands more attention in the world than the British government or Britain itself. How has this come about? In the first century or so after the transformation from absolute to constitutional monarchy, British power was reaching out to distant continents and was being exercised, in the name of the Crown, by an oligarchy of territorial magnates. But in the 1830s two great changes occurred. At home the process of franchise extension began, very tentatively at first, while overseas Lord Durham's report on Canada (resulting from unrest there) recommended that the principle of responsible government be applied to that country, which had hitherto been a wholly dependent part of a centralised empire. This opened the way to a Commonwealth of self-governing nations, bound together only by language, sentiment, shared interests and common institutions: in particular, the supremely emotive bond of a common crown.

Strictly speaking, it was not the crown that was common to all, but the person wearing it. The crown was – and is – peculiar to each of the self-governing dominions (as they were originally called), which became separate monarchies under a common monarch. Nevertheless, so long as Britain remained a superpower by virtue of its accumulated wealth, its dominant position in world trade, its vast dependent Empire, especially India, and the undiminished strength of the Royal Navy, the splendour of the monarchy continued to reflect that of metropolitan Britain, not to outshine it. At the time of Queen Victoria's golden and diamond jubilees, and even at the time of George V's silver jubilee (in 1935), the prestige of the monarchy was scarcely, if at all, distinct from Britain's own. But after two world wars – in which, be it noted, the British Commonwealth was united in active participation from first to last – Britain was bankrupt and rapidly ceased to be a superpower. Soon the dependent Empire dissolved and Britain reverted to being a medium-sized nation off the north-west coast of Europe.

The British monarchy, however, was not cut down to size. On the contrary, its position was enhanced, not only relatively to that of the British nation, its home base, but by acquiring an entirely new dimension. When independent India decided to become a republic without wishing to leave the Commonwealth, a new office was created, that of Head of the Commonwealth, which the present Queen's father, George VI, was invited to occupy. At his death soon afterwards, she was invited to succeed him in it, but one must stress that the office is not hereditary. If in due course her successor as sovereign follows her as Head of the Commonwealth, he will do so by invitation. Today, the Queen presides over a worldwide association of 54 nations, large and small, in 17 of which she is also the monarchical head of state.

Despite a few imperfections, the British monarchy enters the new millennium in excellent shape. During the last century it performed, on the whole, remarkably well. Too much has been made of two occasions when, according to some, it was in dire danger: the Abdication Crisis in 1936 and the recent death of Diana, Princess of Wales. The Princess, like the previous Prince of Wales (who abdicated as Edward VIII), was a brilliant but unstable star in the royal firmament. Both did much good, as well as some harm, to the monarchy. Neither would have been heard of if they had not been royal personages; the emotions that both aroused were part and parcel of the romantic aura surrounding the institution. Neither posed any threat to the monarchy's existence. Republican sentiment was a more serious factor during the middle years of Queen Victoria's reign than at any time in the 20th century.

The idea, peddled by some, of 'slimming down' the monarchy is utterly misconceived if it means depriving it of its traditional splendour. The pageantry associated with it is cherished by most people, including many citizens of republics where such an aesthetic and historically resonant dimension to the political system is absent. It is anyway absurd to talk of slimming down a monarchy which belongs to nations in every continent. Some British sourpusses may be resentful that our monarchy has to such a large degree outstripped the confines of Britain. But it is surely more natural for us to rejoice in its universal success.

Overleaf: *A group of peers leaves Westminster Abbey after the coronation of Elizabeth II, 1953*

The Martyrdom of Thomas More
Peter Ackroyd

The death of Thomas More by beheading, on Tower Hill in 1535, marked a climacteric in English history and English society. The facts of the matter are perhaps well enough known. In the long process through which Henry VIII sought to annul his marriage with Katherine of Aragon and to marry Anne Boleyn, the sovereign gradually began to understand the possibilities of his own power. He had been a loyal servant of the Pope, having even been granted the title 'Defender of the Faith' in the battle against Martin Luther; but when the pontiff refused to accede to the King's wishes, their relationship was thoroughly changed. Rome was in the way of the royal will, and that will was not to be thwarted.

Thus in the very earliest period of the Reformation in England, when Thomas More was the King's faithful knight and Lord Chancellor, Henry VIII proclaimed himself head of the Church of England; the clergy, and the congregations, were to look to him for inspiration and leadership in spiritual affairs. Those who espoused the old faith were at first astounded and then afraid. Those who refused to accept the King's new status were summarily imprisoned and tried on charges of treason. Certain monks were tortured, and public rituals of execution by disembowelment served to remind those who wavered in their allegiance that the wrath of the King meant death.

Thomas More himself suffered from the agonies of private fear, but public conscience and pious study prevailed over human weakness. He had investigated the matter well and adjudged the consequences of the King's actions; in that respect he saw what his contemporaries could not, or would not, see. In particular, the sudden accession of Henry to spiritual as well as temporal power effectively meant that England was parting from the European communion of faith and that a thousand years of unity and loyalty were coming to an end. It was his abiding belief that no one man, however exalted, could set himself above these fundamental ecclesiastical principles and conditions; it would mean, in practice, turning away from the divinely appointed apostolic succession and treating with contempt the testimony of the saints and martyrs.

It has to be remembered that More's training and education were those of a lawyer; he had served the law all his life, whether in church or at Court, and his whole existence can most plausibly and generally be seen as an attempt to fulfil all the various duties and obligations placed upon him. He was also a deeply pious man, who had for a while withdrawn from the world into the Charterhouse and who practised mortification; so strong was his commitment to the established religious order that he harassed the books and bodies of the Lutheran 'heretics' who were preaching reformation even before the King's proposed divorce.

So for More, the abrogation of the Pope's authority meant no less than everything. He had a duty to the King, of course, but he had a higher duty to Christendom itself; he could not repudiate the traditions which he believed to have been instituted by God and maintained by written and unwritten authority. For him, there was no choice in the matter. To sign the document stating that the King was supreme head of the Church was, in the

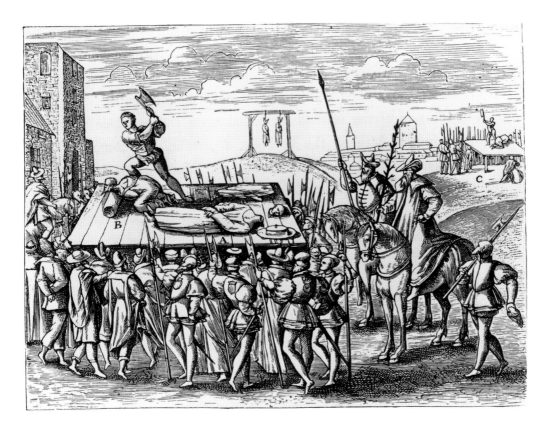

strictest sense, an illegal and unprecedented act, which no court or congregation could possibly justify. To sign such a document would also mean the forfeiture of his own soul, and thus eternal damnation within the pains of Hell. He had only one course. He refused to sign, and was promptly put on trial in Westminster Hall, where he fought for his life with characteristic legal skill and nicety. But no force on earth could withstand the King's anger, and of course More was found guilty of treason. His first sentence was that of death by drawing and quartering, but the King was graciously pleased to commute that barbaric sentence to one of simple beheading. He was taken to Tower Hill where, in front of a large crowd, he protested that he died a true son of the Roman Catholic Church.

All then took place as he had foreseen – the people were stripped of their rituals, the churches denuded of their ornaments, the monasteries destroyed, and England itself torn apart from the main course of European civilisation. It marked the beginning of Protestant England, as defined by nationalists to this day, but it also signalled the profound demise of an ancient civilisation.

The execution of John Fisher ('A'), Thomas More ('B') and the Countess of Salisbury ('C')

The Introduction of the National Health Service
Barbara Castle

Blackburn was a drab place when I became its MP in 1945. The depression of the 1930s, and four years of war, had left it with rows of working-class houses without gardens, where the children had nowhere to play but the street, and with unrepaired schools and forbidding mills. There was not a decent café or hotel in the place. Poor diet had made its textile workers famous for their stunted growth. As I went electioneering, I found that the faithful workers manning our committee rooms were subsisting on meat pies and mushy peas, except that there was precious little meat under the pies' tough crusts. Above all, the town seemed to be populated with old age pensioners. It was in fact the headquarters of the National Federation of Retirement Pensions Associations, which seemed to be run by Conservatives.

It was with some trepidation, therefore, that I took up my new job. With food and clothes rationing continuing to dominate our lives, there seemed to be few fruits of victory I could offer my constituents.

But a shaft of light illuminated the darkness when the National Health Service was born in 1948. The pensioners who had been forced to buy their spectacles at Woolworths, groping their way among the sixpenny bits of magnifying glass to find something that would help them see less mistily, suddenly found the door to better vision open magically before them. They could have their eyes tested properly for nothing, and they were fitted free with the appropriate spectacles. It was their first glimpse of a new world. They could also be fitted with false teeth which did not wobble painfully as they ate.

A new generation of babies blossomed in their prams on free cod-liver oil, orange juice and cheap milk. Aneurin Bevan, the Welsh rebel, who as Minister of Health fought his way through the hostility of the medical profession to found the NHS, used to boast, 'If you want to see this country's prosperity, look in the perambulators.' Victory seemed to have borne its fruit at last.

The problems I met in my weekly surgeries were still great – housing shortages, low pensions and demob controls – but a new ethic had come into our national life. You paid your income taxes according to your ability to pay, and in return were entitled to receive free at the point of use the best medical care the country could provide.

Cynics who had predicted that GPs would be swamped with unreasonable demands were confounded. In areas like Blackburn, people were stunned with gratitude for the medical largesse which was heaped on them. One prominent cynic alleged on the newly emerging TV that people were bombarding their doctors with demands for free rolls of cotton wool with which to stuff their cushions. To my constituents, her claim was a sick joke. The realisation began to take root that, rationing or no rationing, what we were rearing was the healthiest generation the country had ever known.

As austerity diminished, Blackburn was transformed. So was the NHS. The demands made on me for healthcare became more sophisticated: improvements in our local hospital,

The healthiest generation the country had ever known: a beneficiary of the NHS wears his free glasses

more intensive care units and better antenatal provision. This time, the demands were led by the middle class, which had begun to be aware of what the NHS could offer them. So powerful was this new ally that no government since then has dared to attack the NHS frontally or suggest we should return to the old 'flag days' to keep the voluntary hospitals afloat.

The development of the NHS was epitomised for me when, in the 1960s, my husband had to have open-heart surgery. He was referred by his GP to the National Heart Hospital, where the prestigious heart surgeon Mr Donald Ross was due to operate on him. When I visited my husband in his bed in the public ward, he announced to me gleefully: 'There is a constituent of yours a few beds away.' When I talked to my constituent, I found he had been referred from Blackburn to get the same top treatment as my husband in the country's most famous heart hospital. Of course, the NHS then as now was strapped for cash. The busy nurses had no time to look after the flowers brought by well-wishers and they were dying in their vases. I spent some of my visiting time topping them up with water.

Food was hardly lavish. As the precursor to open-heart surgery, my husband, who had neglected his teeth, had to have them all extracted, and when I visited him he mumbled toothlessly that he had been given salad for his lunch; so I had to ferry into him an endless stream of egg custards. None of this mattered when he emerged safely from his operation, as did my constituent. I felt like kissing the hem of Mr Ross' surgical gown. When I thanked him profusely he said to me with quiet satisfaction: 'Do you realise what this operation would have cost you in America?' My husband and I could not have raised that money easily, and I knew that my constituent would have found it impossible. All that counted was that the NHS had got its priorities right.

It is not surprising, therefore, that the virility of the seed that Aneurin Bevan sowed in 1948 has survived all attempts to uproot it. In a world in which privatisation was spreading in other fields, the NHS, together with the concept that healthcare is the right of everyone, old or young, insured or uninsured, has embedded itself in the national consciousness. Some have tried to nibble away at it, but the ethic it enshrines has become part of our national life. Most significant of all, at a time when political parties are vying with each other to promise tax cuts, the new Labour Government has been forced to inject the biggest cash increase in NHS expenditure for decades. The middle class has won, and so has the NHS.

Newton's Laws
John Gribbin

Newton's law of gravity and his three laws of motion provide the foundations of modern science. Not just because of their importance in their own right, but because they are the archetypes for other scientific laws, and established the scientific method as a way of finding out how the world works.

The law of gravity provides the best example. Isaac Newton proved mathematically that the planets could only be held in their observed elliptical orbits around the sun if there was a force (gravity) which pulled them towards the sun with a strength inversely proportional to the square of the distance between the planet and the sun. This is a universal law – any two objects, anywhere in the universe, attract each other with a force inversely proportional to the square of the distance between them (and proportional to the product of their masses, but we need not go into that here). There is no escaping a law of science; it is a universal truth. But there is nothing in Newton's law of gravity to tell you *why* things should behave in this way. For that, you need a theory, or an hypothesis, and Newton specifically said *hypotheses non fingo* ('I do not make hypotheses'). The best *theory* of gravity we have is Einstein's general theory of relativity, which explains gravitational forces in terms of the curvature of space. There might be a better way to explain this – although nobody has yet found one; Einstein's theory may not be the last word in theories of gravity. But any theory of gravity has to 'predict' inverse square law, or it is just plain wrong.

One of the great things about laws of physics is that once they have been discovered, they can often be applied in circumstances that the person who discovered them never dreamed of. Newton's three laws of motion exemplify this feature of the triumph of science. The laws are so familiar today that it is hard to appreciate that discovering them required considerable skill on the part of Newton and his predecessors, such as Galileo and Descartes. The first law says that any object stays still or keeps moving in a straight line at the same speed (that is, at constant velocity) unless it is acted upon by a force. The second law says that when a force is applied to an object, it accelerates, and keeps accelerating as long as the force is applied. Acceleration means either a change in the speed of the object, or a change in its direction, or both; so the moon is continually accelerating in its orbit around the earth, even though it moves at roughly the same speed all the time, because it is constantly changing direction. The third law says that when one object exerts a force on another, there is an equal and opposite reaction back on the first object (as anyone who has ever stubbed a toe has painfully found out).

Newton discovered his laws in the context of things like planets orbiting around the sun, balls rolling down inclined planes, and apples falling from trees. They apply perfectly to snooker balls moving around and colliding with one another on a frictionless surface. When the idea of atoms began to gain ground in the 19th century, the pioneers of physics developed a model known as the kinetic theory of gases, in which the behaviour of gases is explained by treating them as made up of atoms and molecules which can be thought of as

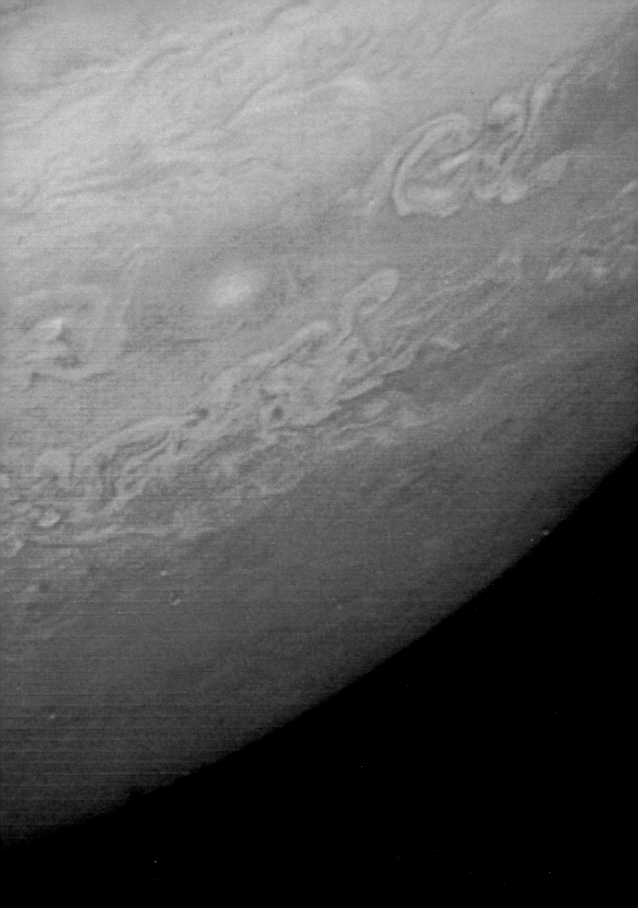

little hard billiard balls, moving around and colliding with one another and with the walls of the container. This kinetic theory explained the behaviour of gases beautifully if the behaviour of the individual atoms was described by Newton's laws of motion, even though Newton had no inkling that gases worked like this, and his laws had been established in a different context well over a hundred years before.

The law of gravity can be ignored on the scale of atoms and molecules, because the masses involved are so tiny. But at the other extreme, when astronomers look out into the universe at large, they have to take account of the inverse square law of gravity to explain the motion of stars, galaxies and the whole expanding universe itself. Again, Newton never dreamed that the universe began in a Big Bang, and has been expanding for the past 13 billion years or so. The expansion itself was only discovered in the late 1920s, and models (or theories) to describe the expansion are still being developed at the beginning of the 21st century. But those models share a common feature – that the expansion of the universe has been slowed down over the time since the Big Bang by gravity acting in accordance with Newton's law. There has been great excitement among astronomers recently with the discovery that the expansion may be proceeding slightly faster than they had thought – but this in no way pulls the rug from under Newton, since the explanation seems to be that there is another force at work, a kind of antigravity, which only operates on very large scales and cancels out some of the Newtonian gravitational influence.

Newton's laws were worked out from studies of middle-sized things on the scale of the universe – objects accessible to the human senses. But they work even for particles within the atom, and even for the entire universe. Even though theories and hypotheses may come and go, the laws will remain the same – if and when Einstein's theory of gravity is superseded, apples won't suddenly start falling upwards out of trees, and the planets won't leave their orbits around the sun. Nobody does it better than Newton, and nobody ever will.

Darwin's Origin of Species
Richard Dawkins

The *Origin of Species* must be a contender for the title of most revolutionary book ever written, anywhere, in any language. If it had been published in a little country with no other literature at all, the *Origin* would alone have been enough to put that country on the cultural and scientific map. As it happens, it was written and published in Britain, and it is as British as any book I know. On one level, Charles Darwin was an English naturalist who travelled adventurously around the world and then settled down to become a country gentleman of reclusive habits. Captain Fitzroy almost rejected him from the *Beagle* (he found Darwin's nose phrenologically unsound), but changed his mind at the last minute, thereby saving Darwin from his destined career in the Church. But for Fitzroy's relenting, Darwin would presumably have become that other very English institution, the botanising, beetle-collecting country parson, a sort of 19th-century Gilbert White. In the event, he became arguably the most influential scientist of all time, not just in Britain but in the world.

Arguably, perhaps, but it is a hard argument to lose. The distinguished American philosopher Daniel Dennett is in no doubt:

> Let me lay my cards on the table. If I were to give an award for the
> single best idea anyone has ever had, I'd give it to Darwin, ahead of
> Newton and Einstein and everyone else.

That idea, of course, was evolution by natural selection. All living things are cousins, related by branching descent from a remote and much simpler ancestor. Each branching event is an origin of species. Descent with modification proceeds very slowly and gradually by human standards, under the guidance of natural selection – the non-random survival of randomly varying hereditary information. Every creature is descended from a literally unbroken line of successful ancestors, and has inherited what it took to be successful. That is why all species are so good at what they do: swimming in the case of fish and dolphins; flying in the case of birds, bats, insects and pterosaurs; digging in the case of moles, mole crickets and mole rats; climbing in the case of monkeys and squirrels; thinking in our own case. Those successful ancestors outcompeted large numbers of unsuccessful rivals, whose unsuccessful hereditary attributes therefore diminished through the generations. This principle of non-random success is natural selection. It may not be the only force that guides evolution, but it is the only force capable of guiding it in the direction of improvement. It is the force responsible for the compelling illusion of design in the world of living things, the illusion that has been such a mainstay of religious faith down the ages. Before Darwinism there were a few atheists, but they can't have felt very satisfied about it.

Natural selection is not one of those plodding ideas that might be right or might be wrong, and you have to wait for the evidence to settle it. Natural selection is one of those ideas which is so elegantly simple yet so shatteringly powerful, you know it has to be right the moment you understand it. As T H Huxley, 'Darwin's Bulldog' (what could be more British?), sighed, on closing the *Origin*, 'How extremely stupid not to have thought of that!' Of course, there is plenty of evidence as well.

One other person can be securely credited with arriving at the same idea independently. That was Darwin's younger contemporary Alfred Russell Wallace, who had his inspiration while in a malarial fever on one of his collecting expeditions in South East Asia. Two other 19th-century writers, Edward Blyth and Patrick Matthew, also have their champions as independent foreshadowers of Darwin and Wallace. I find their claims rather less convincing. They certainly understood the principle of natural selection as a negative, weeding-out process, but I suspect that, unlike Darwin and Wallace, they did not clearly see the positive power of natural selection to build up all the complexity, diversity and apparent design of life. For the purposes of this book, though, the salient point is that all four of these men were British. Moreover, both Darwin and Wallace recorded that their moment of inspiration came, independently and by an eerie coincidence, from reading the same book, the *Essay on the Principle of Population* by Thomas Malthus, another Englishman.

I do not know if there is anything to be made of the fact that the historical origins of modern evolutionary ideas are almost entirely to be found within these islands. The same cannot confidently be said of physics, despite the towering figures of Newton, Faraday and Maxwell. The other puzzling thing about the history of Darwin's great idea is that, although it waited in fact until the 19th century, there seems no obvious reason why nobody thought of it in any previous century. This is quite unlike, say, Maxwell's theory of electromagnetism, which needed a long history of experimental and theoretical physics before it could spring into a mind – and that mind had to be one skilled in mathematical techniques which themselves needed a long history of step-by-step development. The principle of natural selection could have occurred to anyone, with no mathematical skills, and with no more factual knowledge than this: individuals vary; like begets like; and individuals in their reproduction are on average more prolific than is necessary for replacement – many die young. Such knowledge had been commonplace among farm labourers, gamekeepers, dog fanciers, racehorse breeders and pigeon racers for centuries before Darwin's time. Some of it would surely have filtered up to the great minds of any age. Why did this stunningly powerful yet simple idea evade all those brilliant minds, from Plato to Goethe, from Aristotle to Hume? Why did it wait all that time before springing, independently, into two – or it may have been four – minds in the 19th century? And is it just coincidence that all four were British minds?

Darwin and a distant cousin: a cartoon from The London Sketch Book, *1874*

PROF. DARWIN.

This is the ape of form.
Love's Labor Lost, act 5, scene 2.

Some four or five descents since.
All's Well that Ends Well, act 3, sc. 7.

Oxbridge
Simon Heffer

In the era of the common man, the institution of Oxbridge – that frightful term used to evoke our two old universities – has come in for some aggressive pummelling. A 'conspiracy' of its graduates is supposed to run our country, and to run it, by implication, for the worse. It suggests a cold and ruthless élite, and one established not by merit but by birth and privilege. Despite attempts to broaden its intake, the institution now offends against the egalitarianism which supposedly informs the present day by selecting people on academic merit, thereby discriminating against those with an inadequate secondary education. As any fool knows, however, it is precisely that pursuit of excellence which has made the institution the force in the land – indeed in the world – that it is.

Perhaps it was once true that thick hoorays could buy their way into Oxford or Cambridge. However, the universities would not have survived since the 12th and 13th centuries respectively had it not been for their prodigious attachment to learning and research, and the vast contribution they made to the life of our country. Even at the time – notably the 18th and 19th centuries – when the universities were most susceptible to a charge of being simply finishing schools for the aristocracy and moneyed classes, they were still pushing forward the frontiers of erudition and discovery. They contained men (for, until Girton opened in 1869, they were run by and for men) who sought always to discover more about their disciplines, be they arts or sciences, and to expand human understanding of our world and its culture. Why, otherwise, would Jude the Obscure have been so keen, as an artisan determined to improve himself, to study at Oxford?

The role of the old universities in equipping Britain and the world with statesmen, churchmen, scientists, engineers, industrialists, economists, teachers, artists, writers, explorers and historians cannot be overstated. British culture rests to a large extent not just on the products of the old universities, but on the way of life propagated from them. Oxbridge is – or should be – about the best sort of liberalism. The pluralism and moderation of our society and polity rests on the academic and moral freedoms inculcated in generations of undergraduates at Oxbridge. At a time when there were no other seats of further education, Oxbridge produced the missionaries of a civilisation that gripped not just Britain, but the world. Today, when universities of varying standards proliferate, Oxbridge still draws on its history of excellence, research and innovation to lead the academic community in Britain. While it no longer has a monopoly on the best – indeed, in league tables Imperial College, London, is rated above Oxford – it still commands academic and intellectual resources without which our culture would run aground. It also uses its brains to keep ahead of the times, as the development of Cambridge as a world centre for scientific and technological research amply proves.

Then there is the more spiritual, less practical side of Oxbridge in our culture: the 'dreaming spires', the glory of King's College chapel, cricket in the Parks, punting on the

Heading for the top? An Oxford student on his way to Finals

Cam, Boar's Hill, the Grantchester grind, gaudies and feasts, the constant and enduring celebrations of a history whose own millennium is now not far off. There is, on all levels, an indissoluble link between what England stands for and what Oxbridge stands for. Both are ancient, and replete with monuments to their antiquity. Both evolve, and the visitor to either sees abundant evidence of their evolution. Both pride themselves on the maintenance of certain values, rooted not just in Christianity but in reason, and Oxbridge, over the centuries, can lay claim to having been the fount of those ideals. Until the late 19th century, when learned men went abroad in Britain or from Britain, whether as teachers, clergymen, administrators, lawyers or politicians, they more often than not started their journey from Oxford or Cambridge. No wonder this amalgam is everywhere in our sights; no wonder it recurs again and again in our own inquiries into where we came from, or why we are what we are – and how we are.

The institution must be praised, too, for having perfected the very British art of mutability. When, in the mid-20th century, it became clear that the grammar schools were producing so many of the country's finest brains, their products were assimilated into Oxbridge almost effortlessly – and from there they took their places in parliament, the civil service, the professions and the arts. When, a little later on, it became clear how absurd it was for Oxbridge to offer such limited opportunities to the growing number of highly educated and able women seeking a tertiary education, old colleges that had educated only men for up to six or seven hundred years suddenly welcomed women. In both cases, the institution realised that in a modern, free society nobody has a monopoly on the provision of learning – and that they as institutions would fade and die if they remained anti-meritocratic. Similarly, unthinking radicals who today try to prevent the admission to Oxbridge of brilliant public schoolboys – simply because they *are* brilliant public schoolboys – will soon find that the universities to which those students go instead will, if such prejudice continues, challenge Oxbridge's superiority.

For all the genius of Oxbridge, for all its pre-eminence, for all the roll-call of the great in nearly every walk of life that it has produced, it will continue – also in a very British way – to be a target for criticism. Its dons will be caricatured as otherworldly, bitchy and effete, its collegiate system as inefficient, its architecture as insulation from the modern world, its research as occasionally self-indulgent and its attitude as destructively arrogant. Yet it works: it is still regarded by many as the pinnacle of the nation's educational achievement and it is still a by-word for excellence. Young graduates find that an Oxbridge education remains, even in these egalitarian times, a passport to success in the real world. For so long as this is so – and that it is reflects as much on other seats of learning as on Oxbridge – Oxbridge will matter, and will thrive. We should rejoice that it does, and that it always has, for our country and our world would be immeasurably poorer without it.

The Oxford English Dictionary
Simon Winchester

I bought my first set in a bookshop hidden in a rabbit-warren of streets in Hong Kong during a massive typhoon back in the early 1980s. Seventeen tombstone-sized volumes, all with gold-lettered dark blue bindings, many wrapped in slipcovers the colour of clotted cream. Too heavy, I supposed, for some expat to ship all the way back home: I promptly snapped up the lot for 9,000 local dollars, though the Chinese saleswoman insisted she wouldn't or couldn't deliver. I had to find a taxi and cram the books into the boot in sheeting rain, the thunder roaring and the gales whipping through the canyons of Wanchai. It was a memorable beginning to my life with the *OED*.

Since then, 20 or so years ago, no house I have ever occupied has been without at least one copy of this extraordinary book. If I can be permitted a mixed metaphor Sir James Murray, the best-known editor of the *OED*, would probably in this one case allow, I thus live, breathe, swim and otherwise take my ease in a limitless, Oxford-provided ocean of words: the entire English vocabulary, *aa* to *zyxt*, is on eternal hand, silent and ubiquitous like the very oxygen itself. It is a book I cherish and I love, both for serendipitous joy and for reasons essential.

So essential, for me and for anyone whose passion, need or fancy is for English and its words, that it sometimes seems as though the dictionary in general, and this dictionary in particular, has been around for ever.

And yet, most decidedly, it has not. The dictionary as we now know it is a relatively new invention. Four hundred years ago, such dictionaries as existed were mere books of translation, offering the English equivalents of words in Latin (of which *dictionarius* was one) or French or German. The notion of an alphabetical list of English words was wholly unimagined. When Shakespeare wrote, he did so unaided by a handy volume on one side. A few small word-books were made in the 17th century, but all were specialised – lists of the names of birds, flowers, furniture, or the kind of long words to use at parties and impress.

It took that most energetic of parliamentary journalists Samuel Johnson to create the first true and truly grand catalogue of the English language – a language which by 1755, its publication date, was well on its way to becoming the dominant speaking-tongue of the planet. His two-volume work, with its 40,000 entries, became in quick time the defining standard for the lexicographer's art.

Until, that is, one foggy Guy Fawkes' evening in London in 1857, when a learned divine named Richard Chenevix Trench issued a formal challenge: Johnson was limited, and Johnson was unreliable. The book defined only a small fraction of what philologists believed was out there; countless of those definitions were either wrong or too eccentric for use. The definition of oats, for example – a grain commonly given to horses, but which in Scotland feeds the people – was hardly the kind of disinterested entry that a proper dictionary should have. The English language, mighty and mightily important as it was, deserved better.

And so a grand project, the kind of project that only Victorians might have the nerve to undertake, was set in motion. A great new dictionary was to be created, in which every English word – every nuance, sense, meaning, variant spelling, every obscure, forgotten and forlorn word, along with all the new, vulgar and popular words – should be included. Crucially, no rules should be laid down as to what the nation should speak or read or say. Unlike French, our English was, the editors of the great new book insisted, inviolably flexible, inclusive and delightfully anarchic: all of those merits that allowed it to become so widely used should be illustrated in and by the new dictionary.

And more: for every single word there should be, as it were, a biography – a collection of quotations that showed just how every word had been used over the centuries, how its meanings had twisted and turned over hundreds of years of usage. And to do that, everything ever written must be examined, and millions of quotations needed to illustrate the uses must be culled, amassed, catalogued and, if suitable, entered into the book.

A huge army of volunteers was therefore required; people were invited and persuaded to help and, in their tens of thousands, did. The *OED*, under Murray's heroic editorship, thus turned into an exercise in lexicographical democracy, where the people's language was prepared by and for the very people who spoke, read and wrote it.

It took 70 long years to produce the First Edition – and when in 1928 the first 12 volumes came thundering from the presses in Wolvercote, the American lexicographer-wit H L Mencken declared the day so important that it should be celebrated 'with military exercises, boxing matches between the dons, orations in Latin, Greek and the Oxford dialect, yelling matches between the different colleges and a series of medieval drinking bouts'.

There has since been a Second Edition, with 20 volumes and well over half a million words; and now there are plans for a Third, due within the decade. This edition, fully 40 volumes and nearly a million words long, may never, Oxford says, be published as a book at all. Maybe no more blue bindings. No more gold lettering. No more slipcovers the colour of clotted cream.

If this is to be, then I for one shall regret it. True, half a forest would go to make it. True, it wouldn't fit in the boot of a car, and no sensible person would buy one in a Chinese typhoon unless guaranteed delivery. But truly, too, the book itself will be a thing of inestimable beauty, an enduring symbol of greatness, and a monument, writ very, very large, to perhaps the greatest instrument for good – the English language – with which Britain has ever endowed the world.

Heroic editorship: James Murray in his Oxford scriptorium

The Palace of Westminster
John Cole

The House of Commons first met in a part of the Palace of Westminster called St Stephen's Chapel. It is now the broad corridor on whose padded benches people queue to be admitted to the public gallery. In medieval times, it was a gift from the King to his faithful Commons.

The significance of these topographical origins is that, from the very beginning, two groups of MPs faced each other from what had been the stalls of the Chapel. When the Commons got a purpose-built chamber, they carried these seating arrangements with them. By contrast, in many European countries the parties sit in a semicircular chamber, shading from far Right to far Left. Each system doubtless suits its own country.

Critics say the shape of the House of Commons, with the lines between its two front benches drawn, symbolically, two swords' lengths apart, has made British politics more adversarial than that of other countries. Yet when I first visited the French National Assembly in 1948, the usher who showed us round, a *mutilé de guerre*, gave a graphic account, in rapid French and with gestures of his one arm, of recent fisticuffs in the semicircular chamber.

Since democratic politics is about choice, the adversarial system has much to commend it. There are dangers in reducing the right of voters to choose their government from a clear selection of parties and policies.

The fashion in political commentary in the last quarter-century has been for more consensus, more coalition. Businessmen repeat their hoary complaint that changes of government make it impossible for them to plan ahead. Some in the 1970s called for a 'Businessmen's Government'. Columnists pretend that our economy has suffered, over many decades, not so much from manifest weaknesses in our industrial and commercial behaviour and talents, but importantly from changes in direction at Westminster. Politicians have become a convenient whipping-boy for failures in which we all share.

This critique of our political institutions is largely based on ignorance. Sadly, even the admission of television cameras into the Palace cannot convey the magic of the place. I have been privileged to spend time there, as a journalist, over many years. The old building imposes many inconveniences on those who work in it. Offices for the Press would certainly not qualify under the Shops and Offices Act, but Westminster enjoys exemption as a royal palace. Yet the Palace imposes its own intimacy, through inevitable contact among politicians of different parties and with journalists and lobbyists. It is an arena for politics that is hard to equal.

The craving for coalition has evoked demands for change in our voting system, for Proportional Representation in one of its many forms. Advocates of change give conflicting reasons. In the 1980s, it was to ensure that a Labour Party controlled from the Left should not gain power. At the end of the century, many spoke of PR as a means of keeping the Conservatives out of office forever. The implicit message in both cases was that you cannot trust the voters.

'The mother of parliaments': Monet's 1903 painting of the Palace of Westminster

There are attractions in coalition. Indeed, many non-political citizens would instinctively go further, and aspire to a 'Ministry of All the Talents', a device to which Britain has wisely turned in two world wars. Why, they ask, should we not mobilise the best men and women from all parties to govern the country in peacetime?

The problem is one of democratic choice. Any democracy needs not just a government, but an alternative government. The adversarial system, including the possibility of changes of government at quinquennial general elections, is surely one of the glories of Britain. There is a wise political aphorism: 'When in danger, or in doubt, / Turn the sitting member out.' I would amend that to 'sitting government'. Frequent rotation between two principal parties – first Whigs and Tories, recently Labour and Conservatives – has been a guarantee of our liberties, without recourse to revolution, for a longer period than in any other democracy. As Edmund Burke said, writing at the time of the French Revolution, 'a state without the means of some change is without the means of its conservation'.

Many British people seem to me unduly complacent about the stability of our democracy. Freedoms have to be fought for, and more particularly thought for, in every generation. I would not draw many conclusions from events in my native Ulster, but one is the need, in any country, to devise a party structure that offers the possibility of alternative governments. For demographic reasons in Northern Ireland, no such party structure exists. Power-sharing is a sensible alternative in a desperate situation. But nobody seems to notice that until sectarian voting is eroded, there can be no alternative government, no choice for voters. That is second-class democracy. The Commons chamber at Stormont, carefully modelled 68 years ago as Westminster-in-miniature, has changed its shape and is now semicircular.

Westminster, with its rectangular chamber, can *choose*. Britain has been able, for most of the last two centuries, to change its government by peaceful exercise of the franchise. For the voters, General Election Day is make-your-mind-up time. They may have told the opinion pollster that they don't know or don't care. Yet on election day a government still has to be chosen.

Central to the argument against PR is the belief that the supreme democratic choice is that of a government, rather than of an MP. Of course, some voters will decide to concentrate on the merits – or, indeed, weaknesses – of their constituency candidates. But most people want to determine who will form the government. On occasion, the collective view will be indecisive. Paradoxically, that also is a decision; the electorate will have refused untrammelled power to either big party, and the third party, at present the Liberal Democrats, will influence what kind of government Britain has.

Over the past century, our system has shown remarkable flexibility. It is surely a negation of democracy to devise a voting system to give advantage to coalition. Choice is for the sovereign people, not for politicians, whether in smoke-filled or smoke-free rooms.

These are the values enshrined in the Palace of Westminster. It stands for tradition, rather than for political fashion. I believe that the British ought to take pride in how long our working democracy has lasted. Not for nothing did John Bright say that 'England is the mother of parliaments'. For all the 'animal noises' that occasionally sound out during what *Hansard* calls 'turbulence' in the House of Commons, the Westminster village on which Big Ben looks down remains a bulwark of peace, and of government of the people, by the people, for the people.

The English Parish Church
Simon Jenkins

The smallest church in England lies buried in thick woods where the slopes of Exmoor fall towards the Bristol Channel. The church of St Culbone lies a mile from any road, silent relic of a long-lost settlement of lepers and prisoners, left to fend for themselves in the forest. Today, worshippers still walk from Porlock to kneel and pray amid the shades of their forebears, surrounded only by the sounds of the woods. The place is deeply moving. At Culbone, the Christian God somehow communes with the older gods of tree and forest.

I am told that every breeze passing over a meadow leaves some memory of its passing in the lie of the grass. Likewise, the walls of England's churches bear the imprint of the passing of history. To me, they are the true museum of the nation, a collective memorial to the English people, especially to those who lived far from London, from court, cathedral and commerce. They display what Thomas Gray in his churchyard elegy called 'the homely joys and destiny obscure… the short and simple annals of the poor'.

Ever since the Middle Ages, and despite Reformation and Civil War, the Christian church has been the patron of the best British vernacular art and craftsmanship. It guards the best stone and wood carving, the best screens, bench-ends and sculpture, the best stained glass, the best metalwork, calligraphy and embroidery. After the great cathedrals, parish churches are the noblest manifestation of medieval art extant. Their bells are the music of the landscape, their steeples its punctuation marks.

For most people today, the church means little more than a tapering spire rising above a skirt of trees and cottage roofs. It is a symbol of antiquity and conservatism, seldom entered and always in need of repair. Villages and towns with surviving medieval churches tend to be those avoided by the Industrial Revolution and by Victorian zeal. Stonework still crumbles to the touch. Graveyards are filled with tumbling headstones and ryegrass. Rooks bustle about the oaks and beeches. The scene seems laden with nostalgia for something irretrievably lost; yet the church remains a fixed point in the English landscape.

Seeking the best churches is like nominating 'winners' in the National Gallery. Some 8,000 Anglican churches survive in England from before the Reformation, and roughly the same number have been founded since. (Parish churches are less prominent in Wales, Scotland and Ireland.) They stand alongside countless churches of other denominations, mostly erected in the past century and a half. The British may have become a godless society, but England is far from being a churchless landscape.

No student of ecclesiastical architecture could fail to appreciate the masterpieces of non-cathedral church architecture. Beverley, Tewkesbury, Christ Church, Selby and Sherborne are relics of medieval monasteries which failed to make cathedral status after the Dissolution, yet were miraculously saved from destruction. While they rank with the finest of cathedrals, they are parish churches, no more or less, and must be supported by their communities as such.

More typical are the great town churches, most of them the products of mercantile patronage from the 14th century onwards. The magnificent church of St Mary Redcliffe,

The Kingdom of God is at hand. Repent ye, and believe the Gospel

The Blood of Jesus Christ His Son cleanseth us from all Sin

Holy, Holy, Holy Lord God Almighty, Which was & is & is to come

As many as are led by the Spirit of God, They are the Sons of God

All Scripture is given by Inspiration of God, and is profitable

Bristol, still holds the ghosts of Bristolian sea captains in its north porch, the arch modelled on a Seljuk portal whose design boasts of some distant voyage. The soaring tower of St Peter Mancroft in Norwich challenges the local cathedral in splendour, as does that of St Cuthbert in Wells. The towers of Somerset display a fierce civic pride, a virtuoso collection of late-medieval art. Those of East Anglia are stupendous works of medieval engineering.

The true church enthusiast often prefers not the spectaculars but the small 'atmosphericks', churches seldom visited and thus considered private discoveries. My favourites include the Norman St Aldhelm's Chapel, alone on its seaside clifftop at Worth Matravers in Dorset. It defies both the elements and the passage of time. At Willoughby in Nottinghamshire I found a rare figurine of the Madonna of the Rose, barely six inches high, that had escaped the attention of the iconoclasts. The 12th-century church of Kilpeck sits silent on a Herefordshire outcrop, its red stone grotesques glowing like embers until fired into life by the setting sun. In a fold in the North York Moors lies the ancient crypt of Lastingham, its giant capitals harking back to the architecture of the Roman conquest. On a rainy winter's evening, I found that someone had laid a copy of Eliot's 'Little Gidding' on the lectern. The marriage of archaeology and poetry was deeply moving.

Churches are among the last traces of county England. They define counties as do no other works of art. Soaring stone spires speak of Northamptonshire and the East Midlands. Humble drovers' chapels speak of the Sussex Downs. In the West Country, gnarled pews still honour Charles the Martyr as if the Reformation had never happened. In London are the post-Fire churches erected by Wren, Hawksmoor and others, more splendid than anything of their time in Europe.

In every county is an eccentric. Shobdon hides in the backwoods of Herefordshire, a riot of rococo Gothick like a boudoir in the *Marriage of Figaro*. In Wreay in Cumbria lies the only church designed by a woman, Sarah Losh, in memory of her family and a young soldier killed on the Afghan frontier. The church is an inspiration to any visitor and Losh is architecture's Charlotte Brontë.

We approach churches with different emotions. To T S Eliot they were places of intense holiness, 'tongued with fire beyond the language of the living'. John Betjeman required a church 'to bring us to our knees in prayer'. Others see churches as a sort of museum, a place of local history, art and craftsmanship. They lock within their walls not just the handiwork of their communities, but the story of their faith. They are custodians of the hopes, fears, joys and agonies of English people for over a millennium. Churches are witnesses to England's history, both spiritual and secular. They are the nation's most enduring and endearing institution.

The 15th-century roof of the church of St Mary, Woolpit, Suffolk

The Discovery of Penicillin
Thomas Stuttaford

Sir Alexander Fleming, who is credited with the discovery of penicillin, was, like Admiral Nelson, accorded the special honour of being buried in St Paul's Cathedral. However, Fleming's contribution to Britain's glory, although developed during a war, was essentially one of peace.

Few people would have guessed, if they had met Alexander Fleming as a boy, that he would one day be internationally renowned. His early career was unremarkable. His education was not guaranteed to lead to academic greatness. He went to Kilmarnock Academy and then to Regent's Street Polytechnic. On leaving the polytechnic, he didn't immediately go into medicine, but became a shipping clerk. By dint of working in his spare time, and although older than the other entrants, he won a scholarship to St Mary's Hospital Medical School in London, where he displayed a brilliance which had previously lain hidden, and won virtually every prize the school had to offer.

Fleming's name will forever be synonymous with the discovery of the first antibiotic, which heralded the post-war revolution in drug therapy and the advent of modern medicine. The actual discovery of penicillin was fortuitous, but the element of chance shouldn't diminish the importance of Fleming's contribution. He was a punctilious and precise scientist, who had been taught to be very observant and to record everything he observed. However, Fleming was not only a painstaking worker; he was also a seminal thinker. Six years before he noted the antibacterial effects of one of the penicillin moulds, he had recognised the importance of an enzyme called lysozyme, which is found in tears and some mucous fluids, and has a role in countering infection.

If Fleming hadn't had a summer holiday in 1928, penicillin might never have been discovered. Before he went away he had, by chance, left some staphylococci growing on an uncovered petri dish by an open window in his laboratory. (Petri dishes are glass dishes, rather like saucers, containing a nutrient jelly on which bacteria will flourish.) On his return, Fleming noted that where a mould had blown in and grown on the culture plate, it had competed with, and destroyed, the staphylococci.

Fleming failed to identify the type of penicillin correctly, even if his earlier work in the First World War, during which he had been involved in counteracting cross-infections in war wounds, enabled him to see its potential. The antiseptics used in the 1914–18 war had been toxic and destructive of healthy tissue. Fleming realised that penicillin, although an anti-microbial, was neither destructive nor even irritant, but that it was effective against the whole range of gram positive bacteria. Unfortunately, preparations made from it in the traditional way were highly unstable and therefore therapeutically useless.

Fleming never worked again on his discovery. He recorded and published it, and then – with the exception of Professor Harold Raistrick's research in 1936, which repeated Fleming's

A chance discovery: the Penicillin chrysogenum *fungus used in the production of antibiotics*

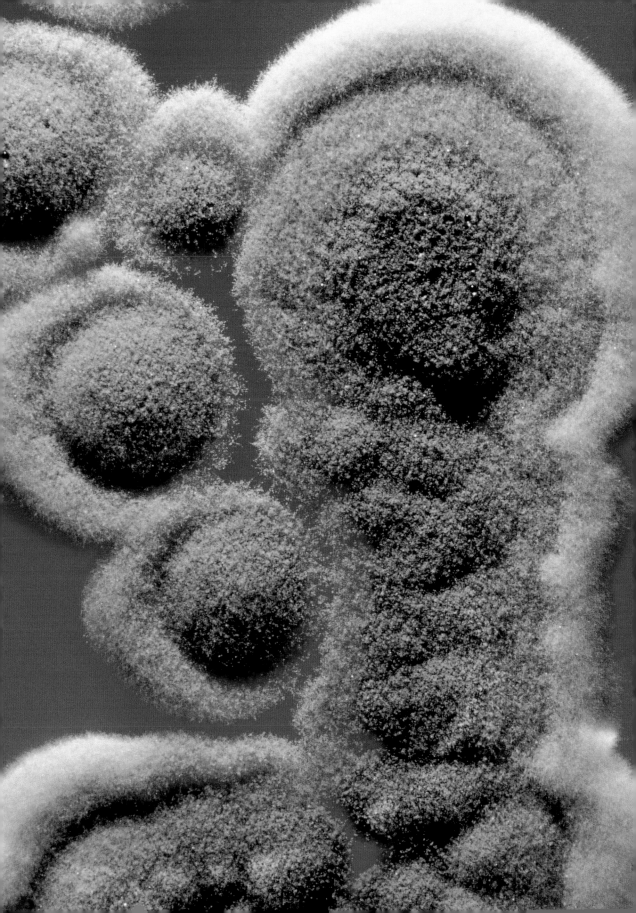

work and confirmed both penicillin's antibiotic powers and its instability – it seems to have been forgotten. When the Second World War became imminent, the search was on for a better anti-microbial treatment than had been available in the First. A team working in Oxford, which included Howard Florey and Ernst Chain, undertook the project. As scientists are wont to do, they combed the literature for anything which might be relevant before starting their own experiments, and came across Fleming's paper on penicillin. Fleming was approached and was only too keen to lend his support.

The Oxford scientists isolated the antibacterial component of penicillin, found a means of producing it by chemical synthesis, and started animal experiments with eight mice, which were inoculated with streptococci. The four mice which received penicillin injections survived, the four which did not died. Encouraged by its effect on mice – which often respond in a very human way to drugs – the scientists looked for someone who would be doomed without some dramatic intervention. In the Radcliffe Infirmary there was a policeman who had scratched himself while pruning his roses. These scratches had become infected with staphylococcal bacteria – the same organism which had grown on Fleming's petri dish when he was on holiday 12 years earlier. The effect of the penicillin on the policeman's septicaemia was dramatic: from being moribund, he started to recover. For a time it looked as if the story would have a happy ending, but the penicillin manufactured in Oxford's laboratories ran out and the patient died.

Florey realised the enormous potential of penicillin as an antibiotic, but he also recognised the limitations of pathology and chemistry laboratories as pharmaceutical factories. Although he and his team utilised old bathtubs, milk churns and, it is said, even bedpans, they couldn't hope to produce penicillin in commercial quantities; and the British pharmaceutical industry was already weighed down producing drugs for the armed forces. The Oxford team asked one of their number, Norman Heatley, who had done much of the fundamental work on the manufacture of penicillin, to go to America. There he, and an American called Andrew J Moyer, improved the manufacturing technique still further, and persuaded three American companies to apply it commercially. By 1943, manufacture was well enough established for penicillin to be used very effectively in treating the Allied war-wounded.

Harold Florey and Ernst Chain had very different, but difficult and determined, characters. Florey was tough and exuberant; Chain, who had had a well-established career in Berlin before coming as a refugee to Cambridge in 1933, has been described as teutonically practical. He was efficient and far-sighted, even if he had the habit of changing his mind while pursuing his research. One of the major disputes between Florey and Chain was over patents. Chain wanted Oxford to patent penicillin, but Florey felt this was a discovery for the whole of mankind and adamantly refused. As a result, the American pharmaceutical companies who manufactured the first commercial batches patented it themselves, and the British later had to pay huge royalties to use their own invention. By then, however, penicillin, the first antibiotic – discovered only because an observant scientist had mistakenly left a petri dish uncovered during a summer holiday – had changed medicine forever.

Pets
Julie Burchill

Every 20 seconds the RSPCA responds to a call from the public; with no government funding, just 320 inspectors investigate the hundreds of calls they receive each day. They looked into more than 132,000 cruelty complaints last year – every one they received – and brought more than 2,700 successful convictions. These are the first statistics one must take on board whenever considering the alleged British love affair with animals.

But then there is also the fact that in most other countries in the world the phrase 'cruelty to animals' would not raise an eyebrow. Bullfights? *Foie gras?* Bear-baiting, cock-fighting? Sure. Right this way.

Although the British often fall short of their ideals when it comes to treatment of our furry friends, the very existence of those ideals marks us out from the rest of the world, and informs our view of other nations. At least part of our antipathy towards the French (where vegetarians are routinely mocked in a manner that died out here in the 1950s) comes from the fact that they eat horses; snails too, thereby breaking the second British taboo on which animals it is OK to eat. Ideally, neither the really beautiful ones nor the really ugly ones should go under the knife – only the moderately attractive should be masticated.

It was the French philosopher René Descartes who decreed that animals were literally automata, and this idea appears to have stuck there. But even in allegedly civilised Switzerland you can buy dried dog meat, while in Spain *caldo de gato Extremadura* features cat cooked in white wine with bay leaves and thyme. The Ancient Greeks and Aztecs ate both dogs and cats, as do the Chinese, Ghanaians, Burmese and Koreans. The Filipino addiction to dogmeat is so great that the government have had to limit its consumption by law after rabies entered the human population *via* dinner *à deux*.

But the British are different. 'I had a slice of spaniel the other day,' wrote the English journalist and MP Henry Labouchere during the siege of Paris in 1870, when over 1,000 dogs and 5,000 cats were eaten by the starving population, 'and it made me feel like a cannibal.' Perhaps it is the British sense of fair play that makes us reject the idea of eating those bred for companionship, or perhaps our famous lack of ability or inclination to show our feelings to our loved ones finds a welcome release in the mute compadre. Whatever the cause, pets play a part in British life which is both comical and touching.

Perhaps I, like many other people, am over-attached to my pets. But these Anglo-Saxon attitudes don't just come out of the blue. Human history is a veritable vale of tears, and one day you just hear about one developing country too many where they can't afford food but can somehow afford endless state-of-the-art weaponry, and your string snaps. This is why young people here are so massively disillusioned with even humanitarian politics, but will happily throw themselves under a lorry in order to better the life of a veal calf. That is why the young honeymoon couple fell in love with a mangy Greek stray, came home and could not get him off their minds, so packed in their jobs and went back to Greece to look for him. Six months later, financially ruined, they found the unprepossessing mutt and were pictured

with him in the newspapers, tears of joy running down their faces, declaring 'It's all been worth it!' Love that illogical, that mad, seems wonderfully refreshing in this sensible, penny-pinching world of ours.

'People who love animals hate people.' There's always some misery-bucket lurking around muttering this whenever the human love of animals comes up in conversation, usually in conjunction with the amazingly original observation that 'Hitler was a vegetarian, you know!' So? Hitler was also a man, a European and a house-painter, and if we were to conclude that just because *he* was criminally insane then so are the constituents of each of these groups, we'd rightly be accused of being total bigots and alarmists. The statement also implies, of course, that people who don't like animals spend their entire lives working for the betterment of the poor, sick and wretched people of the earth, dividing their time between the Samaritans hot-line and soup-doling front-line when they're not going round hospices holding the hands of the terminally ill. Whereas in reality it means that they're just too tight to spring for a 39p tin of Kattomeat. It really is time to nail once and for all the myth that every time one feeds a duck in Sussex, a fellow human being dies in Ethiopia. One has absolutely nothing to do with the other.

No, if someone has no time for pets, what it reveals about them, in my opinion, is not an all-embracing love of humanity, but rather an absolute lack of a sense of humour – the sense of humour that the British are famous for, in fact. For it is the very *preposterousness* of cats and dogs that is so enriching and enlivening. In a world where, increasingly, human beings are bred to live their lives like beetles on a dungheap, scurrying around attending to their own ordure with no glimpse of a greater plan, the very existence of pets is proof that some things actually prove their excellence by *not* being a profit-making concern in this rational, rationalised society of ours.

To be born with a leg at each corner, and a tail – a *tail*! – and to exist solely to be stroked and loved; well, it makes a lot more sense to me than putting a bomb under somebody because you want to see a different piece of material fluttering from the flagpole. The British have lost their faith in politicians and put their faith in pets; I'd say it was a pretty good deal.

Previous pages: *A preposterous pet investigating a dinosaur at the National Musueum of Wales*

The Proms
James Naughtie

No event has more trouble with its climax than the Proms. That Last Night… those balloons… the funny hats… the juvenile chants. It is safe to say that for everyone who loves it and cherishes it as some piece of Britannia that must never be allowed to crumble, there are a dozen and more who flee at the very thought of it. This is a pity, one of the great pities of our time, because the Proms at their best – away from the Last Night – are an example of how music should be enjoyed. They are fresh and they are challenging.

Every summer, thousands of people chance on the Royal Albert Hall or hear a vague recommendation that they should give the Proms a try. They drift in from Hyde Park across the road, or from the steps of the Albert Memorial where they've been enjoying the golden glow that its restoration has given back to us. They squat on the floor of the arena or drape themselves high up in the gallery for a price unknown in any other concert hall – still only £3 in 2000 for each of 72 concerts – and they can hear for nearly two months during the summer some of the best musicians enjoying the experience of playing to up to 5,000 people who fill that great amphitheatre and have only one rule: listen to what's being played.

How strange it is that the Proms should be regarded as so 'British', because this kind of cultural experience is one that our tradition has often tended to strangle. It has sometimes been thought right to fear serious music, and though there are spectacular exceptions – think of Manchester's relationship with the Hallé – it has often been considered a near-private experience for an élite, something best done away from the public gaze.

In all the argument about 'accessibility', which sometimes takes such tortuous ideological turns and ends up back where it started, the Proms are the example to be celebrated. You can hear almost anything here, from the Germanic symphonic repertoire played in a given year by the Berlin Philharmonic or the Vienna, or maybe the New York or the Chicago Symphony, to the new commissions which have always been a pillar of the Proms and are still wheedled out of our younger composers by the BBC, now the sole and determined guardian of the season. The point is breadth. The spirit is of discovery. The atmosphere is emphatically relaxed.

How difficult it sometimes seems for people to think of that relaxation together with artistic seriousness, and yet it is the whole point. There is no more silly fallacy than the belief that the smarter an audience is, the more likely it is to listen attentively to the music or to enjoy it. The Proms give the lie to that nonsense, night after night.

There is hardly a tie to be seen, but the silence is profound. Artists who come for the first time tend to boggle at the way the audience, particularly those standing or sitting in front of them on the floor, is absorbed by the music. Even some of those who will be blunt about the Albert Hall acoustics, which can't compare with an engineered concert hall's, tend to talk of the energy they get from the audience. The ones who are apt to fall asleep in concerts are tucked away up in the boxes; the ones you see are there to listen to every note. And if you are trying to wrestle with Rachmaninov on a dodgy piano – quite a common experience not too long ago in this hall, though no more – that helps.

Since Sir Henry Wood started the festival, a little more than 100 years ago, it has introduced generations of people to the magical quality of live music. Performance is the thing. Once felt, that immediacy isn't easily forgotten. Even a slightly ropey concert can feel special there, and I have seen artists who are fumbling get strength from the faces in front of them, enough to recover and get through it with a flourish. And orchestral players from some fabled stables look forward to their visits with an almost childish glee. They don't see audiences like this anywhere else.

The idea of the promenade, which Sir Henry perpetuated with his own orchestra in the Queen's Hall next to Broadcasting House until one of Hitler's bombs moved the show to the Albert Hall, was to establish that kind of intimacy. They weren't stuck in their seats. And still, in the arena and the gallery, they sprawl and move around. They bring rucksacks and books, water bottles and bulging briefcases from the office. All sorts of things go on, and as long as it stays quiet no one minds. The atmosphere of the late-night Proms, which have become a regular part of the season in the last couple of decades, is one that you hardly find at a classical concert anywhere else. If only those who see the Last Night on television once a year could feel this, instead of having to cringe when the front 10 rows do their bobbing up and down to Wood's own arrangement of British sea songs, or gag at the balloon-popping and manic flag-waving. A former director, Sir John Drummond, tried to cool it all with an order banning strange devices. It didn't work. And the awkwardness of his position had been illuminated a few years earlier when the Last Night conductor, Mark Elder, then at English National Opera, attacked the excessively nationalistic atmosphere and was promptly replaced. When it comes to the Last Night, you can't win.

The antidote is the rest of the season. New compositions, authentic baroque performance, the symphonic repertoire at its best, soloists from the top drawer, jazz and now children's proms. From a rather flabby post-war period – there were no foreign conductors until the late 1950s, believe it or not – the Proms in the last 40 years have become a festival of a kind that isn't matched anywhere else in the world, even in some of the finest European temples of music. And on every night except one you wouldn't know that the trainspotter element in the audience is there at all.

Anyone who feels pride in that achievement knows that it is worth more than a thousand flags, even if they are all waving in time.

Music for all: a poster for a 1922 Queen's Hall concert conducted by Henry Wood

QVEEN'S HALL

Sole Lessees— Messrs. CHAPPELL & Co., LTD.

TWENTY-SIXTH SEASON, 1921-22.

SATURDAY, JAN. 28TH, 1922,
AT 3 O'CLOCK.

SOLO PIANOFORTE—
BUSONI.

THE NEW
QUEEN'S HALL ORCHESTRA
(Proprietors—Messrs. CHAPPELL & Co., LTD.)

PRIN. VIOLIN - MR. MAURICE SONS
ORGANIST - MR. FREDK. B. KIDDLE

CONDUCTOR:
SIR HENRY J. WOOD

SYMPHONY CONCERTS

FRANK NVDD

ANALYTICAL PROGRAMME, ONE SHILLING.

The Pub
Rowan Pelling

> There is nothing which has yet been contrived by man, by which so
> much happiness is produced as by a good tavern or inn.
>
> (James Boswell, *Life of Johnson*)

The British public house is at the heart of the nation's social life. And the prefix 'public' is as misleading in this context as it is when attached to a British school. The implication seems to be that any old Joe is welcome, when precisely the opposite is true. The British pub is run like a club and the landlord can blackball people on a whim. Kim Tickell, late, lamented patron of the Tickell Arms in Cambridgeshire, tacked the following to his door: 'No bare feet, dirty hair, gym shoes or lefties.' In Britain we have no written constitution, we have the unwritten understanding that no one is born equal; within the four walls of any establishment, be it a cottage, a pub or MI5, the resident chieftain has feudal rights over you. No matter who you are, the British publican reserves the right to be completely unimpressed.

Pubs are the melting-pots of British society; in front of the bar, queuing patiently for a pint, social boundaries fall away and all men stand equal before the landlord. How different that equality is, though, from the egalitarian freedom enjoyed by drinkers beyond these shores. The American dream is one of wide open spaces, roadside diners and individual freedom; the British vision celebrates the crushed snug bar and the petty tyranny of the landlord. The French take pride in chic city bars which serve 30 brands of Armagnac to Catherine Deneuve lookalikes; the British quietly relish a faded lounge with two draught ales, one bottled lager and Lambrusco served up by Barbara Windsor's spiritual cousin. And no culture celebrates drunkards to the degree that Britain does. Where else would Oliver Reed, Jeffrey Bernard and George Best have been so fêted for their capacity to drink a barrel dry?

I was born and bred in the perfect British pub. Shepperton Studios could have shipped it over to their back lot and Alex Korda would have given an approving nod. Built in the centre of a hamlet in the early 19th century, and little changed since, it has a front lawn studded with tables and skirted by beech trees. Access to the bar is gained by stepping gingerly over an enormous hound, but not before a vigorous session with the shoe-scraper by the door – 'Take that bloody mud off your boots,' someone roars from the gloom. The leaded windows, thick with dust and pollen, filter little light through. The bar runs the length of the long, low-ceilinged room and a row of polished dark wood stools prop up a meeting of the local philosophers. Away from the bar, by the big open fires that punctuate each end, is a motley arrangement of old family furniture, sofas that sag, tables that lurch and chairs with scarred legs. Just as important is what there isn't: no jukeboxes, no chips, no piped music and no fruit machines.

The hub of British life: down the pub in the 1950s

For many years the sole source of entertainment was my father: a trim silver-haired major in a sports jacket, with a Clark Gable moustache and strawberry-tinted nose, glaring at interlopers with barely suppressed rage. How dared people saunter into his bar uninvited trying to buy drinks? Didn't they have homes to go to? Had he fought a war so that rabble like this could sip lemonade shandy on his lawn? It's a curious fact that a nation which sets such store by genteel manners so applauds their total absence in its landlords. The ruder my father was, the more the punters loved him. A London headmaster and his gentle wife drove a round journey of 50 miles every Friday to be told to 'Bugger off'. My father retained the right to ban men with long hair, to call favoured clients 'rat' or 'hooligan', to serve pints topped by dead insects, ploughman's lunches covered in mould ('Turn the lights down, they'll never notice'), to make up prices as he went along, and to threaten undesirables with a loaded shotgun. One New Year's Eve, he surpassed himself and chucked out all the revellers at a quarter to midnight (he said it was 'the law'), and they had to sing Auld Lang Syne in the carpark. He was a mine of information, a maestro of the well-placed insult, and uniformly kind to women, children and dogs. At his funeral, grown men approached me in tears and told tales of secret generosity, money loaned and jobs secured, sound advice and great tips for the Derby. My father's coffin carried his last copy of the *Sporting Life* and he was buried next to a man who owed him a large bottle of brandy.

The British pub is all about character. The quirks of its structure's vernacular should be matched by its proprietor's and clientele's sheer looniness. People will scour the wildest dales of Yorkshire and the bleakest stretches of Exmoor looking for a scenario akin to the opening scene of *An American Werewolf in London*. They want to walk into a bar and find a bunch of inbred locals tying garlic to their jerkins. They want to be stared at with simmering malice as all conversation ceases. And after they've stayed at the local b & b two days, they'll be best friends with the landlord and engaged to his daughter. Because pub life is essentially a soap opera. It's no coincidence that *Eastenders*, *The Archers* and *Coronation Street* place pubs firmly at the centre of their action. Pubs make the perfect backdrop for romances and infidelity, feuds and skulduggery. Ever since Chaucer sent his pilgrims off to Canterbury with a stirrup-cup from the Tabard, pubs have been crucial to the British narrative tradition. From the hostelry of Mistress Quickly in *Henry IV Part I* to the inns of Henry Fielding's *Tom Jones*, pubs are the forum for debating the action of the external world.

All epic journeys should start from a pub, like the Battle of Britain fighter-pilots who were scrambled over Kent after a pint in the White Hart in Brasted. And when the foe's defeated and the golden prize is won, the journey's end should find you with a pint of best bitter, pulled from a handpump by a woman with the loveliest breasts in Christendom. As one wistful and anonymous British poet wrote, '*Meum est propositum in taberna mori*' or 'I desire to end my days in a tavern drinking'. It's hard to disagree. When my time comes, I hope the Grim Reaper carries a handbell and calls out to me softly, 'Last orders, ladies and gentlemen, please.'

Punk
Ian Rankin

I was 17 in 1977, just about the perfect age for punk. The time and the mood were right. Unemployment statistics, racism, Northern Ireland, and the plight of youth: topics and concerns not exactly dealt with by the behemoth of 'Prog Rock'. At 14 I'd been cherry-picked for one of Fife's better comprehensive schools, where I met fans of ELP, Yes, Genesis, Focus, and the like. But my roots were working class: after school was out and I'd swapped my blazer and tie for a Target shirt, I'd be mixing with friends from my old school. They all wore regulation Doc Martens and Skinner jeans, suede-head haircuts with long sideburns. They all read 'Skinhead' books and *A Clockwork Orange*. They listened to the same music: heavy metal, Status Quo, Alex Harvey. While to Prog Rock fans the 'three-chord wonder' of Status Quo sounded banal, to me it always sounded cleaner and more honest than something like Van der Graaf Generator. But it didn't matter whether the band in question was Quo or Genesis: the one thing we could be clear about in Fife was that none of them would be heading our way. It was a long time since Dunfermline's Kinema Ballroom had played host to bands like Deep Purple, or David Bowie had played Glenrothes.

As the 1970s progressed, it seemed that the bands were intent on distancing themselves from their fans. The giants, such as the Stones and Led Zeppelin, would play huge stadiums, with massive TV screens so that most of the paying public weren't reduced to watching a group of spindly, ageing ants hundreds of yards away. Rock was trying to grow up, toying with classical arrangements, its lyrics becoming ever more opaque and cerebral, the cover designs of the likes of Roger Dean and Hipgnosis striving for mainstream acceptance as works of art… All the time forgetting that the essence of rock is the antithesis of the grown-up and the 'brainy'. It's about being young and being rude, about shocking your elders and betters. About rebellion.

Enter punk rock. Being 500 miles from London, our first sightings of the beast came through salacious media reports and grainy photo-shoots. The rock weekly *Sounds* was an early bible, to be read, memorised and passed around. Soon we discovered that to form a punk band, all you needed were instruments and a dollop of chutzpah. No experience required. I decided to buy a punk record at my local record shop, Bruce's in Kirkcaldy. The old rockers behind the counter sneered at me as I shelled out for the Damned's *New Rose*. A couple of months later, Bruce's had its own punk fanzine, *Cripes*, and boss Bruce Findlay was on his way to managing Simple Minds. A bunch of us started taking the train to Edinburgh on Saturdays, where we'd slouch around and buy punk records in Virgin on Frederick Street. We knew we'd cracked it when a well-dressed elderly lady confronted us on Cockburn Street and shrieked 'Can't you walk like human beings?!' Punk was dangerous all right. Back in our home town, a friend of mine was head-butted by a crash-helmeted biker, just for 'looking different'.

Influenced by seminal fanzine *Sniffin' Glue*, I would sneak into the economics class at school when no one was looking and use the copier to produce my own fanzine, *Mainlines*. Then we got someone to take our photo as we posed in the boys' toilets. We sent a letter to *Sounds* along with the photo, and both were printed. It was probably the highlight of any of our lives to that date. It was the same issue which had the Pistols on the cover, signing to A & M outside Buckingham Palace. By this time, punk didn't seem so distant. Every town in the country had its own resident punk band.

Every Sunday we'd head off to the Pogo-A-Gogo club in Kirkcaldy. I would sneak out of the house with my punk gear in a bag. An enlightened parent drove us to our destination, while we all changed in the back. I had purloined a blue boilersuit, which I'd laid out on my bedroom floor before dripping neat bleach onto it. It looked fine, but smelt terrible, and my mother was always puzzled by the large white stain which had appeared on my bedroom carpet.

At the Pogo, there was usually a live band, and if we were lucky they'd be the Skids, Fife's first and best. One night, the pogoing got so bad that the wedding party from downstairs in the hotel came to complain that the ceiling was about to come down. We all looked at each other and grinned: right time, right place. The only thing left to do was form our own punk band, so that's what we did. It was an *ad hoc* affair, put together for the December '77 Christmas school dance. Our drummer had never picked up a set of sticks in his life. Our guitarist was classically trained, and more used to playing with the Scottish Youth Jazz Orchestra. And the singer… well, that was me. I'd penned a little ditty titled 'Cowdenbeath's Burning', based none too subtly on the Clash's 'London's Burning'. Everything was fine until the guitar solo, which sounded like a Mike Oldfield B-side…

From the ashes of that evening, a band did eventually form. We called ourselves the Dancing Pigs, but we weren't punk; we were New Wave. The tunes were all written by the keyboard player, who liked David Sylvian and Japan. Punk was already in its death throes, only the news took a little time to reach us north of the border. Reading and watching the histories of punk rock now is a disorienting experience, because they all concentrate on the Pistols and Malcolm McLaren, on the fact that punk was created as a tool for selling clothing and merchandise. Or else they insist that punk was a political movement. But at the time, it was a brute necessity, a way of clearing away the musical detritus and bringing rock back to the people (and *vice versa*). It got us back to the drum/guitar/bass sound which is integral to rock and roll, and it intimated to a lot of young people that they had a chance, that they were worthwhile, that they didn't have to conform. Go make a band and make a noise, go write a magazine. Go and perform. The trickle-down effect from those days is still being felt. And in the process punk has become part of the iconography of Britain, as witness every third postcard outside London's tourist booths. It'll be a cold day in hell before I stop listening to punk.

The public face of a grass roots movement: Johnny Rotten of the Sex Pistols

Queuing
Shyama Perera

I wasn't born British, I had Britishness thrust upon me. Thrust, in the sense that one day I was somewhere else, the next I was here in the country of pea-souper fogs, *Rule Britannia* and Lassie. It was an age of pinstripe suits and bowler hats, of boiled beef and carrots, and Anita Harris going on a tuppeny bus ride. For a small Asian girl, however, the quintessential spirit of the country was enshrined in an Enid Blyton phrase that peppered her Mallory Towers and St Clare's books: the British sense of honour. The British sense of honour was something characters were always trying to impress on visiting Americans and wild Spanish circus girls who crept out of the dorm to ride horses bareback in the moonlight. It was a quality which I immediately recognised and understood; and I saw it best embodied in the practice of queuing.

More than the church, which represents the past, or the City, the present, the queue captures the timeless essence of the British spirit. This is because, while the way the queue is constructed may change, the way it operates doesn't. Thus we have multi-queuing at cashpoint machines and inside banks; parallel queuing at bus stops equipped with both seating and standing space; allocated queuing at departure gates or the London Eye; and standard queuing at theme parks, ticket booths and supermarket tills.

Whichever mode is preferred, the underlying principle remains the same: first come, first served. Woe betide the dodgers who try to ingratiate themselves further up the line. Almost inevitably, someone will politely redirect them to the back as the polymorphous straggle suddenly condenses into a tight, single formation, squeezing out shoulder space and becoming instantly impenetrable.

The queue is a totem of patience, practicality and a sense of fair play, which starts in the playground and the school dinner-hall and continues in the endless queues that start to form early outside Post Offices on pension payment day. The signing-on queue and the welfare queues are demonstrable examples of these qualities in practice. People who may be desperate for work or money, people who are often on the brink of despair and loss, wait politely for hours in forlorn expectation of succour. This is Britishness at its most impressive. Which is not to say that everyone appreciates it. In the multicultural hotchpotch of the city centre, we occasionally see members of more assertive or less organised races trying either to test or to buck the system. With each new basket of immigrants, there's a period of trial and error. People rushing for the doors as the Number 8 draws up, or trying to slip a trolley through the baskets checkout at Asda. Ultimately, the penny drops. They literally fall into line. How could one not, when it's one of the fairest and gentlest ways of ensuring parity?

My first memory of marathon queuing is standing in line with my mother to enter Selfridges on the first day of the sale. Outside were people who'd spent two or three nights sleeping by the main doors to buy a half-price colour television or a bargain Wedgwood dinner service. I often wondered how they could guarantee getting them, when the tenth person down the line might have faster legs or longer arms with which to gather the item.

There was never any problem. The first queue I joined voluntarily was outside the Rainbow in London's Finsbury Park. It was around 1974, and I wanted to see David Bowie in concert. The Who's rock opera *Tommy* was on around the same time with an all-star line-up. Crazily, both sets of tickets were released on the same day. I was 14, and nobody in the queue was over 30. It would have been so easy to slip in unnoticed between groups of stoned hippies, to complain about the ridiculously inefficient box office with only two tellers, or to create an aggressive disturbance in order to discourage some of the punters. The thought never entered our heads. Instead, we maintained a cordial ambience. For a full nine hours, standing in the rain on a cold and miserable day.

Queuing is an inherent part of being British. Now that I'm older and on a more rigid timetable, with responsibilities for children, home and work deadlines, every minute lost has consequences. None the less, I will sit silently in unmoving traffic for hours, thinking unprintable thoughts, but never once tooting. The British are one of the few races for whom road rage is alien – that's why it receives so much coverage. I have sat for 30 minutes on a one-way city road in the middle of the rush-hour while a scaffolding truck unloaded. Getting out to stretch my legs, I could see the line of traffic behind me stretching for several blocks. Not one person complained or sat on the horn, despite the fact we were all office-bound. Given that we had no choice, and that, if the truck didn't hold us up now, it would merely inconvenience a different group of drivers in an hour's time, we took the delay on the chin.

The queue represents the qualities of justice and righteousness that have fuelled British thought and action from the centuries of empire to the days of equal opportunity and multiculturalism. I contend, however, that, more than any scientific or cultural invention, more than any rule or right enshrined in statute, more than any other social construct or convention, it literally stands alone as a beacon of success. The fundamental principle does not lend itself to either criticism or revisionism. That is the queue's triumph.

Overleaf: *Falling into line: a rationing queue in Camberwell, South London, 1947*

The Red Telephone Box
Andrew Graham-Dixon

'There are signs that the telephone Kiosk will soon become as familiar an object in our highways and byways as the more historic red pillar box,' announced an editorial in the *Telegraph and Telephone Journal* of 1933. 'With its cheerful hue by day and its welcoming bright light at night, its promise of ready communication, its form as a friendly figure in the scene whether it stands in one of a row in a busy railway station or shopping centre, or solitary in a suburban High Street… it is undoubtedly a persuasive standing advertisement of the telephone service.'

The author of this prescient panegyric to Giles Gilbert Scott's classic red British telephone box was writing less than a decade after examples of the first prototype model – the K2, as it was known – had begun to appear on the streets of London. In its even more successful later incarnation, as the lighter, cheaper but equally solid and well-designed K6 (the 'Jubilee Kiosk'), Scott's classic example of 20th-century street furniture would become rather more than 'a persuasive standing advertisement of the telephone service'. It would become a ubiquitous feature of the national landscape and an instantly recognisable symbol of Britain itself.

The much loved telephone cubicle was the product of a rare moment. As the Victorian era came to a close, there was a general reaction both against the eclecticism of 19th-century taste and against what was widely regarded as the chaotic, free-for-all 19th-century attitude to city planning and development. The classical style made a comeback, as did the supposedly 'classical' values of a centrally planned and organised urban environment. The Great War, which killed so many, further intensified the general public desire to improve the lot of the living.

Spare but unmistakably classical in inspiration, capped by a saucer dome supported by four segmented pediments, Scott's elegant red telephone box was one of the most enduring products of this unusual time (other prominent manifestations of the same utopian spirit of civic improvement being the lettering and station designs commissioned for the London Underground by Frank Pick). The 'Jubilee Kiosk', manufactured in many thousands, is an object lesson in the combination of form and function: instantly recognisable, almost perfectly soundproofed and eminently well suited to shelter its users from the harsh British weather. The only regular complaint made about it concerned the heaviness of the teak door and the difficulty of gaining sufficient purchase on the rather shallow 'cup' handles provided to open it. But just as every Turkish rug is said to contain a deliberate mistake to propitiate God, Scott should be allowed his one tiny flaw.

Scott was a practising architect who thought of the Bankside Power Station as his finest work (it too has become a Great British Landmark, having been converted into Tate Modern, the world's largest modern art gallery). The primary inspiration for his telephone box was – aptly enough if one considers such a construction to be a miniature building – architectural. He

A secular confessional: Giles Gilbert Scott's classic red telephone box in a rural landscape

based his design partly on the mausoleum which the great Georgian architect Sir John Soane built for himself and his family in St Pancras Churchyard. There is a very close resemblance between Scott's saucer dome and the dome that caps the Soane tomb, and given that Scott was a trustee of the Soane Museum this is unlikely to have been merely coincidental. British films and television dramas have often contained scenes where people get shot or stabbed to death in the telephone box, perhaps in subliminal recognition of its origins in graveyard architecture.

Scott originally intended his telephone box to be neutral in hue, but the GPO persuaded him to make it red and in doing so made one of the few really brave British colour decisions of the 20th century. Colour has made the British people terribly nervous ever since the 16th and 17th centuries. It was then that the reforming zealots of the Church of England (followed by the Puritans) tore all the paintings out of the nation's churches and cathedrals, smashed all the brightly painted statues which adorned their exteriors, and whitewashed everything over. Up until that time, hard as it may be to believe, the British had been regarded as among the most passionate and colourful of the European peoples. People came from far and wide to purchase English red pigments and dyes, said to be the reddest and brightest to be found anywhere. But ever since the Reformation, strong hues, like strong feelings, have been viewed with great suspicion in Britain. Especially red.

The telephone box was a wonderful exception to the long tyranny of British chromophobia. It is a particular pleasure to come on examples, as one sometimes still does, in the middle of the countryside. Red being the complementary of green, they make an especially vivid effect in rural locations – and, incidentally, prove how wrong all those silly country conservatives are in their belief that man-made constructions should be designed to 'blend in' with the scenery. Truly great designs assert their own presence and before you know it they have become *part of* the scenery. Proof that the telephone box has done so is to be found in the fact that people up and down the country now want to conserve them. They have become Heritage. Passionate battles are fought on their behalf.

I suspect there is more to this curious national attachment to Scott's telephone box than a simple love of the principles of good design. As is the case with so many aspects of national life, I think the true explanation for this British love affair is ultimately to be found in the deep recesses of the nation's troubled religious history. Britain is a Protestant nation brutally cut off from a Catholic past for which it cannot help secretly yearning. We want to be passionate and colourful and outgoing and all the things that we were before the Church of England reinvented us as dour introspective introverts. We want to be able to sin and confess, to be forgiven and shriven at a stroke. Perhaps it is this which ultimately accounts for the deep appeal of Giles Gilbert Scott's telephone box. I think it was one of the Surrealists who described the telephone as 'an implement of confession'. Scott, who designed his telephone box while Surrealism was in its heyday, gave the proposition tangible form. His ubiquitous, papal-red cubicle for confidential communication was nothing less than a modern, secular confessional – a capsule into which the British people could step, as one, as if to return, miraculously, to their repressed Catholic origins.

Robin Hood
Ruth Padel

Every fairy-tale needs a forest. The forests of northern Europe were the crucible of folk imagination, magical, confusing, a tangle of dangerous dark sexuality (see the thorns around Sleeping Beauty), where you stray off the path (like the Babes in the Wood or Red Riding Hood); where (like Snow White) you meet figures you never encounter elsewhere. Britain had all that too, but by the 13th century had its own extra take on the legendary forest. The Norman kings imposed a law which made all forests the king's 'secret place', whose animals were ferociously protected for him alone to kill. This, plus post-Conquest Saxon-Norman conflict, is the background to the Robin Hood legend.

The films faithfully reflect all that. Robin is a Saxon lordling (as in Walter Scott's *Ivanhoe*): Kevin Costner or Patrick Bergin standing up on forest land he thinks of as his to champion a peasant caught poaching deer against a foul Norman baron enforcing the king's law. Then, outlawed, Robin sets up court in the forest. This is the peculiar British spin on fairy-tale forest (reflected in *As You Like It* and *A Midsummer Night's Dream* as the forest of Arden or Oberon's fairies): the alternative woodland court, a fairer society at the heart of the king's secret domain. In T H White's *The Sword in the Stone*, Robin is not Hood but Wood. 'What else should un be,' says Little John, 'seeing as he rules 'em?' As the wood's guerrilla 'ruler', Robin exists between the king's justice and injustice. His earliest screen appearance (in a British film, *Robin Hood and his Merry Men*, 1909) lined him up, like most films since, with Richard the Lionheart (absent on crusade) against the wicked Regent Prince John, to a backdrop of brutal taxes and tortured peasants.

How true is that?

If Robin lived, it was in the 12th or early 13th century, for he figures in songs and chronicles of the late 13th and 14th centuries. A portion of the Pipe Roll of 1230, relating to Yorkshire, mentions a 'Robertus Hood fugitivus'. Other traditions say he was born in 1160; or (it was a common medieval name) is in prison in 1354, awaiting trial for offences committed in Northamptonshire woodland. He died on 18 November 1247 – or in 1325. Or he was Robert Fitzooth, Earl of Huntingdon, from Locksley, Nottinghamshire, who fled to the woods in disguise. Or Robin and Little John were defeated with Simon de Montfort at the battle of Evesham. Or Robin is yeoman stock, hence his woodcraft. He turns up in Barnsdale in Yorkshire; in Nottinghamshire; in Plumpton Park in Cumberland; or in Sherwood Forest.

But whoever, whenever, wherever, behind his woodland existence is a politics of disaffection which made him the folk hero of over 80 14th-century ballads, the 'Rymes of Robyn Hood'. They are full of James Bondish fights, adventures, and escapes, but also that longing for a people's hero who plunders the rich to give to the poor. And they emerge around the time of the Peasants' Revolt (1381). Robin is against nobles, the law (the Sheriff of Nottingham), fat corrupt churchmen and feudal injustice. He is a matchless archer: generous, brave, imaginative; a medieval Batman or Scarlet Pimpernel. And also monumentally chivalrous: 'I never hurt woman in all my life / Nor man in woman's company.' Womankind responds

by killing him. He is bled to death by a treacherous nun suborned by his cousin, prior of Kirkless in Nottinghamshire. But his men – Allen-a-Dale, Will Scarlet, Little John, Friar Tuck – though they often start as antagonists (the fight on the bridge, the challenge in the cart), end by adding their own special qualities to his band.

Hollywood (Douglas Fairbanks in 1922, Errol Flynn in 1938) fell on Robin as the forerunner of the cowboy outlaw with different talents (like the Magnificent Seven) in his support team. But Robin came from deep in the British countryside and its idioms. There were country sayings like 'go round Robin Hood's barn' (get to the right conclusion the long way round), 'sell Robin Hood's pennyworth' (sell half-price), 'Robin Hood's feather' (a hatband), 'Robin Hood's bargain' (a pennyworth). Hundreds of hills, plants (especially flowers) and trees throughout England and Scotland bore his name.

For he also flickers out from a far earthier layer of folk imagination and life. From very early on, Robin Hood was also 'King of the May'. By the 15th century, he is the hero of many folk-plays which were assimilated to Morris Men's danced stories and the May Day pageants in which Maid Marian was also a character. (In later tradition, she gets drawn into his exploits because she was Columbine to his Harlequin in dances and May Day partying.) Behind Robin Hood are the springtime rites of village sex, pushed out of sight to the greenwood. The night before May Day you spent with lovers in the woods. As Amiens sings in *As You Like It*,

> Under the greenwood tree
> Who loves to lie with me...?

When Theseus (about to get married himself) sees the lovers of *A Midsummer Night's Dream* asleep in the forest, he guesses that 'they rose up early to observe / The rite of May'. Robin (the only 'merry' man in that wood who has a woman) is lord of spring lust and lustiness. The 'Lincoln Green' clothes were not just camouflage. Giving 'a green gown' for May Day spelt sex, as in Herrick's poem 'Corinna's Going A-Maying':

> Then she became a silken plaid
> And stretched upon a bed,
> And he became a green covering
> And gained her maidenhead.

And finally, green is fairy-tale's favourite colour for magic, too: as in the Green Knight (from a 'Green Chapel' in the forest) who disturbs King Arthur's midwinter revels. Robin Hood in green is also the 'spirit of the wood': a wood demon, the Jack-in-the Green or 'Green Man', whose leaf-ringed face glimmers at you on carved cloister bosses in the village church. So his woodland powers are over-determined. They come from every aspect of medieval British village life – well, all the big ones: ballads, politics, magic and sex. He is a hero-figure created by nearly 10 centuries of British folksong, fairy-tale, dances, and village theatre. Plus, of course, that achingly British longing for 'the greenwood'.

The forerunner of the cowboy outlaw: Errol Flynn as a Hollywood Robin Hood, 1938

Salisbury Cathedral Close
Edward Heath

I have lived for more than 15 years in the cathedral close in Salisbury, which throughout that time has retained both its charm and most of its sense of tranquillity. That is not to say that we are secluded, or play a less than wholehearted part in local affairs. Like most similar sites, the Close is a huge tourist magnet (with 750,000 visitors a year), and each year the ever-growing Salisbury Festival makes its presence felt, with a wide variety of exhibitions, concerts and massive *son et lumière* extravaganzas.

The Close contains a great array of English architecture. Some buildings, like the cathedral itself, date back to the 13th century. Others have sprung up more recently. All are set well back from the cathedral and between them they create an aura within the Close not only of peace and quiet but also of quintessential Englishness.

The cathedral close is not a uniquely British concept, of course. The stern cathedral in Lübeck, in northern Germany, has environs that would be recognisable to any denizen of an English cathedral city. However, the combination of grandeur with architectural and natural balance in Salisbury has, in my view at least, no equal either outside Britain or within it.

Originally, the area forming the Close was overwhelmingly allocated to members of the clergy connected with the cathedral. The priests, canons and clerks were given an acre and a half of land, with the more senior clergy receiving three acres. These days, only a tiny handful of the Chapter are resident in the Close, and the former Bishop's Palace has been turned into a school. Most of the houses in the Close are now leased by the cathedral to private residents, and a wide variety of people, many of whom have no direct connection with the Church of England, now live in them.

It was in the spring of 1985 that I first saw what is now my home in Salisbury Cathedral Close, and it was love at first sight. I learned of its existence when Robert Key, the MP for Salisbury and my Parliamentary Private Secretary at the time, telephoned to tell me that it had become available because its occupant had died, at the age of 94. He also told me, in no uncertain terms, that I must hurry down and see it the next day.

'Arundells' is primarily a 13th-century house built during the construction of the cathedral and has its origins in a medieval canonry. The first canon of the cathedral to use it as a home was probably Henry of Blunston, Archdeacon of Dorset, who died in 1316. The resident canon was deprived of the house in 1562 for practising magic, an archetypally exotic 'Close tale'. After that, the house was understandably leased by the Chapter to secular tenants, who continued to adapt and add to it, especially in the early years of the 17th century and again in the early years of the 18th. 'Arundells' is also one of the few houses in the Close which is well set back not just from the cathedral itself, but also from the narrow road surrounding most of its lawns. This gives it an ideal view of the cathedral, from a north-westerly angle, particularly from the main windows in the front bedrooms.

Gateway to the Close, Salisbury *by J M W Turner*

Salisbury Cathedral is considered by many to be the loveliest in Europe and is generally agreed to be the finest example of a Gothic cathedral in the United Kingdom. It has two great virtues. It remains as it was built during the 13th and 14th centuries, without appendages or other disfigurements, and, thanks to the loving care of almost 800 years, its fabric has survived more or less intact. It is also set in a spacious close of well-mown lawns which enable one to see it to full advantage from a decent perspective, without interruption from other buildings. Around the lawns are residential buildings constructed in a variety of styles in different ages, but all giving way to the Gothic grandeur of the cathedral itself.

The main reason for the homogeneous style of Salisbury Cathedral is thought to be the fact that, incredibly, its body, including the tower and the west front, was completed in under 40 years by around 300 men. The most notable feature, however, soaring above the Close and indeed the surrounding area, is the legendary spire. Commemorated by Constable in his paintings, this spire was the highest in Europe until Ulm's was built in the 19th century. It was completed in 1315, some 95 years after work on the cathedral began, and at 404 feet (123 metres) is not only the highest (and arguably the most elegant) in Britain, but also the tallest medieval structure in the world.

During the 1980s, we all feared for the spire. The wear and tear of the centuries had taken its toll, and the cost of putting matters right was astronomical. That the necessary support was found, however, was not only a measure of the spire's fame. It also showed that people right across the world treasured and cherished those values of community and continuity of tradition which, in Salisbury as elsewhere in Britain, both the cathedral and the cathedral close represent.

The Saturday Afternoon Football Results
Michael Palin

One of my earliest memories of shared family activity is of clustering round the radio with my father and mother to listen to the classified football results at five o'clock on Saturday afternoon. Tea would have been prepared for half-past four. Bread and butter, chocolate and Digestive biscuits, possibly a pikelet (as they called crumpets up in Sheffield) and blackcurrant jam. Tea would have been eaten by ten to five and cleared away by five to five. Even though my mother knew or cared little about football, she recognised the importance of this particular family ritual and would never dream of disrupting the scores with the clatter of crockery.

During the six years of the Second World War, access to a radio, or wireless as my father called it, had become virtually indispensable. Even in the early 1950s the words 'It's five o'clock and time for *Sports Report*' brought on a palpable sense of national bonding. There might have been people who didn't listen to the classified results at five o'clock on Saturday, but then there might have been human life on Uranus.

Listening to the 'classified' results (these were not just any old results, they were the ones on which football pool payouts were based) was more than a ritual, it was a quasi-religious experience. As five o'clock struck, the sounds of 'Out of the Blue' played by the Central Band of the RAF rang out like a clarion call to the nation. Next to the national anthem, 'Out of the Blue', played at the same time every week for the last 52 years, must be the most recognisable of all British themes. Indeed, it could have been a national anthem itself, were it not so jaunty. It stiffened the sinews and summoned up the blood as effectively as any pre-Agincourt pep-talk and set up a delicious sense of expectation and anticipation. These were the days before half-time scores and instant link-ups. Aside from those who actually went to the games, the information on *Sports Report* was imparted to a nation united in ignorance.

As the music faded, the results were read out, as they still usually are, by the majestically named James Alexander Gordon, a man whose very name rang with a sense of historical continuity – Khartoum, Culloden, the Conquest of Persia and the football results all rolled into one.

His delivery was impeccable. There was never a fluff, even when he entered the tricky nether regions of the Scottish Third Division South. There was never the slightest hint of personal preference or prejudice. Events at Raith Rovers were revealed with the same precisely modulated clarity as those at Manchester United. Only a consummate professional, or someone who hated football, could maintain such persistent disinterest.

There was, and still is, an almost musical lilt to the way Gordon read the results and a careful student of his inflection patterns could guess the outcome of the game as soon as the first part of the result had been uttered:

Sheffield United three…

Everybody's Weekly, May 1, 1954

FOURPENCE

Everybody's

TOM FINNEY
Up for the Cup
WONDERFUL WEMBLEY—See page 24

PHYLLIS BENTLEY on   REUNION   £1,000 MUST BE WON

'WHAT THE BRONTËS MEAN TO ME'   AT TOBRUK   CROSSWORD

Which might have sounded promising, but equal stress on all the words was ominous, and as soon as James Alexander's voice (the voice of all our hopes and fears) shifted up an octave you knew you were done for:

Ars-enal [tell-tale pause] four.

I often wonder if he realised quite how powerful a grip he had on the nation. If Hitler had had any sense, he would have put him on the radio instead of Lord Haw-Haw and made him feed false football results to demoralise us:

Leicester City nil, Stuttgart… eight.

For five minutes every Saturday afternoon, the nation was to James Alexander Gordon as flies to wanton boys. In his wake he left a trail of emotional havoc – joy, despair, pride, shame, all-encompassing misery and delirious elation – a huge psychic force-field, which if harnessed could probably have provided enough electricity to light a small city.

There was a significance to the ritual which went beyond the results themselves. The weekly recital of the 60-odd names that made up the Football League was like a beating of the national bounds. A roll-call of the kingdom. Places like Alloa and Accrington, which seemed to have no existence outside football, had their moment of glory alongside their more cosmopolitan cousins in London or Birmingham. It was a time to be reminded of the diversity of the country as the great melting-pot of the FA fixture list threw up ill-assorted couplings, like Gillingham and Cardiff, Sunderland and Stockport. It was a time to rejoice in our sturdy eccentricity as results came in from teams with names like Sheffield Wednesday and Hamilton Academicals.

Being there, by the wireless, when the results were read out gave me a chance to share unfeigned emotion with my father on a weekly basis. A mutual gasp of horror and disbelief or a swell of vicarious achievement moved us both, however briefly. Victory guaranteed a happier evening in the house.

Forty years on, much has changed. Saturday afternoons have been robbed of their uniqueness. Television has led demands for games to be played on Sunday and Monday as well. The five o'clock moment has lost its significance as instant information is available at all times on radio, TV, telephone and the internet. No one seems to stop for afternoon tea any more, and today's fragmented family life means that I am usually alone as the afternoon draws to a close.

But I still can't hear the strains of 'Out of the Blue' without succumbing to that exquisite combination of pain and pleasure which used to accompany the classifieds at five o'clock on Saturday. It remains for me, and I suspect for many others of my generation, the most quintessentially British time of the week.

Tom Finney featured in Everybody's Weekly, *1954*

The Savile Row Suit
Judith Watt

The suit is an English invention and a British icon. The best suits are still made in London's Savile Row, in an historic collaboration between the English gentleman and his tailor. Each one is different and reveals precisely what its wearer desires. It can denote status, be a suit of armour in the cut and thrust of business, be sexy, conservative or subversive: all of these, but *never* ostentatious. That, according to the Savile Row tradition, is the art of being well dressed, not dressing well. And the suit can never truly escape from tradition.

The power of Savile Row lies in imagery and perception. Together, establishments like Henry Poole, Huntsman, Gieves and Hawkes, Hardy Amies and Richard James can muster Nelson, Winston Churchill, Balenciaga and Tom Cruise amongst their customers. All have been drawn to the tradition and craftsmanship of their tailors, the ambience of the fitting-room and the immaculate quality of the suits they produce.

The suit was originally intended to be subversive, a British challenge in cloth to the dominance of French fashion. It was invented by Charles II, Samuel Pepys noting in his diary on 15 October 1666: 'This day the King begins to put on his vest, and I did see several persons in the House of Lords and Commons too, great Courtiers, who are in it, being a long cassock close to the body, of black cloth, and pinked with white silk under it, and a coat over it… it is a very fine and handsome garment.' Louis XIV first mocked, then adopted it.

Although court and formal dress returned to silk, the three-piece suit in cloth remained for sporting and country dress. Non-ostentation and excellence in tailoring were crucial to its development. With this went the philosophy of the English gentleman, personified by George 'Beau' Brummell, who arrived in London in 1798. 'If John Bull turns round to look after you,' he said, 'you are not well dressed, but either too stiff, too tight or too fashionable.' His quiet perfection in dress set him apart from the dandies who aped him and the vulgarity of the Prince Regent. There was, wrote Lord Byron, nothing remarkable in Brummell's dress, except a 'certain exquisite propriety'.

Brummell's trousers, coat and waistcoat transformed into the 19th-century lounge suit, an informal and sporting outfit. Although it remained unacceptable in town, after the First World War Edward, Prince of Wales, whose tailor was Scholte of Savile Row, made the suit fashionable. (However, there was disapproval in certain quarters for the Prince's innovations. P G Wodehouse's sartorial barometer Jeeves expressed distaste for his charge's new suit in *Carry on, Jeeves*. Wooster: 'But lots of fellows have asked me who my tailor is.' Jeeves: 'Doubtless in order to avoid him, sir.')

So popular was the suit that in 1926 Gieves and Hawkes shocked some customers by launching a ready-made service. As Robert Gieve has said: 'That idea of "bespeaking" a suit is a very British thing: charming in its fading glory, along with the frayed carpet and curtains that needed new linings.' In the 1920s, a gentleman didn't wear anything new. The bespoke

A classic in the lexicon of British style: a Savile Row suit in the making

suit was given to the valet or gardener to be worn in. New customers required a formal introduction to grander establishments and a young man's first suits would often be made by his father's tailor. The suit became conventional business dress. Fashion was largely ignored and the Savile Row suit, superbly crafted and made in the finest cloth, maintained its classic status. Innovation was discreet.

In 1969, with the 'peacock revolution' in full swing, Tommy Nutter, working with tailor Edward Sexton, brought a much needed dose of fashion to Savile Row when he opened his premises there. Together, Nutter and Sexton subverted the classic suit, using large checks or contrasting fabrics, highlighting the contours of the body, with narrow waists, huge lapels and baggy trousers. Their customers included the Beatles, Ossie Clark and Mick Jagger.

In the 1980s, the loose-fitting, label-blazing designer suits of Paul Smith and Armani made the suit an international fashion item. Bespoke suits continued to express both personal nuance and traditional values, but were increasingly perceived as old-fashioned by the young. Then, in 1992, Richard James opened his shop on Savile Row, aiming to make bespoke exciting for the new fashion-aware generation. His suits are contemporary, in innovative tweeds and pinstripes, silks and twills, and rule-breaking colours. He made bespoke relevant to men aware of the latest designer collections, but who want to be individual and smartly classic.

Today, Savile Row customers wear two-piece single- and double-breasted suits, with the waistcoat that traditionally made up the three-piece single-breasted suit seldom featured. But the trademarks which are the legacy of earlier days remain important indicators of bespoke: the double vents at the back of the coat which originally featured in the riding coat, allowing it to part over the back of a horse; four buttons on the cuff which can be undone (but never should be: that is ostentatious); a hand-stitched buttonhole on the lapel, with the loop behind to hold a carnation; pockets within pockets which don't spoil the silhouette, but which now may accommodate a mobile telephone.

It takes an average of three fittings from bespeaking one's suit to its completion, around 20 measurements for the coat and a minimum of five for the trousers. Between 275 and 300 separate pieces go into making a suit, almost entirely hand-sewn, with the coat interlined with canvas and horsehair, basted to mould to the figure and move with it. Cloth suitings have become finer, flattering the body and making it possible for them to be worn in most climates – essential for international travel in the modern world.

For more than a century, the Savile Row suit has allowed for (almost) every sartorial wish to be granted and rule broken. In true British fashion, it enables a man to look impeccable while indulging in idiosyncrasy and eccentricity. In all its variations, it remains a classic in the lexicon of British style.

Captain Scott's Last Expedition
Fergus Fleming

'Great God! This is an awful place…' With these words, Captain Scott arrived at the South Pole on 17 January 1912. It was awful not just because of the weather – strong winds, the temperature -30°C – nor because he and his team were physically and mentally exhausted. It was awful because, instead of a pristine wilderness, he found an abandoned tent from which flew the Norwegian flag. Roald Amundsen had beaten him to the Pole by 34 days. It was the loser, however, who emerged triumphant; for while Amundsen's journey made him a hero, Scott's made him a national icon.

The Britain to which Scott belonged had a peculiar self-image. Behind its confident façade there lurked a niggling fear that the nation was going downhill. Modern men and women were demonstrably smaller and weaker than their ancestors. Serious discussions were held concerning the physical degeneration of the race. Britain, whose empire covered a fifth of the world's landmass, was described (by a Briton) as 'a weary Titan'. Look at what had been achieved before, said the men of stiff collars and mahogany desks: look, for example, at Sir John Franklin, who in 1845 had bravely led 136 men to their doom in search of the North-West Passage; look at Captain Nares, who in 1875 had reached farther north than any human being in search of the North Pole; look at the glory days of imperial conquest. Since then a Norwegian (Amundsen, 1905) had crossed the North-West Passage, an American (Robert Peary, 1909) had reached the North Pole, and as for imperial honour – well, the four years it had taken the world's mightiest power to put down an army of South African farmers spoke for itself. Men of pluck and deeds of heroism were needed to stop the rot – men such as Scott and deeds such as the conquest of the South Pole.

It was Sir Clements Markham, President of the Royal Geographical Society, more than any other, who encouraged Britons to seek and capture the South Pole. In his youth he had been an explorer of sorts – he had taken part in the search for Franklin during the 1850s – and the experience had given him very definite ideas about how polar exploration should be conducted. Man-hauled sledges, as had been used in Franklin's day, were in his view the only way to travel. Dogs and skis may have been more efficient, but Markham considered them in some vague fashion unnatural. Several people thought him wrong, but Markham took care to choose for his expeditions a leader who agreed with him: a naval officer named Robert Falcon Scott.

Scott sailed for Antarctica aboard the *Terra Nova* in 1910. As a leader he inspired awe in his followers. He was almost superhumanly tough and he had already proved himself in the southern ice. But, alas, he shared many of Markham's misconceptions. Aboard the *Terra Nova* were dogs, skis, horses and even a novel form of motor-sledge. In the event, however, only the skis found favour. The dogs were rejected as unreliable, the motor-sledges did not work and the horses were used only to haul depots of food into the Antarctic continent. It was his men on whom Scott would rely for the achievement of the Pole. As Markham liked to say, man-hauling was the British way.

Amundsen departed for the Pole on 20 October 1911, Scott on 1 November. While Amundsen zipped southward with his dog-teams, Scott's team trudged patriotically in the same direction with their horses. On a daily basis they covered a half to two-thirds of Amundsen's mileage. They left caches of food as they went, the main one being One Ton Depot, some 130 miles from their base at Cape Evans. On 11 December they reached the foot of the mighty Beardmore Glacier. Ten days later they were at the top, and Scott sent the main body of men home. For the next 300 miles it would be traditional man-haul. Joining him in harness were Dr Edward Wilson, Captain 'Titus' Oates, Lieutenant Henry Bowers and Petty Officer Edgar Evans.

The trek south was a miracle of endurance. Instead of furs they wore chill-inducing wool and waterproofs. Their tents let in the snow. Their rations were insufficient. They suffered from vitamin deficiency, and in Evans' case scurvy. Their sledge was weighed down with unnecessary geological samples. The pace Scott set was unremittingly fierce. What was surprising was not that Amundsen beat them to the Pole but that, in their exhausted, half-starved condition, they reached it at all.

The extent to which Scott had overreached himself became apparent on the way home. Rapidly weakening, his team struggled from depot to depot, still strapped to their overburdened sledge. For a while it seemed as if they might make it, but on 7 February they reached the Beardmore Glacier. As they floundered through its crevasses – Scott had neglected to mark his trail on the way out – hope began to slip away. Evans died on 17 February. Exactly one month later, Oates remarked casually, 'I am just going outside and may be some time.' Then he walked alone into a blizzard, never to be seen again. On 21 March they were just 11 miles from One Ton Depot. It was a distance they would never cross. Confined to their tent by a storm, the three remaining men succumbed to cold and starvation. On 29 March, Scott wrote his last diary entry: 'We shall stick it out to the end, but we are getting weaker, of course, and the end cannot be far. It seems a pity, but I do not think I can write any more.'

The bodies were discovered eight months later. The tent was collapsed on top of them and a cross of skis erected to mark the spot. Among the few items removed were their diaries, letters and a roll of film. When developed, the film produced an arresting image: there stood the five men, travel-stained and weary, their faces stretched in despair; and behind them at the Pole flew the Union Jack. It was a picture of defeat that became an emblem of triumph. Here was the true face of victory. These haggard men had died for their country and for their beliefs. Some bold souls said they were largely the authors of their own misfortune, but this was dismissed as defeatist talk. To the British public, Scott stood on a pinnacle of glory compared to which Amundsen's achievement was a soulless pimple.

Scott's expedition entered British mythology as an exemplar of sacrifice and devotion. It came to epitomise a host of national traditions: monumental understatement – nowhere better displayed than in Oates' last words; the struggle against overwhelming odds; the adulation (however perverse) of amateurism; support for the underdog; and in later years, ironically, nostalgia for a past toughness. When the weary Titan finally collapsed in clouds of imperial dust, memory of the Antarctic lived on. On occasions of marvel or incredulity, Britons still uttered the phrase 'Great Scott!'

Previous pages: *Captain Scott's birthday party at the McMurdo Sound base in Antarctica, 6 June 1911*

The Beatles' Sergeant Pepper
Hunter Davies

I was there when *Sergeant Pepper* was being made, as I am always boasting, even if my children yawn, and I was there when England won the World Cup at Wembley – two moments from the Sixties, two defining events, the like of which I can't see happening again.

Both have improved with age, as memories get polished, more memorabilia appear, comparisons are made, research done, books published, theories honed, and we all nod our heads sagely and say, Yeah, those were the days, good ole Sixties, eh?

Did we realise then that both events would be seen as so momentous in our social and cultural history all these decades later? I think so. But at the same time I thought – I hoped – both would soon be equalled and then bettered, so that, while they would not be forgotten, we would have gone on to further and better achievements in music and sport, which the rest of the world would be envious of. Didn't quite happen that way.

Our World Cup win has long been put in the shade by the achievement of other countries. Unlike *Sergeant Pepper*. That has grown stronger, more significant, regarded all round the world as one of the defining moments of modern times – always there at the top, or near the top, when experts, or pseudo-experts, get asked to list their all-time faves.

Totally justified, so I believe. And for five different reasons – five ways in which *Sergeant Pepper* broke the mould.

First, and very simply, for the time it took to make. The Beatles' first LP *Please Please Me*, which was released in 1963, took one day to make and cost £400. They just knocked off in the studio, mostly in one-takes, the songs they had been doing on the road. Four years later, in the early part of 1967, they spent four months creating *Sergeant Pepper*, spending 700 hours in the recording studios at a cost of £25,000. This was unheard of, breaking all records for time and expense. It marked the beginning of the rise of pop musicians, if considered of sufficient commercial or musical worth, to the status of creative artists, who could not be bossed around by producers or record companies, who did it their way, even at the risk of self-indulgence.

Secondly, the techniques. Ample time meant better, more advanced, richer recording techniques. The Beatles were able to use a system of four-tracking all the way through, rather than just one-tracking, as on their early records. This meant the sound could be built up and onto, layer after layer. The backing track was laid down first; then the singing; then extra musicians, like trumpeters or a whole orchestra, were brought in. Finally, they were able to add on any sounds they fancied – which they did, from farmyard noises to laughter. All this was revolutionary, state-of-the-art at the time, the forerunner of what is now commonplace in the computer age. Tracks can now be laid forever, or stolen, or repeated till we all die of boredom.

Thirdly, the cover. It still gets acclaimed as the Best Cover in the History of Civilisation, Record Covers Division; but it wasn't just that well-known front image which was and still is so memorable, but the whole package and presentation.

Included inside the cover was a cardboard moustache, the Sergeant's stripes, a picture postcard of him, plus the words of all the songs – things which had not been assembled before in that format. It made the cover into a work of art in itself.

I was there when the cover was being shot, when the final cut-out figures were lined up. I remember John being talked out of having a cardboard Hitler in the line-up. Hitler was there, standing to attention in the corner, but was never used. Just as well. We all still remembered what happened around the world when John thought he was making a light-hearted remark about Jesus.

If you look at the front cover carefully, you'll see at the front, amongst the flowers, inside the letter L in the word BEATLES, there's a funny little statue which looks like an egg-shaped globe on a plinth. No idea what it was – but I put it there. As we left Paul's house that evening, he said 'Grab a few ornaments which we can shove in the front of the picture to fill up any gaps.' Something else I've told my children, oh many times, and had many yawns.

Fourthly, it was the first ever concept album. All the songs were connected, purporting to be from *Sergeant Pepper*'s concert, hence the laughter or applause linking all the songs so there is not a sound gap between them. Neither EMI nor Brian Epstein liked this idea, saying the public were used to a properly marked break between numbers. Later, it became a cliché for major performers to have their concept album, with a running theme or created as a whole.

Fifthly, and by far the most important, the contents. That clever cover and amusing presentation would not have been sufficient to make the album still marvelled at today if the music itself had not been so good. Not just good: tinged with genius. George was inspired at the time by his Indian experiences. Paul had emerged as a brilliant organiser, co-ordinating most of the *Pepper* innovations. John was on a high, for reasons we need not go into, out of it a lot of the time, but still very creative. Ringo was, well, Ringo, loved by all, hence their little song for him, one of the best he ever sang, 'With a Little Help from My Friends'. They were still friends at the time – no dramatic frictions yet – and at the height of their powers.

There are many other individual Beatles songs, from other albums, which I'd want on my desert island, but *Sergeant Pepper* is the one album I could not be without. I still think the music, words and images of 'She's Leaving Home', however simple, are some of the finest created in the Sixties.

And of course the final song, 'A Day in the Life', with its shattering climax, is now standard funeral service fare. It will be at mine…

Previous pages: *The Beatles at the time of* Sergeant Pepper

The Plays of William Shakespeare
Anthony Holden

No writer, no individual in history has seen more deeply into the human heart and soul than William Shakespeare; no one has had more truths to tell mankind about itself (if it would but listen) than still he does. That he happened to be a son of Warwickshire does more honour than any other quirk of fortune to a nation sometimes overproud of its chequered past.

To see Shakespeare's face, in the words of his admirer Anthony Burgess, 'we need only look in a mirror' – a variant on the time-honoured critical conceit that we do not so much read Shakespeare as he reads us. Whether rewriting English history or age-old fables, or merely noting and processing the current events of the momentous times through which he lived, Shakespeare brings a uniquely timeless, universal perspective to the interplay of individuals and the sometimes random, usually judgemental, often self-inflicted forces of destiny. Works first performed on the Elizabethan stage, its conventions artificial enough to have boys playing women's roles, live on so vividly four centuries later as to provide the West End with some of its most compellingly relevant drama, Hollywood with some of its most powerful contemporary screenplays. 'He was', as his friend and rival Ben Jonson was the first to perceive, 'not of an age, but for all time.'

Shakespeare lives on because, unlike Jonson and his other great contemporaries, he was neither a social satirist nor a propagandist so much as an impartial but laser-sighted seer of the human condition. He took no topical position, argued no party line nor moral point of view beyond man's inescapable responsibility for the consequences of his own actions; the stories he chose to tell, usually recycled from lesser originals, survive as moral fables (richly entertaining, exquisitely lyrical, often unnerving, sometimes devastating) for every generation which has succeeded him, or ever will. Just as the art form of the 20th century, the cinema, found its own inventive ways to recreate him, adapting his vivid scenarios to the spirit of its own times, so will that of the 21st, the world wide web, bringing Shakespeare to a wider audience than ever. No apter tribute could be paid to his uncanny ability to echo so resoundingly through the ages.

There is no explanation for Shakespeare's sudden emergence from the banks of the River Avon, the stews and taverns of rackety Elizabethan London, the liveried cellarage of James I's court, to speak so topically to the rest of time. It is some sort of uniquely British miracle. He came of farming stock, the oldest surviving son of a socially ambitious father who married above his station and left his rural roots, bent on social advancement. While making a decent living as a glover, with a little property dealing (and illegal moneylending) on the side, John Shakespeare rose to become Bailiff (or Mayor) of Stratford-upon-Avon – and thus the council official who invited travelling troupes of players to town. As a boy, well educated at the local grammar school, wide-eyed young William would have had a front-row seat beside his father.

Raised (according to recent scholarship) a recusant Catholic, at a time when adherence to the 'old' religion cost lives, the teenage Shakespeare was secretly despatched to a Catholic household in Lancashire as a tutor, perhaps to train as a priest; but the stage-struck youth

showed more talent for acting, and soon wound up in London as a stage-door ostler, then prompter, then bit-part player, then house dramatist, leaving behind in Stratford his 'shotgun' wife, Anne Hathaway, and their three children. As Elizabeth I's reign drew dangerously towards its heirless close, he had a ringside seat as a member of the household of the Earl of Southampton, to whom some of his cycle of sonnets (never intended for publication) are addressed. When the Queen was succeeded by another theatre-loving monarch, James VI of Scotland, the actor-playwright became a King's Player, and thus a lowly member of the royal household. One of his first, rather risqué works in the new reign was a play about the assassination of a Scottish king, replete with references to the Catholic-led Gunpowder Plot of 1605.

Macbeth survives, along with Hamlet, Othello and King Lear, as the summit of Shakespeare's achievement in tragedy, alongside morally complex history cycles, gently lyrical comedies, the 'problem' plays (so called because of their refusal to be categorised) – All's Well that Ends Well, Measure for Measure and Troilus and Cressida – and the serenely redemptive late works – Pericles, Cymbeline, The Winter's Tale and The Tempest – as the canon of 38 dramas which come down to us with his name attached. Their author would be astonished to know that they had survived him, let alone that they were still being copiously performed, all over the world, 400 years later. Although half were published in his lifetime, none appeared with his consent or co-operation; in an age of intense theatrical competition, and no copyright laws worth the name, the corrupt quartos were the work of unscrupulous pirate publishers relying on the fallible memories of actors. It is to his fellow actors John Heminges and Henry Condell, who spent seven years after his death preparing reliable texts for the 1623 First Folio, that the world owes the survival of Shakespeare's plays.

He had hoped, ironically enough, that his name might live on with posterity as a poet. He did personally supervise publication of his long narrative poems Venus and Adonis and The Rape of Lucrece, written while the plague closed the theatres, both of them bestsellers of their day. Poetry, unlike the theatre, was a respectable profession, conferring the possibility of honour during a man's lifetime and immortality after his death. So it is as a dramatic poet as much as a poetic playwright that we should honour the name of Shakespeare – 'this side', with Jonson, 'idolatry'. Bardolaters who cannot admit that their Swan of Avon ever struck a wrong note, wrote an impenetrable line, became the occasional victim of his own facility, do him needless disservice. He left us more than enough to justify his indestructible stature as the most eloquent, versatile and visionary voice ever to have graced these or any other shores.

John Gielgud makes up before the opening performance of The Tempest *at London's Old Vic, 1930*

The Abolition of the Slave Trade
Hugh Thomas

At the end of the 18th century, about 100,000 slaves were being carried from all parts of Africa across the Atlantic every year. British ships were responsible for about half of these, and Liverpool, Bristol and London were the most important ports involved. The slave trade was an essential part of European mercantile life, and the West Indian sugar industry, which provided the largest single import into the country throughout the century, was the making of innumerable fortunes, as the novels of Jane Austen remind us. The wealth of the noble Mr Rochester in *Jane Eyre* also had a West Indian, and assuredly a slave, base. Enlightened families, such as that of Lady Holland, drew money from sugar plantations in Jamaica, just as did conservative ones, such as that of the Gladstones.

But then all changed. Britain, from being the world's premier slaving nation, became the active crusader for abolition. The transformation was one of the most remarkable in history, and understandably inspired cynical comments by French and other competitors. Still, it was genuine, and resulted, in the end, in a great victory against the institution of slavery itself.

The explanation of how this came about is complex. First, several sea captains and slave traders wrote accounts of their activities in Africa. They were not all denunciations of the traffic, but they told the truth about what was happening. Secondly, the philosophers of the Enlightenment – those in Scotland (Hutchinson, Ferguson, George Wallace) as well as in France – questioned the morality of using labour based on force. Adam Smith speculated on the benefits of free, as opposed to slave, labour. Then poets (James Thomson, William Shenstone, Pope) and playwrights, as well as essayists (such as Horace Walpole), made fun of the idea of slavery. Africans were brought to England and their civilised demeanour convinced those who met them that they were men of reason. Finally, and perhaps most important, the Quakers, both in England and what was until the 1770s British North America, began a campaign against slavery and the slave trade as practised by their own members; and then, in the 1780s, began to attack the institution of slavery itself. Others, such as the young Cambridge graduate Thomas Clarkson, were drawn into the campaign.

The pamphleteers and agitators realised that, to have any legal effect, they needed a parliamentary presence. They approached a rich and well-connected young MP, William Wilberforce, who, after talking to his close friend the Prime Minister, William Pitt the Younger, agreed to direct a political movement against the trade in slaves from Africa. The campaigners decided to try and end the trade first, not slavery itself, since they did not want to become concerned in innumerable arguments about compensation. Also they thought, rightly, that the institution of slavery would eventually die once the trade ended.

The campaign to abolish the trade took 20 years, from 1788 to 1807. Wilberforce's persistence was exemplary. Documentation was provided by the campaigners, above all Clarkson. Pitt was consistently supportive, though for reasons of internal politics he never

Pity the Poor Negro!: *an abolitionist poster, c.1827*

Pity the poor Negro!

made abolition a governmental issue. The reformers were thrown off course by the French Revolution, fear of which made the attempt at any kind of reform unpopular. Pitt's friend Henry Dundas helped the slave traders by urging delay, while royal dukes led the opposition in the House of Lords. But eventually Wilberforce's arguments, supported by all the important Whigs (as well as by Fox, Grenville, Grey, Sheridan, Philip Francis and Burke) won the day.

The slave trade was prohibited for British traders as from 1 January 1808. A few captains assisted Portuguese merchants to continue the traffic, and British goods were used as cargoes to be exchanged for slaves in Havana and Rio de Janeiro. But in general, the merchants of Liverpool and elsewhere turned over new business in Africa, palm oil soon becoming as productive of wealth as slaves had once been.

1808 was, however, only the end of the long first act of the campaign against the traffic in slaves. Although the United States Congress also moved against the trade in 1808, Britain's continental competitors were mostly deeply imbrued in their traffic. United States commitment against the trade remained legalistic for some time. Britain, however, adopted a foreign policy after 1808 in which opposition to the trade played a capital role in both Tory and Whig administrations. This had three elements. First, a West African naval squadron sought, within the sometimes narrow limits which maritime law made possible, to seize slave ships and to destroy the bases of slave traders. Second, British diplomacy in European capitals put the case against the trade, and gradually gained from France, Spain, Portugal and Holland condemnations which led to a moral change (if far from as immediately complete as it had been in Britain) everywhere – despite accusations that the British were seeking command of the seas by their putatively philanthropic actions. Third, Britain spent money in bringing African kings and merchants to abandon the slave traffic, though, in some places, for example Dahomey, it had provided an important source of revenue. There was also some high-handed action by British naval captains off Brazil, as well as liberal spending of secret funds, in order to end the slave trade there.

A case can be made for thinking that the slave trade to Cuba would not have ended had it not been for the tardy action against the traffic of the United States Navy in the days of Lincoln. But in Washington as in London, British diplomatic pressure against the business over several generations played the decisive part.

The internal slave trade in Africa did not end as a result of British action and, to a limited extent, survives. But the name of Wilberforce was cited by Nelson Mandela as an inspiration in his speech to the two houses of Parliament in 1996; and few of those who know any history would question that the policies with which that name is associated were among the most dazzling ever realised by the British.

The Sleeper to Scotland
James Naughtie

The sleeper is a train that still respects the romance of the railways. Somehow its hissings and clankings and creakings in the night speak of the great age of British train travel, and at the moment when it starts to move into the dark and gather speed you feel drawn back into a world where you might still catch a cinder in the eye if you looked out, and where the engine's effort on the long climbs near the Border seems to have every carriage heaving and straining in support and sympathy. This is the real thing.

Growing up far enough away from London to need the sleeper was a privilege. I remember the moments on Aberdeen station by the harbour, the one where the seagulls and that morning's fish will always remind you where you are, when the sleeper was ready to go. People posted last-minute letters in a special box on the side, with an extra halfpenny stamp, to have them sorted by invisible hands in the night; you watched blinds being drawn and nightgowns being unpacked; and the guard always seemed an especially awesome figure, because it was he who would send this whole little world off into orbit in the dark. I can feel the excitement now.

There were rituals. You checked your name on a printed list stuck on the window. The conductor would remind you how to undo the catches and bolts in your little room, and in those days show you the decorous china pot which sprang out from beneath the sink. You'd catch a glimpse of a dressing gown sweeping past your door. And before you left you would breathe that particular kind of steam that oozed out of the grilles at your feet, steam that on this train seemed tangy and different. This was no ordinary journey.

I can understand why people still wanted to take the sleeper from Edinburgh even after the air shuttle started in the 1970s and it all seemed so much quicker. Waverley near midnight had that same excitement. A few carousers would tumble into their carriages, there would always be some official government briefcases stowed away, there would be the sense of going on an adventure, even if you would be at King's Cross in less than six hours and the train would stop a couple of times on the way to make sure you didn't arrive too early. In this country it was – and is – the way to travel from north to south, and a journey big enough to match the business of going from country to country within these islands.

Going north in the summer you might see the Forth Bridge at dawn, or on the Inverness line the mountains of Perthshire and then, away to your right as you rolled into Aviemore, the massive rocky heights of the Cairngorm plateau itself. And as for the part of the train that separated and found itself pulled into Fort William, is there a more thrilling way to leave the city behind than to wake being ferried across Rannoch Moor into the folds of the Nevis range?

This is a fascination that can't be expunged, and wasn't even when the authorities took against the sleeper in the early 1980s and started trying to turn it into something ordinary. The different trains to Scotland were amalgamated so that passengers for west, north and east all started together and separated at Carstairs. All the trains went up the west coast line, thus abandoning King's Cross for Euston – which has no feeling now for the great age

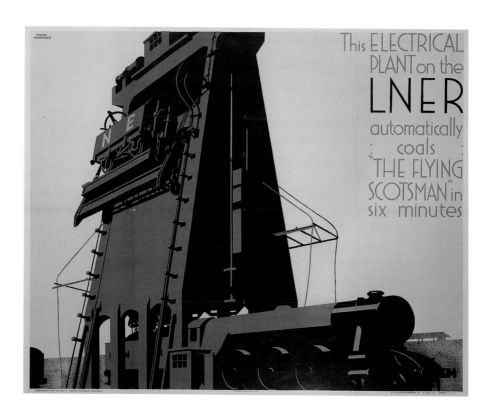

of the railways – and avoiding the long hill in north-east England that used to wake you up because you could feel the engine trying so hard and where, quite often, the whole thing used to come to a thrilling halt. To abandon the route of the *Flying Scotsman* seemed mean. Even in the dark that way was the best.

But by the late 1990s there were signs that the lure of the sleeper was being recognised again and that a new generation will be allowed to discover the irreplaceable uplift of the sight of the Highlands from your bed, the same bed that you collapsed on in the middle of the city a few hours before. They have even organised kippers again, not to mention the bar that is open most of the night.

Everyone who knows it will hold the feelings close. I think of stations with wicker baskets, and heavy trolleys with rumbling metal wheels. They carried parcels, boxes, fishing rods, guns, bikes, cases and trunks, at least once in my memory a coffin that seemed to be occupied, dogs and cats and budgies. No one was left out. Guards vans on the sleeper were places of mystery and excitement. Skimbleshanks, you will remember, was the cat of the night train who checked the platform at Crewe, greeted the stationmaster at Carlisle and then:

> You saw him at Dumfries, where he speaks to the police
> If there's anything they ought to know about…

This is not a faked-up romance. Things happen when you race through the dark. I know a distinguished MP who says he was conceived on the sleeper – 'involuntarily, where you hit all those points at Crewe' – and I have often sensed strange goings-on in the to-ings and fro-ings from carriage to carriage. When those doors close you inch away from the platform to who-knows-what.

And think of how it must look to someone out late in the fields. Out of the dark comes the night train, a patchwork of lights from its windows where some sleep and some don't. For a moment you feel its presence and then it's gone. In his commentary for the inspired Post Office documentary about the night mail, W H Auden said:

> In the farm she passes no one wakes
> But a jug in a bedroom gently shakes.

Somehow it is secretive and bold at the same time. It's a will-o'-the-wisp train because it is always being swallowed up in the dark. I can't explain why that should still be an electric feeling in our age, two generations after steam. But it is. Give me the sleeper, any night.

The night train: London and North Eastern Railway posters from the 1930s

Teatime
Jane Pettigrew

British social life and tea have been intertwined for so long that it has become almost impossible to think of the one without immediately calling to mind the other.

What would we do on Sunday afternoons without tea in the garden or around the fire, neat sandwiches and scones piled high with strawberry jam and spoonfuls of thick clotted cream? What would Victorian and Edwardian nannies have fed to their young charges up in the nursery if banana sandwiches and sticky gingerbread and cupfuls of milky tea had not been the children's favourite meal? What would get us going in a good mood each day if not an early morning 'cuppa'? How would exhausted workers satisfy their hunger at the end of a long day without a robust 'high tea'? How would the progress of a cricket match be measured without the teatime score? And how could unions have secured the statutory 'tea-break' without the significance and importance of tea to all British workers?

Say the word 'tea' and the memory fills with images of picnic teas, birthday teas, Wimbledon teas with strawberries and cream, warm soothing cups of hot sweet tea administered in times of shock, Mad Hatter's tea parties, mugs of tea and a gossip over the kitchen table, Lyons Corner Houses, village teashops with low beams and willow-pattern china, and hotel lounges with chintz armchairs, tuxedo-clad waiters and dainty porcelain cups and saucers.

Teatime is so British that its oriental ancestry is often forgotten. Introduced to Europe by the Dutch and the Portuguese in the early 17th century, the herb slipped quietly into England in the 1650s, unannounced and barely noticed. Like a timorous guest, it attracted little attention except from those who recognised its unusual qualities and took the trouble to get to know it better.

The prices made it an indulgence available only to the very wealthy. At between £6 and £10 a pound, it was well beyond the reach of footmen and maids, unskilled labourers and farming folk, and even the aristocracy bought tiny amounts at a time. In palaces and country mansions, quarter- or half-pound measures were guarded carefully in fine Chinese porcelain jars and displayed on shelves in private closets alongside the fine porcelain tea wares that were used in its brewing and serving.

The liquor was served particularly as a *digestif* after the main meal of the day, which began at midday and ended at three or four o'clock in the afternoon. As soon as the last dishes of food had been consumed, the ladies withdrew to a closet and left the men to their pipes and bottles and loud conversation. Well away from such masculine indulgence, the ladies prepared tea and gossiped quietly together until the men were summoned by a servant to join them for a refreshing bowl of the brew.

By the end of the 17th century, the pattern of tea drinking had been established as an after-dinner ritual, presided over by the ladies in elegant surroundings away from the dining

The cup that cheers: taking a tea-break in 1939

room. Its associations were with idle feminine chatter, stately homes and gardens, fine porcelain and genteel behaviour. The incredibly high cost and the skill needed to brew the beverage meant that servants were never allowed to handle the leaf. Their responsibility was merely to deliver the tea-making equipment to the appropriate room with a plate of bread and butter and leave the lady of the house to carry out the brewing ritual.

Little changed through the 18th century, except that prices dropped a little and even those who could ill afford the still expensive leaf, replaced their earlier preference for ale and beer with a passionate love of tea. By the late 1700s, while wealthy aristocrats entertained visitors to a 'dish of tea', servant girls were surreptitiously slurping the dregs from their mistresses' teapots, harvesters and labourers were eagerly quenching their thirst with bottles of cold tea in the shade of their haystacks, and even beggars were discovered lurking in country lanes brewing mugs of tea from cheaper smuggled and adulterated leaf.

Afternoon tea, the most British of all our tea occasions, is said to have been invented in the 1840s by the 7th Duchess of Bedford. The development was more an adaptation than an invention, and resulted from the gradual shifting of the main meal from early afternoon to late evening. Breakfast at nine o'clock, newly created luncheon at midday and dinner at 8.00 or 9.00 p.m. left a long afternoon with no refreshment. What better to fill the gap than cups of tea with the customary platefuls of thin slices of bread and butter? And so dinner and tea quietly swapped places.

As the Victorian period progressed and the middle classes grew, tea became an ideal focus for social occasions amongst all ranks and in all corners of Britain. The aristocracy continued as before, the middle classes pretended that their lives and tea parties were just as grand, while the poorer classes pooled their meagre supply of china and brewed weak but comforting pots of tea that made their harsh days less dreary.

Heady Edwardian days brought palm court lounges with string quartets to entertain the elegant rich while they sipped their tea at four o'clock. And the arrival in London of the tango in 1910 led to the somewhat eccentric addition of tango tea-dances to the teatime repertoire. Hands of whist, music and 'dancing on the carpet' had long been features of both after-dinner and afternoon tea drinking, but now the colourful combination of tea and dance moved out of the home and onto the floor of the hotel lounge and fashionable restaurant.

Two world wars, radical shifts in lifestyle and the arrival of instant coffee and fast food brought about a temporary demise in teatime activities in the 1950s. But since the early 1980s, tea has shown its determination not to be ignored or rejected. It has become a special guest, welcomed by us all at every social event, and as comfortable at royal garden parties as by the fire in a simple country cottage. What other drink refreshes and revives, comforts and calms, provides a focus for quiet communication with such ease and simplicity as tea? Should it ever be replaced by less elegant and palatable beverages, we will have lost a trusted and loyal friend who has kept us company and improved our lives for 350 years.

Theatreland
Ned Sherrin

First there is tradition: lively, living tradition.

If you take the Elizabethans and Shakespeare as our arbitrary starting point, you have introduced Marlowe and Ben Jonson, and very soon the Jacobeans and Webster and Ford and Beaumont and Fletcher – the last two names still a sufficiently vivid presence to enable Noel Coward to correct Dame Edith Evans when she persisted in misquoting a famous line in his *Hay Fever*: 'No, Edith. The line is "On a clear day you can see Marlow." On a very clear day you can see Marlowe and Beaumont and Fletcher.'

And already, with Burbage and Alleyn, a line of actors and actor managers is established to interpret the playwrights. The roles they created are still being played today on many of the same sites in Theatreland every time an actor rediscovers Hamlet or Rosalind, Falstaff or Viola, Benedick or Beatrice.

Down the ages, Garrick and Siddons and Kemble, Betterton and Macready, have given way to Kean and Irving, Olivier, Gielgud, Wolfit, Thorndike, Evans and Ashcroft, who in their turn hand on the baton to Dench and Smith, Tutin, Rigg, Jacobi and McKellen, who observe the emergence of Branagh and Fiennes, Stevenson and Shaw.

In one family, the Redgraves, we can trace a Theatreland line from a Drury Lane ticket tout, whose operation eventually flowered into the Keith Prowse ticket agency, *via* his son Roy Redgrave, the 'Cock of the North', a roistering barnstormer who toured Australia after siring Sir Michael, who begat Vanessa, Corin and Lynn, who begat among others Natasha and Joely and Jemma.

These generations of theatre people are doubly blessed with a rich variety of theatres in which to practise their craft. It is hard to imagine a more imposing playhouse than the Theatre Royal, Drury Lane, successor to three earlier buildings on the same turf. Which is the prettier, 'the little theatre in the Hay' (the Theatre Royal, Haymarket) or Sir Charles Wyndham's eponymous playhouse in the Charing Cross Road? Which is the warmer house in which to play, the red plush of the Apollo or the Lyric on Shaftesbury Avenue? Both stand firmly beside the Queen's and the Gielgud, which until recently was the Globe. On reopening the building now honoured by his name, Sir John, then aged 90, remarked that he was now so out of touch that he was relieved to see one name which he could recognise in lights on the famous theatre street.

Another reason for changing the name was that Sam Wanamaker's herculean task of funding and building the recreation of Shakespeare's Globe in Southwark has been miraculously achieved, and it now packs in full houses of eager students and tourists every summer for a stirring experience in the heart of Shakespeare's original Theatreland.

Then there is another tradition, the speaking of the verse, a practice which shows how tradition is modified and adapted to the taste of different generations. At the turn of the century, William Poel's rigorous examination of Shakespearean verse stripped it of the vocal accretions of years of Victorian excess. Poel formed the Elizabethan Stage Society in 1894

and laid the foundations of an approach to Shakespearean speaking and staging which is still being built upon. Where tradition had favoured the declamatory style, 'full of sound and fury, signifying nothing', Poel wanted the words to be spoken 'trippingly on the tongue'. He cast Edith Evans as his Cressida in 1912 when she was still a milliner. (Hermione Gingold was Cassandra.) In a recent play by Nicholas Wright, *Cressida*, there is a fascinating scene where Michael Gambon as a trainer of boy actors 50 years after Shakespeare emphasises 'modern' modifications. The great Wolfit, the greatest Lear of the last century, often considered by the ignorant as a 'ham', also benefited by being produced by Poel, his role as Cato in a conflation of *Julius Caesar* and *Caesar and Pompey* earning the review: 'his elocution was admirable, so devoid of histrionic declamation that every line he spoke was natural'. Poel and the actor-director-playwright Harley Granville-Barker were to influence the splendid director Tyrone Guthrie and, in a direct line, Professor Rylands at Cambridge, who was to instil the message in Peter Hall and John Barton when they started the Royal Shakespeare Company, and on down through the ranks of the Royal National. Even in a thin month in the West End, there is invariably something richly to be enjoyed in these two great forcing houses.

Then there is the line of playwrights who followed the Elizabethans and Jacobeans – Sheridan, Congreve, Farquhar, Wycherley, Vanburgh – interrupted only by a curious drought in the 19th century and re-established by Wilde and Shaw (note how many of the names are from Ireland). In the 20th century, Priestley, Coward, Maugham and Rattigan provided revivable classics. T S Eliot and the magical Christopher Fry produced a spirited short revival of poetic drama, and after 1956 the floodgates of a new wave were opened by John Osborne and the Royal Court. Pinter, Wesker, Bolt, Nichols, Ayckbourne, Frayn and Stoppard offered and still supply a rich variety – and again the Irish flourish.

How could a theatre which can draw on the accumulation of these years of acting experience handed down and revised, a body of writing so diverse and so exciting, a variety of playhouses so handsome and so beckoning, fail to provide a sumptuous contemporary Theatreland? It can rise above the sordid mess of West End streets, the villainous taxes on tickets, the pettiness of parking regulations and even the spiralling cost of dinner after the theatre. Indeed, the stomachs of visitors to Theatreland are now served better than ever before in this new heyday of the Ivy, the Caprice, Elena's Etoile, Quo Vadis, Joe Allen, Orso, the Mirabelle. Even in the artfully restored Royal Court there is a new restaurant burrowed out beneath Sloane Square.

In an amusing conceit in Nicholas Wright's *Cressida*, the Carolean actors repair after a first night to celebrate at a tavern which is a witty period pastiche of Joe Allen. The acting strain in Edward Alleyn and his son has given out in the grandson – the restaurateur 'Joe Alleyn'!

As Tevye would say in *Fiddler on the Roof* – 'Tradition!'

Noel Coward with his designer, Gladys Calthrop, c.1924

The Poems of Dylan Thomas
Paul Ferris

As poets go, it would be hard to find a practitioner, living or dead, who was more eloquently aware of being one than Thomas. He could be self-deprecating about his powers, once describing himself as 'top of the second eleven', but the career he wished upon himself as a mildly wicked young man in South Wales in the 1930s was sustained, complete with appropriate boozing and ribaldry (as well as private tears and agonies), throughout the not very long life that ended in a New York hospital in 1953.

The poems that first made people notice him were published in the mid-1930s. The best of them had a fierce, nervous quality of self-awareness that showed itself in the opening words:

> The force that through the green fuse drives the flower
> Drives my green age; that blasts the roots of trees
> Is my destroyer…

What this force was, exactly, the poem didn't say. What mattered was a kind of morbid relish at energies seething under the human skin, in particular the skin of Dylan Marlais Thomas. He was 18 when he wrote it, the son of the English master at Swansea Grammar School, Jack Thomas, a disappointed man who wished his own lost hopes of literary achievement on the child.

The Thomases were rooted in rural, Welsh-speaking Carmarthenshire. The 'Marlais' came from the pen-name of a clergyman-poet in the family, the 'Dylan' from a book of medieval Welsh legends that appealed to Jack Thomas. But the poetic tradition that the father ingrained in his son was purely English, the heritage from Shakespeare to Milton to Keats. No Welsh was spoken in the suburban house (two and a half bedrooms, view of Swansea Bay) where Dylan Thomas, born 1914, grew up.

A few solemn little poems, probably written before he was 10, show a grasp of rhyme and metre. He soon developed a taste for comic verse. Showing off in a letter when he was aged about 11, and newly enrolled at the grammar school, he calls himself, tongue-in-cheek, a 'bred & born philologist' and constructs a series of neat couplets about the ambiguity of language: 'If it freezes when it's frosty, is it squosty when you squeeze? / Would you have to buy a biograph to write biographies?'

But comic verse was a sideline. A series of four notebooks (others have been lost) contain about 200 poems of increasing sophistication and complexity, the earliest dated April 1930, when he was 15 and still at school. The last notebook ends four years later, in April 1934, by which time he had left school, where his academic record was dismal, worked briefly on the local newspaper and experimented with beer and girls; he had still seen little of the world outside South Wales, and home was still his father's house on the hill.

The young Dylan Thomas, by Augustus John

Of the 90 or so pieces that make up Thomas' *Collected Poems*, almost half originate in those early years, though many of them were revised later. 'The hunchback in the park' was suggested by a real hunchback in Cwmdonkin Park, near his home, and first drafted in May 1932. 'After the funeral' mourned one of his Carmarthenshire aunts, Ann Jones, who died in 1933. The notebook version, which went through many revisions, was dated 10 February: as it happens, the day before her funeral. Mrs Jones and her husband ran a small farm, Fern Hill, where Dylan stayed as a child, laying down memories that surfaced in less happy times, just after the Second World War, when he wrote one of his best-known poems.

> Now as I was young and easy under the apple boughs
> About the lilting house and happy as the grass was green,
> The night above the dingle starry,
> Time let me hail and climb
> Golden in the heydays of his eyes...

From time to time, Thomas was attacked as an impenetrable modernist. Some of his poems were unarguably difficult, although from the start he leavened them with what he called 'simples', and in the end it is the 'simples', like 'Fern Hill', that have endeared him to his readers. Inside the supposedly wild young Celtic lyricist was always an orthodox English poet, struggling to get out. Not that the self-image of hopeless bohemian, which Thomas cultivated to the point of caricature, has done anything to harm his popular reputation; on the contrary.

In fact Dylan Thomas was not a serious hell-raiser. He told endless funny stories, many of them against himself; was feckless and unreliable; became emotionally dependent on his wife Caitlin. His real task as he saw it was poetry, though broadcasting and other hackwork deterred him from it. Even *Under Milk Wood*, his romantic comedy about a Welsh village that never was, he regarded as a potboiler.

After the early 'Swansea period', his output was small. His poems were written slowly, often painfully, and in the end were not written much at all; touring America for dollars, reading poetry to rapturous audiences, sucked him dry at the end. He always saw the writing of poems as a vocation, and some of them dwelt on the business itself, his 'craft or sullen art'. The structure of his verse was formal and traditional. One of the last pieces he wrote, to his dying father, the celebrated 'Do not go gentle into that good night', is in the rare style of a villanelle, which employs only two rhymes, arranged in a particular pattern. Few notice except the poet.

Throughout his life, much of his time was spent in or near London, but the poetry was mostly written in Wales, and he lived there, at the Boat House in Laugharne, Carmarthenshire, for the last four years of his life, 1949 to 1953. The dream of childhood in 'Fern Hill' was already in the shadow of the future. The words are carved on a stone in Cwmdonkin Park:

> Oh as I was young and easy in the mercy of his means,
> Time held me green and dying
> Though I sang in my chains like the sea.

The Letters Page of The Times
John Grigg

Letters to *The Times* have a unique status in British life. Though this famous feature has inspired the paper's competitors to develop lively correspondence columns of their own, the original has somehow managed to retain its primacy. Having a letter published in *The Times* still carries more prestige than having one published anywhere else.

All my life I have been aware of this curious phenomenon, but never more so than when I was writing the most recent volume in *The Times'* official history, covering the period 1966–81. As I immersed myself in back-numbers of the paper, the quality and variety of its correspondence was fully brought home to me. It was obvious that, day after day, some of the paper's best copy was produced free of charge by its readers in the form of 'Letters to the Editor'.

The subject-matter ranges from the nationally important to the quirkily intriguing. The prototype of the latter category of *Times* letter was, perhaps, that written on 4 February 1913 by R Lydekker FRS, reporting that he had just heard a cuckoo in his Hertfordshire garden. Though he had to confess a few days later that he had been deceived by a bricklayer's labourer imitating the bird's call, the theme of the first cuckoo caught on – and incidentally, Delius' *On Hearing the First Cuckoo in Spring* was first performed later in the year. When four anthologies of *Times* letters were published between 1976 and 1987, they were entitled *The First Cuckoo*, *The Second Cuckoo*, *The Third Cuckoo* and *The Last Cuckoo*.

Some *Times* readers seem to have made a career of writing to the paper. One, named Hockley Clarke, had almost 40 letters published, on such subjects as tomato plants, bats, caterpillars, hotels, the Christmas post, chemical sprays, railway closures and wintering in England. Another correspondent, annoyed at the non-appearance of what he thought a good letter, complained to a friend that one had, apparently, to be a member of the Athenaeum Club to get a letter accepted. So how did one become a member of the Athenaeum? The friend's reply was that he thought the first step towards membership was to get a letter published in *The Times*.

The effect of the paper's correspondence column is similar to that of a Greek chorus, commenting upon the affairs of the day, and also upon the views and editorial decisions of the paper itself. When, in March 1971, a whole-page picture of a naked girl appeared, ostensibly advertising a well-known chemical firm, some readers were outraged. One, writing from Cuckfield in Sussex, asked if the editor was trying to drive readers away by pandering to the commercial exploitation of sex: 'If you want to maintain the position claimed by your own advertisements, surely you had better eschew the nudes and pay more respect to womanhood.' But a schoolmaster from Leatherhead, with a former *Times* publicity slogan ('Top People Take *The Times*') clearly in mind, wrote simply: 'Topless People Take *The Times*?' And a correspondent from Bletchley showed an equally light touch: 'I hope this delightful picture has the same effect on *The Times'* circulation as it does on mine.'

On the whole, *Times* letters – at any rate those selected for publication – do not have the 'Disgusted, Tunbridge Wells' tone. Even indignation tends to be expressed with a certain dignified restraint. A high proportion of the letters are written by obscure people, whose capacity to be interesting comes to the world's notice only through *The Times*' correspondence column. But the feature also serves as an outlet for statements on matters of public concern by people with established names, occupying important positions in every conceivable field. MPs or ministers of the Crown may choose to make a point in a letter to *The Times* rather than in parliament. Moreover, a controversial issue raised by some notable figure writing to the *The Times* may be taken up elsewhere and so become a major item of news.

The most remarkable example of this was the letter published in the paper on 7 May 1918 from Major-General Sir Frederick Maurice, until recently director of military operations at the War Office. Maurice wrote at a time of crisis in the First World War, when the Germans were attacking on the Western Front and still threatening the Channel ports. In his letter, he challenged statements made in parliament by the prime minister, David Lloyd George, and the Tory leader, Bonar Law, who was his coalition partner. The purpose of the letter was unmistakable: to pin the blame for the military crisis on Lloyd George and his government.

Maurice was the faithful acolyte of Sir William Robertson, whom Lloyd George had eased out of the post of chief of army staff (CIGS) a month earlier. Naturally, the letter created a sensation and Lloyd George's numerous though ill-assorted opponents felt that it gave them an opportunity to topple him. Matters came to a head in a parliamentary debate on 9 May, in which Lloyd George triumphed. Never again has a letter in *The Times* been quite so momentous in its potential consequences as Maurice's, though many have caused a stir and continue to do so.

The department that deals with *Times* correspondence consists (as I write) of four journalists and three secretaries. They have their work cut out, because on average 400 letters are received every day. An important change that has occurred in recent years is that electronic mail has largely taken over from letters sent to the editor through the post. E-mail and fax now account for 60 per cent of the correspondence received, and 85 per cent of letters actually used. Yet the electronic letters are still dressed up to look like old-fashioned letters, beginning 'Sir' and ending 'Yours faithfully'. These gestures to the past may well be dropped before long. But in essential respects the feature can be expected to remain true to its tradition, appearing on the leader page and providing the same fascinating blend of serious comment, out-of-the-way information and sheer entertainment.

Some of the paper's best copy: a letter to The Times, *written in 1854*

1 Spring Gardens.

London, Decr 27th 1854

To the Editor of the Times.

Sir.

In the Times of
the 10th inst. was published a note from
a correspondent, containing an extract
from a letter purporting to come from
St. Petersburg — in which the writer makes
the following statement:

"Col. Colt has been or is still here
with his Machinery to make Revolvers."
Whereupon, without any further delay I am
attacked by various Journals in terms of
severe condemnation — Through the Times,
I beg the privilege of answering the
statement and the attacks —

It is not true that I have

The Battle of Trafalgar
Andrew Lambert

After an inconclusive naval battle in 1916, Kaiser Wilhelm II boasted that 'the magic of Trafalgar has been broken!' It was his proudest day, the culmination of a lifelong ambition. Fortunately, the magic – unlike the Kaiser – would endure.

The magic reflected the reality. Trafalgar was no mere battle; it marked the final defeat of Napoleon's plans to invade Britain. On 21 October 1805, a British fleet of 27 battleships, commanded by Admiral Lord Nelson, engaged a combined French and Spanish fleet of 33 battleships, led by Admiral Villeneuve and Admiral Gravina, off Cape Trafalgar on the south coast of Spain. Despite his numerical advantage, Villeneuve, who had seen Nelson and his 'band of brothers' wipe out a French fleet at the battle of the Nile in 1798, was resigned to defeat. After six hours watching the British ships approaching, most of his men shared his foreboding. The allies (the French and Spanish) fought bravely that afternoon, but they were amateurs. They faced the finest fighting force the world has ever seen, a navy unbeaten for over 100 years, and men who were masters of their art. Nelson's tactics reflected this mastery. Confident of victory, he used the simplest tactics, abandoning formal rules in favour of a fluid, dynamic approach to battle that simply outclassed the allies. Anxious to make the enemy stand and fight, he elected to attack in two columns. The columns would break the enemy line of battle, forcing the close range mêlée engagement in which his superior officers and men would annihilate the enemy. Nelson expected his captains to use their skill and judgement to out-think the enemy, as well as out-fight them. This 'Nelson touch' had been explained to every captain, and all were struck by its unique power.

Before the battle began, Nelson showed the human quality that made the sailors, and the British people, love him. His signal 'England expects that every man will do his duty' made every man proud to be there, a pride that reflected the confidence he had shown in them. They also knew that Nelson would lead by example. Suitably inspired, the officers and men overwhelmed the allied ships with superior seamanship and speed of fire. As HMS *Victory* broke into the allied line, her broadside guns smashed through the flimsy stern of Villeneuve's flagship, cannon balls, grape shot and canister spreading death and destruction along her decks. Soon afterwards, Nelson was shot and mortally wounded while walking on the upper deck of the *Victory*. A musket ball ripped through his lung and severed his spine. As he slowly suffocated on his own blood, only his indomitable will kept him alive to receive news of complete success. By the end of the afternoon, 19 allied ships had been taken or destroyed. The scale and significance of the victory, combined with the heroic, noble death of Britain's first national hero, gave Trafalgar a sublime quality that can never be equalled.

News of Trafalgar led to a rare outpouring of national emotion, a combination of triumph and grief that would sear the British consciousness. The event was recorded with a symbolism that combined the values of God and man. Nelson was buried in the crypt of St Paul's, flanked by two captains who shared his fate that day. When Benjamin West painted *The Immortality of Nelson*, with a central figure clearly based on Christ being taken down from

The Turf
Richard Dunwoody

To me, the turf is the very stuff racing is made of: the fabric of the racecourses of our country, home of the finest horseracing in the world. Britain can boast 59 racecourses, and, unlike those of many other countries, which often seem almost interchangeable to the rider, each has its own distinctive characteristics. Since this book is intended as a celebration of the best of Britain, what follows is a personal gazetteer of some of my favourite courses. My reasons for choosing them are as different as the tracks themselves and embody something of that living variety which is one of the British turf's most engaging qualities.

So, in the best tradition of gazetteers, let's start with A – in this case for Aintree. Indeed, where else could we start than here in Liverpool with the greatest race in the world: the Grand National? Today, 550 million watch the spectacle in more than 25 different countries, and many more millions of pounds are won and lost on its outcome. The race in its present form – a handicap – was first run in 1843, since when great names like Red Rum have become immortalised by their triumphs in it. (Red Rum actually won his first ever race at Aintree, as a two-year-old in a five-furlong selling race!) The fences are as famous as the horses: the Chair, Valentines, Beechers Brook, Canal Turn and Foinavon. I have been lucky enough to win this race twice, a feat that makes a household name of horse and jockey alike, but my first encounter with the track was probably the lowest point in my career. It was 1985 and I was riding West Tip, who fell at Beechers. The following year, however, we redeemed ourselves when I won on the same horse. I was 22, and such is the prestige of the race that it helped me secure the much sought-after job of stable jockey to the champion trainer David Nicholson and effectively launched my career.

If Aintree hosts the greatest race in the calendar, Ascot is arguably the finest racecourse in the world. The air is heavy with the tradition of the turf. Indeed, the first meeting was held here back in 1711 at the command of no less a figure than Queen Anne. Royal Ascot, which is held in June, is now without doubt the world's most prestigious flat-racing meeting, as legendary for the parties in the carpark afterwards as for the racing itself.

Cartmel, on the north-west coast, is in a different league. It is unashamedly a 'country track'. None the less, it is one of my favourite courses. The carnival atmosphere is unique, especially at the August Bank Holiday meeting, when the noise of the funfair and the smell of barbecues fill your senses as you corner a track less than a mile round, with the winning post only fractionally more than a furlong from the turn into the winning straight. The old village is so narrow that a big horsebox has to unload in the high street, with the runners led through the thronging streets to the course, accompanied by much backslapping and tipping 'enquiries'.

Cheltenham is the home of steeplechasing, and for every jockey the Cheltenham Festival is the highlight of the season. Every race is hard to win, but none more so than the Cheltenham Gold Cup. The roar of the crowd, augmented by thousands of my fellow Irishmen, is unrivalled, and coming into the winners' enclosure afterwards is to navigate

As legendary for its parties as for the racing: Ascot in 1975

an endless sea of spectators, who – uniquely to this race – seem equally enthusiastic about the winner whether they have backed it or not!

Our gazetteer continues with Epsom in Surrey. This course is probably best known for staging the Blue Riband of the turf, the Derby – a meeting almost as venerable as Royal Ascot, having been founded in 1780 by the 12th of the Earls who give it its name. The course undulates dramatically, and the race is perhaps the ultimate test for the thoroughbred, which needs to draw on all its reserves of speed, stamina and temperament to win. Even though flat-racing is not my game, Epsom is in my blood. My mother's father, Dick Thrale, and her Uncle Peter both trained horses on the famous Epsom Downs surrounding the course, and I am told that I first watched the race at my grandfather's house at the age of five months!

Next, to Kempton Park in Surrey – another historical meeting, this time held on Boxing Day. For me, this course will always be the scene of my triumphs aboard that great grey horse Desert Orchid – 'Dessie' to those of us who loved and respected him so much. It was here that we won two consecutive King George VI steeplechases together, the second of which was Dessie's fourth win in the race.

Perth in Scotland, on the other hand, provides an example of the turf as it used to be. The 'craic' is legendary in the annals of British racing, because jockeys, trainers and owners alike all stay in the town for the two- or three-day meetings, which take place at either end of the jumping season. This kind of 'travelling circus' was once characteristic of all horseracing in Britain, and the camaraderie and sense of place still to be found in Perth can make you regret – for a couple of days at least! – that improved roads and railways have made it such a rare survival. The course lies along the banks of the River Tay in the beautiful grounds of the palace of Scone, where the Kings of Scotland were traditionally crowned, and the track itself is about 10 furlongs round, right-handed and a nice one to ride.

Sandown, near London, is synonymous with the Whitbread Gold Cup, a rare mix of flat and jumps, where there is always much leg-pulling in the weighing room between the jockeys from both codes, who otherwise rarely meet. One of the course's most famous features is the Railway Fences, which come in quick succession at the end of the back straight and have found out many a good chaser over the years.

Last but not least, we come to Wincanton in Somerset, a fine rural course which is always well supported. The best-known race is the Kingwell Hurdle, which has served as a stepping stone for many future Champion hurdlers, including Persian War, Bula and Kribensis. It also holds a special place in my affections as the course on which I set records both as the most successful jump jockey (with my 1,679th winner) and, on the same day, as the first National Hunt jockey ever to ride 10 consecutive centuries in a season. Since I retired some months later as a result of injury, Wincanton serves as a fitting place for me to end this short celebratory tour, just as it crowns my own memories, of the glories of the British turf.

The Works of Turner
Andrew Graham-Dixon

J M W Turner was the most intellectually, spiritually, emotionally and technically adventurous artist of the turbulent 19th century. He changed the way in which people saw the world and taught them to find value and beauty in aspects of nature – sunsets, sunrises, light-filled panoramic vistas – to which they had previously paid only slight and distracted attention. He was also one of those rare creative figures who alter, forever, the very medium in which they work. To put it simply, there was painting before Turner, there was painting after Turner, and they were not the same thing.

His origins were not in the least grand – he was the son of a barber, born and brought up in Covent Garden in London – but from the very start of his career, when he earned his living as a humble topographical draughtsman and watercolourist, almost everything he did was touched by a subtle and visionary sense of grandeur. It is as if his intuitive sense of the larger, cosmic cycles of creation and destruction governing the world and universe – his sense of 'the Sublime', to use the aesthetic terminology of Turner's own time – was so strong that it had a way of insinuating itself into his depictions of the mildest and most innocent scenes. Sunlight, in even the earliest of his watercolours of ruined abbeys and other such conventionally picturesque subjects, has a way of eating into the forms that it illuminates, anticipating the great dramas of light and darkness of his maturity. His earliest oil paintings, such as *Buttermere Lake*, done in 1797–8 when the artist was 23 years old, have a similar quality about them. The humdrum – in this case, a couple of boys rowing a boat across a lake – has been invested with a sense of wonder. The most vital element of the painting, the rainbow that arcs across a sunlit vaporous sky, is, characteristically, the most evanescent and insubstantial of phenomena. Turner was already proposing an art consecrated to the moment, to the capturing of a brief and fleeting impression, more than half a century before the term 'Impressionism' had been invented.

Turner was almost unique among British painters in his complete immunity to the disease of self-deprecation. He regarded painting as unquestionably 'the most serious art' and from first to last went at it with the ambition to match the very greatest of the Old Masters. He expressed his own high sense of vocation by painting a multitude of homages to painters of the past as disparate as Raphael, Claude, Poussin, Rembrandt and Ruisdael. But he often seems to be competing with those he idolises, and the result is always inimitably a Turner. He fed on the art of the past, devoured and absorbed it and made it his own (he is very reminiscent of Picasso, in his frankly oedipal relationship to the illustrious dead).

Snow Storm: Hannibal and his Army Crossing the Alps, which Turner completed in 1812, is perhaps the picture which marked most clearly the onset of his maturity and the dawning of the realisation that he did indeed have his own incomparable vision of things. The picture is a 'history painting', a work of narrative art and therefore an essay in what was viewed, by the standards of the time, as the highest of the genres. But that is only the beginning of its ambition. Looking into the maelstrom of Turner's painted storm, we can only just make out the painter's ostensible classical subject, the ant-like army of Hannibal performing its heroic feat of endurance. The human drama, the drama of a story, seems to bore Turner – or to leave him merely indifferent – to the point where he includes it only as a vestige. His subject is a drama of elements, a drama of darkness and light.

As he got older, Turner realised the implications of his own artistic compulsions with ever-increasing clarity and took to painting the world, with stunning audacity, almost in terms of light and colour alone. Single-handed, he turned the order of western painting on its head, treating solid objects as if they were the mere incidentals of experience and lavishing almost all of his attention, instead, on that which is transitory, elusive and ever-changing. In a burst of sustained creative energy the like of which has hardly ever been seen in painting, Turner created a great outpouring of masterpieces during the last 30 years of his life. Many of his most hypnotising works were executed in the delicate medium of watercolour. These include an extraordinary sequence of images inspired by Petworth House and its surroundings, which make an aristocratic English house and garden resemble the world before it was fully formed, a place of elemental flux and chaos – as well as an almost miraculously vivid cycle of images of the burning down of the Houses of Parliament, where the paper itself seems ablaze with colour. Turner spent much of his life attempting to translate the limpid purity of colour and atmosphere achievable in watercolour to the medium of oil painting, and in some of his very last paintings, like the radiant *Norham Castle, Sunrise*, he managed the feat with a dexterity that has never been subsequently matched.

The sense that something strange and unprecedented was happening in Turner's art was instinctively grasped by his contemporaries, although quite what it added up to was beyond most of them. They were at once fascinated and bewildered by what he was doing. But even though much of what they wrote about him was intended as the harshest possible criticism, nowadays it can easily read like the highest and most perceptive praise. This, for example, is William Hazlitt on Turner's pictures in 1816:

> They are too much abstractions of aerial perspective, and representations not properly of the objects of nature as of the medium through which they were seen… They are pictures of the elements of air, earth and water. The artist delights to go back to the first chaos of the world, or to that state of things, when the waters were separated from the dry land, and light from darkness, but as yet no living thing or tree bearing fruit was seen on the face of the earth. All is without form and void. Someone said of his landscapes that they were pictures of nothing and very like.

Turner himself should have the last word. The story goes that one day the author and biographer C R Leslie told the artist of a certain New York collector who had complained of the troubling indistinctness of his latest pictures. Turner's retort was brief and to the point. 'You should tell him that indistinctness is my forte.'

Snow Storm: Hannibal and his Army Crossing the Alps, *1812*

The London Underground Map
Terence Conran

Ever since I was a child, I have loved to look at maps. It is not just their inherent cartographic beauty that captivates me, though they are the most perfect executions of line, form and colour. Rather, it is the fact that all maps seem to me to be portals, a possibility made tangible, redolent with the promise of far-away places. One of the world's best-used and most loved maps, and one of the first that appealed to me, is not of distant mountainscapes, or of a remote island waiting to be discovered. To many, though, it is just as exotic, charting as it does a world winding deep below the streets of London town.

The first map of the combined London Electric Railways appeared in 1906, when Charles Yerkes, an American financier, brought each of his four railways together in one network. Those venerable lines, now known as the District, Piccadilly, Bakerloo and Northern Lines, were soon joined by the Central and Metropolitan Lines, and the Underground as we now know it was born.

As the Underground grew, so did the need for new maps, which would help shoppers, commuters and tourists to navigate their way through this expanding subterranean world. In the first quarter of the 20th century, a number of maps were introduced which charted the system in a fairly traditional way, using street-level topography to define the position of each station. It was not until 1926 that a draughtsman called Stingemore, obviously a lateral thinker, abstracted the diagram, removed the restriction of the streets and looked at the position of stations in graphic terms. It was this revolutionary initiative that created the possibility for today's map – one of those moments that designers dream of, when a totally new idea is conceived, one which changes the direction of all subsequent thinking.

Subsequent sophistication of Stingemore's work, and the development of the map that we know and love today, was carried out in the early 1930s by Henry C (Harry) Beck. Beck too was a draughtsman for London Underground. Often considered to be an obsessive, Harry Beck spent much of his working life struggling to have his map accepted and then, once it was, amending it to allow for an ever-changing network. Beck saw the map as a living thing, real, organic and with its own personality. I find it extraordinary that his wife chose to marry him in the early days of the map, preoccupied and driven as he was by his search for perfection – but maybe she was perfect too. Records and reports certainly indicate that Beck was a good man: humorous, noble and kind.

Beck's first designs for the Underground map, scribbled in his spare time in an exercise book, show the constructive processes of a truly creative mind. Simplifying the routes and stations into a loose grid, with only horizontal, vertical and 45-degree diagonal lines, Beck began to define the map we are now so used to. This initial sketch, allegedly based on electrical circuit diagrams, was soon developed into a full map, which, although nearly 70 years old, is immediately recognisable as the precursor of today's version.

The real beauty of Beck's translation of the Underground was the way it created an elegant, abstracted view of the network, with outlying stations appearing close together and central London, with its more commonly used destinations, being shown on a larger scale. But what was really extraordinary about Beck's map was that, while it modified the appearance of the system to allow clear reading and understanding, it still described an understandable geography of the city; Oxford Circus, for example, remained north of Piccadilly, east of Bond Street and west of Tottenham Court Road. For many people, their whole mental picture of London is based on this layout.

This, I believe, was Beck's real skill: understanding the map as a piece of communication, as pure information, and creating the most simple and understandable solution possible. Like all good, functional design, it has its own beauty, an inherent aesthetic which transcends its obvious usefulness. Other versions of the map, by other designers, have been tested or introduced for short periods, but it was to Beck's template that London Underground constantly returned, and the map we use today is based directly on his designs.

Along the way, numerous improvements have been made. The blobs which once denoted each station were replaced by 'ticks', which not only introduced visual levity, but also pointed directly to the station's name, making the map even easier to understand. It is this kind of thinking which elevates the practical into genius, and which I constantly try to instil in designers, chefs and writers. *Faites simple*! Strive for elegance and simplicity; be economical, and enjoy the results! Other notable changes have included the changing of the map's lettering (Johnston's Underground Sans – sublime) from capitals to lower case, which had a subtle, informalising effect. And of course the lines themselves have been through a spectrum of changes in their varied histories.

Today's Underground map, or journey-planner as we are encouraged to call it, carries more information than ever before. The Jubilee Line has (finally) opened. New stations continue to appear while redundant stations still maintain their territories. Proposed routes, restricted lines, peak hour possibilities – they all jostle for position and prominence. And yet the map remains flexible enough to accommodate them. Copied in many countries, revered by many designers, the Underground map is, and has always been, a triumph of design; a simple, informative guide to the largest, most complicated tube system in the world. And, like those countless maps I gazed at as a child, it is quite beautiful.

Overleaf: *Henry Beck's 1933 map of the London Underground*

247

Village Cricket
Mihir Bose

George Orwell once described the typical English village green cricket match as an occasion when a blacksmith playing in braces is called away in mid-innings and, as the light begins to fade, a ball hit for four kills a rabbit on the boundary. Much has changed since then, but village cricket, which is how the game began, retains a purity and an appeal which marks it out as a uniquely English creation.

The English can be rightly proud of the fact that most of the games now played around the world were conceived in these isles, but it is in developing cricket that the English sporting genius reached its peak. Cricket still enshrines the three great English attributes: a love of irony, a general desire to avoid hype, which can almost make an art-form of understatement, and above all a deep distaste for anything that smacks of too much effort and detailed premeditation. The truly great cricketer is still the man who can display magical gifts with the bat or ball, but never feels the need to practice or break into a sweat in order to hone his skills. That, by definition, is for lesser mortals.

Cricket's intricate structure imposes an obligation on players and spectators which is unique in ball games. Unlike nearly all other games, the two teams opposing each other are actually trying to do two very different, indeed opposite, things: the batsman is trying to score runs, while the bowler and his fielders are trying to stop him scoring runs and get him out.

Add to this the fact that while all sports extol the virtues of sportsmanship and fair play but acquiesce in cheating, cricket cannot function without a certain sense of inherent integrity. So until a few years ago the umpires for Test matches, the highest form of international match, always came from the country hosting the matches and, although one of the two umpires is now from a neutral country, there is still a home umpire – a situation that would be inconceivable in any other international sporting contest.

But more even than that, there is the unique role of the umpire. He is not merely the official who has the final say, but acts like a judge in a Court of Appeal hearing. Unless the bowler has clean bowled the batsman, in order to get a batsman out he has to appeal to the umpire, who then judges whether to uphold the appeal or not. In other games, an appeal by the player for a favourable decision makes no difference or can actually be counterproductive; in cricket, a bowler has to judge whether it is worth appealing and then hope to convince the umpire.

George Trevelyan wrote that if only the French lords had followed the example of their English counterparts by playing cricket with their servants, they could have avoided the French Revolution. That may sound like English whimsy, but the way village cricket developed – the squire playing with his workers and all of them taking part in the social side of the game, the drink in the pub before and afterwards, the tea with cucumber sandwiches during the game – meant the match was also a very special social occasion. And it retains this aspect, this bracing egalitarianism, even today.

As much a social occasion as a game: village cricketers break for tea

The many village matches I have played in have been memorable not so much for their cricket as for their setting and the eccentricity of the players. And if at one recent match there were no blacksmiths on the field, then their modern equivalents, the political lobbyists, were there in full force. One of them even played in braces – with a red tie holding up his trousers – and gave every indication of expecting to be called away at any moment on his mobile telephone. And the sheep that grazed just over the boundary occasionally had to move quickly to avoid the fate suffered by Orwell's rabbit. For much of the afternoon, while not dodging cricket balls, they gazed in total bemusement at a man in a white coat, who was meant to be the umpire – he even had the coins in his pocket to count the balls – but spent the entire afternoon lying very still on the grass just beyond the boundary, having consumed the local brew with some relish at lunchtime.

As the match progressed, every cricketer seemed determined to prove that, on the English village green, sportsmanship was still alive and well – you never claimed a prize unless you genuinely deserved it, and even then you did not crow about it. So when a bowler got a dubious LBW decision against a batsman, there were no high fives from his fieldsmen. Instead, they gathered rather sheepishly round him, and there followed a long silence as if everyone were embarrassed by the taking of this wicket, convinced the bowler had not deserved it. Later, back in the pavilion, the bowler apologised to the batsman for appealing in the first place.

This sense of English decency was matched by that other great principle of village cricket: always put a man at ease, even if he is the one who has behaved stupidly. Late in the match, with the side batting second chasing victory, one of the main batsmen got out to a dreadful shot. As he came back rather nervously to the pavilion, not sure how his teammates would greet him, the captain said, 'That was the seven o'clock dinner shot, was it not, Bill? I know why you played that. You have guests coming for dinner at seven and Mary will kill you if you do not get back home in time. I once had three of my main batsmen play such seven o'clock dinner shots and we lost a match we should have won with some comfort.' In the laughter that followed, Bill's horrific shot was completely forgotten and all the talk turned to Mary and her legendary dinners. The result mattered not at all.

An Obsession with the Weather
Ray Connolly

As every foreigner mocks, the British are obsessed with their weather. That's all right. We don't deny it. We are. From the cot to the coffin we carefully observe the vagaries of our clouds, silently implore their kindness, and curse their careless wrecking of our plans. A nation of amateur meteorologists, we follow like racegoers the procession of high- and low-pressure areas across the Atlantic, place bets on the likelihood of snow on Christmas Day and make celebrities of our homely weather professionals on television. Some of the more sophisticated amongst us consult household barometers for signs of change, while the more traditional observe the standing up and lying down of cattle, the flights of swallows and the behaviour of midges, gazing often into the setting of the sun for the delight of shepherds. In all, the weather simply fascinates us.

But more than just watching, anticipating or surviving the weather, what we really like to do is to talk about the weather. To a Brit, weather-talk can be an ice-breaker, a tension-easer or a bond-maker. 'Turned out nice again,' we remark as an opening, cheery gambit in conversation with a stranger; 'Cool for June!' interrupts the slightest difficult lull between friends; while an indignant 'And they call this summer!' will make comrades in scorn of the most singular members of a gale-lashed bus queue.

While the French make love, the Italians make music and the Americans make money, we make do for every occasion with our weather. We know we're laughed at by other nations for what they perceive to be an eccentricity. But we don't mind: the other nations don't know what they're missing.

The British talk about the weather because they realise that, more than anything, the weather made them the people they are. It is one of the essential keys to being British, a capricious but ultimately enabling factor which, through generation upon generation, glues the nation together in national stoicism. 'Rain, rain, go away, come again another day,' we teach our children to recite as soon as they can talk, thus preparing them for the lifetime of wet games days which lie ahead, the frustrations of 'rain stopped play', and the disappointments of Bank Holiday outings spent playing Monopoly or Nintendo while outside the downpour resumes. There's nothing like a British summer holiday for preparing the child for the uncertain realities of life.

But because we cannot rely upon the weather to give us sunshine on the day of the picnic, that doesn't mean we don't have the picnic. We do, because we can't rely upon it not to be a scorcher either.

Thus, because of this temperate, baffling climate, where it's often chilly but practically never too cold, sometimes warm but rarely too hot, and frequently wet but not often to the point of flooding, we have become the world's leaders at 'making the best of it', a people programmed from birth to be ready for anything. Long before the Scouts adopted the motto 'Be prepared', cautious preparation was part of the British character. 'Better take a raincoat, just to be on the safe side,' we've been telling ourselves for so long that some of us founded Lloyds of London

and created a worldwide insurance industry – further encouraged, admittedly, by the Great Fire and the South Sea Bubble. But there it was. Caution was in our blood.

Hoping for the best, while being ready for the worst, pervades British history. Our unreliable weather saw to that – though more often than not it seems to have been on our side. Francis Drake didn't beat the Spanish Armada alone in 1588. A gale in the North Sea finished the job off for him. The Duke of Wellington is reputed to have said that the Battle of Waterloo was won on the playing fields of Eton. But the poor bloody infantry probably took another view. Waterloo was also won because (not to mention the Prussians) the much fancied French cavalry waited for the rain-sodden mud to dry out, leaving the British foot-soldiers free to yomp right through it as they would through a field of potatoes back home. And the weather in the English Channel was hardly impartial in either 1940 or 1944. An obsession with the weather then meant the difference between defeat and eventual victory.

Nations differ in character according to the geographical circumstances in which they find themselves, so surely it cannot be coincidental that these north-western islands of Europe, where extremes of climate are rarely experienced, have, certainly in recent history, been a part of the world where extremes of behaviour attract little following. Even in politics, this 'better not to risk a sudden downpour' nation likes to carry an umbrella.

As for sex, no wonder we got a reputation for being either timid or frigid, or more interested in cricket. While the nearby Continentals, with their warm, dry summers, might doff their few, slight clothes to lie down in the long grass with a partner of choice, our partners would be trussed and tied like waterproof parcels, risking an attack of rheumatism should pale British limbs ever be exposed to the elements. At least with cricket we could always make a dash to the pavilion between maiden overs.

Of course with so much foreign travel these days, and the unsheathing of once modest British flesh to foreign weather and, dare we say it, sunshine, sexual behaviour has begun to change, as a fortnight in Ibiza with a group of 17- to 23-year-olds would apparently demonstrate. Perhaps that was only to be expected. With every day a guaranteed scorcher, and the point of conversation about the weather therefore somewhat lost, British holidaymakers have obviously had to find something else to do with their time.

Indeed, with people flying off to find the weather they think they prefer, rather than staying at home and defying it to do its worst, there was until recently a very real threat that the British obsession might be in danger of dying out.

Not to worry, the threat is no more. With global warming now exaggerating every cyclone and anti, with monsoons in Bridlington, droughts in Swansea, hurricanes in Montrose and heatwaves in Londonderry, the future of the great British art of weather conversation has never looked more lively.

Now, what will it be, snowboots or suncream? Better take another jumper… just in case.

Previous pages: *Whatever the weather: Morecambe holidaymakers in the 1950s*

Whisky
Charles MacLean

As we look about us, Scotch whisky may not seem to qualify as a badge of Britishness any longer. Even strolling between bars in what our grandfathers termed 'North Britain', we learn that more vodka is drunk here than whisky, although the bars themselves are better stocked than ever before with malt whiskies. Yet furth of this sceptr'd isle – and let us not forget that 90 per cent of Scotch is drunk abroad – whisky is the greatest, best-loved and most conspicuous ambassador for Britain in general and Scotland in particular; Scotch contributes over £2 billion per annum to our balance of trade, and is among the top four British exports. So any book celebrating British greats would be incomplete without a mention of Scotch whisky.

The paean is easily inspired: whisky appeals emotionally, intellectually, and – dare one admit it – physically.

The emotional appeal is romantic. Whisky is no mere industrial confection; it is the lifeblood of Scotland and recollects the place of its creation with every sip. Its flavour – and I will say more about this later – embraces the very smells of Scotland: tangled hedgerows and heather in bloom, oatcakes and country kitchens, peat smoke and iodine, polished mahogany and old books.

But more than this, it reminds us of its creators, past and present: the hardy Highlanders who developed the art of distilling and made it part of their culture; the desperadoes who continued to distil in the face of oppressive legislation during the later decades of the 18th century; the canny entrepreneurs who invented the art of blending malt and grain whiskies to create a drink which had broader appeal; and the remarkable salesmen who created a world market for this drink at the end of the 19th century.

During the late Victorian era, blended Scotch, along with tartan and bagpipes, became the icon of a Scotland which had been largely invented by Sir Walter Scott – an image coloured by Queen Victoria's passion for all things perceived to be Scottish, and eagerly adopted by Scots at home and abroad, often with their tongues in their cheeks and an eye to the main chance. Such an image is now deeply unfashionable – and Scotch whisky has suffered by association in its home market – but it is saturated with sentiment, and is much more fun than the colourless Euro-identity that revisionists and modernists would have us adopt.

Happily, Scotch continues to play an important role in the contemporary re-evaluation of 'Scottishness', for in the search for authenticity malt whisky has been rediscovered. This, the original and most flavoursome incarnation of Scotch, was completely eclipsed by the beginning of the 20th century by the phenomenal success of blended whisky. Single malts were simply unavailable until the late 1960s, and even then only a handful were to be found.

But there were stirrings in the Scottish psyche. Beginning with what became known as the 'Scottish Literary Revival', paralleled in music by the rediscovery of folksongs and the serious study of popular culture, burgeoning into a thorough reappraisal of Scottish history and, one might say, culminating in the re-establishment of a Scottish Parliament, Scottish cultural identity took a new and more durable shape. Less romantic, perhaps, but more authentic; and in the quest for authenticity, malt whisky was discovered to be 'the real thing'.

This is where we move from Scotch's emotional charm to its intellectual appeal. Malt whisky is recognised by sensory chemists as being the most complex spirit made on earth, and the most elusive – although made from the simplest ingredients (malted barley and water, fermented by yeast), by a process (pot-still distillation) which can be imitated by children in a school chemistry lab. Over the past 20 years, a huge amount of scientific research has been devoted to investigating why malt whisky tastes as it does and why every malt tastes different, even though made from the same ingredients, by the same process; and although we now know infinitely more about the contributions made to flavour by the individual ingredients and stages of production and maturation, the mystery remains.

Fifteen years ago, when I began to write about whisky, chemists had isolated and identified around 300 flavour-bearing compounds in an average bottle of malt and knew that there were at least as many again to be described. Now they have identified 700, and are still far from concluding the search. Some of the compounds are clearly identifiable by the human nose in dilutions measured in parts per million, parts per billion and in some cases parts per trillion. The enormity of this must not be underestimated: one part per million is equivalent to 10 minutes in 20 years; one part per billion is a click of the fingers in 20 years: and one part in a trillion is immeasurable.

Our noses are infinitely more sensitive than our tongues: while the latter has around 9,000 taste buds, the former has between 50 and 100 million sense-receptors. Furthermore, the taste buds register only the four primary tastes – sweet, sour, salty, bitter. Everything else we 'taste' is in fact 'smelled' *via* the rear nasal passage. This is why we talk of whisky 'nosings' rather than 'tastings', and why blenders and other experts can obtain all the information they need without actually putting the spirit into their mouths.

Sniffing whisky may be the best way to appreciate its subtleties, but you and I consume it – or I do, at least. Which brings me deftly to the final aspect of my appreciation: the physical effect of whisky – a sensitive subject, and one which most books about whisky draw a veil across, although it has been much celebrated in Scottish literature. Whisky intoxicates, yet it is a clean intoxicant, and if you stick with it (and plenty of water) you feel much less pain the next day than you do with many other forms of alcohol. It is a stimulant – inspiring conversation, sharpening awareness, stirring the soul. It exalts more than it depresses; sharpens the wits more than it dulls them; leads to adventure. In short, whisky is an heroic drink – possibly the most heroic drink in the world.

So let us celebrate that greatest of Scottish contributions to human joy – emotionally, intellectually and physically – Scotch whisky.

The lifeblood of Scotland: Dewar's classic 'The Whisky of his Forefathers' advertisement

"The Whisky of his forefathers"

The World of Wodehouse
David Gilmour

My children sigh when they find me reading P G Wodehouse. They whisper and shake their heads and pass the news around, not from any lack of humour or an incomprehensible aversion, but because they realise why I am reading *Right Ho! Jeeves* or *The Code of the Woosters* for the eighth time; they know that for me the Wodehouse world is the best of all anti-depressants.

It is sometimes said that his world was Edwardian, that it vanished, and that he spent the rest of his life trying to evoke it. Yet that world was in fact very much Wodehouse's own creation. He may have retained the apparatus of Edwardian country life, but his cast of eccentric earls, red-faced vicars and supercilious butlers is not real. George Orwell complained that Wodehouse's 'real sin' was to have presented 'the English upper classes as much nicer people than they are'. But he didn't; he just made them fictitious.

Wodehouse was a shy, reclusive and rather naïve man who loved dogs (much more than people) and writing. He expanded his world over 96 books, dividing it into several continents presided over by the imperturbable Psmith, the optimistic Ukridge, Mr Mulliner yarning away in the pub, and that absent-minded pig enthusiast, Lord Emsworth. But the largest and richest continent belongs to that wonderful pair, Jeeves and Bertie Wooster, the Sherlock Holmes and Dr Watson of comedy. When Graham Greene announced that he was thinking of leaving God out of his next novel, Evelyn Waugh warned him that it would be like Wodehouse dropping Jeeves from the Wooster stories.

Hilaire Belloc considered Wodehouse to be the 'best writer' of the age, the master of choosing the right words and putting them in the right order. Waugh also regarded him as a master, because each page contained on average 'three uniquely brilliant and entirely original similes'. Here is Wooster ruminating on the subject of aunts:

> I turned to Aunt Agatha, whose demeanour was now rather like that of one who, picking daisies on the railway, has just caught the down express in the small of the back.

> When Aunt is calling to Aunt like mastodons bellowing across primeval swamps.

> It is no use telling me that there are bad aunts and good aunts. At the core, they are all alike. Sooner or later, out pops the cloven hoof.

'Ages' usually require their best writers to say something about the era and the human condition, but none of that concerned Wodehouse. His only aim was to entertain himself and his readers, and for his own benefit and ours he created an immortal world of bossy aunts, scheming girlfriends and sinister magistrates, all conspiring to thwart a bevy of young loafers (such as Bingo Little, Gussie Fink-Nottle, Esmond Haddock, Catsmeat Potter-Pirbright and of course B Wooster), good chaps who don't know what to make of the ladies, but fall in love (or think they do) and regard a kiss as the summit of their ambition and achievement. There is no sex, no sexual joke or innuendo, and no serious love-scene in any of those 96 books.

After the Second World War Wodehouse wondered 'what the devil does one write about these days, if one is a specialist on country houses and butlers, both of which have now ceased to exist?' But he didn't need to worry: he simply returned to his creations and kept going. In 1974 he was still writing about Jeeves, 55 years after the great butler had first appeared on the page.

In a BBC radio broadcast, Evelyn Waugh declared that Wodehouse's 'world can never stale. He will continue to release future generations from captivity that may be more irksome than our own. He has made a world for us to live in and delight in.' And, one might add, escape depression in. On the radio programme *Desert Island Discs*, guests are invited to choose a single volume to take for their solitary confinement on a tropical paradise. High-minded people would doubtless take Milton or something equally serious to *think* about. But in my case, uncomfortable with myself for very long, I would need better company. And what better than an omnibus volume of Jeeves and Wooster? At least I would be able to identify with Jeeves, whom Bertie could see was 'if not actually disgruntled... far from being gruntled'.

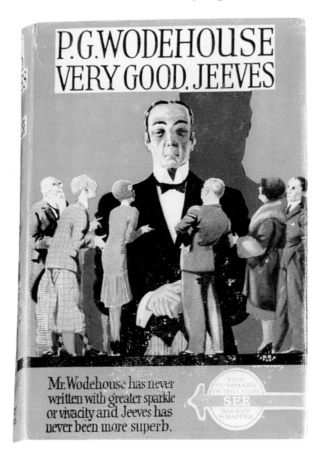

The Sherlock Holmes and Dr Watson of comedy: Jeeves and Wooster make an early (1930) appearance

Author Biographies

Peter Ackroyd's most recent books include bestselling biographies of Dickens, Blake and Thomas More, and the novels *Dan Leno and the Limehouse Golem* and *Milton in America*. He is the winner of a Somerset Maugham Award, the James Tait Black Memorial Prize and the Whitbread Prize for Biography.

Clive Anderson was for many years a barrister specialising in criminal law. More recently he has presented TV programmes for Channel 4 and the BBC, including comedies, documentaries and talk shows. On BBC Radio 4 he presents *Unreliable Evidence*, a legal discussion programme.

Stephen Bayley is an author and design consultant. He was responsible for the Boilerhouse in London's V & A and for the Design Museum that evolved from it. His books include *In Good Shape*, *Sex, Drink and Fast Cars*, *Commerce and Culture*, *Taste*, *Labour Camp* and *General Knowledge*.

Mihir Bose is an author and journalist and senior columnist for the *Daily Telegraph*, specialising in sports business and political stories. He won the Sports Reporter of the Year Award in 1999 and is the author of 20 books, including an award-winning *History of Indian Cricket*.

Melvyn Bragg is an author and broadcaster. He published his first novel *For Want of Nail* in 1965 and his latest *The Soldier's Return* in 1999. His other books include an oral history of England, *Speak for England*. He is currently Controller of Arts and Features at LWT and editor and presenter of *The South Bank Show*.

Asa Briggs is the author of many books on political, social and cultural history, including *A Social History of England*. He was Provost of Worcester College, Oxford, from 1976 to 1991 and Chancellor of the Open University from 1978 to 1994. He was made a life peer in 1976.

Julie Burchill was born in Bristol in 1959 and is a journalist, author and columnist for the *Guardian*.

Barbara Castle was MP for Blackburn for 34 years, during which time she held four Cabinet posts including Minister of Transport and Secretary of State for Social Services. She retired from the Commons in 1979 and was elected to the European Parliament, of which she remained a member until 1989. She was created a life peer in 1990.

John Cole worked for the *Belfast Telegraph* before joining the *Manchester Guardian*, of which he was Labour Correspondent, News Editor and Deputy Editor. He joined the *Observer* in 1975 and remained until 1981 as Deputy Editor. From 1981–92 he was Political Editor of the BBC. His books include *The Thatcher Years: a Decade of Revolution in British Politics* and *As It Seemed to Me: Political Memoirs*.

Joseph Connolly worked in publishing and was an antiquarian bookseller before becoming a full-time writer. He is the author of six novels and many non-fiction works.

Ray Connolly is best known for his journalism, currently being published in the *Daily Mail*. As well as novels and radio plays, he has written screenplays (including *That'll Be the Day* and *Stardust*), TV series (*Lytton's Diary* and *Perfect Scoundrels*), TV documentaries and a biography of John Lennon.

Terence Conran is a designer, retailer and restaurateur. He set up Habitat in the 1960s and The Conran Shop, which now has stores in London, Paris, Germany, Japan and New York. His acclaimed restaurants include Quaglino's, Le Pont de la Tour and Sartoria, as well as Alcazar (Paris), Berns (Stockholm) and Guastavino's (New York). He recently opened the Great Eastern Hotel in London.

Hunter Davies is the author of over 30 books, which include such modern classics as the authorised biography of the Beatles, *The Glory Game* and *A Walk around the Lakes*. He is also well known as a broadcaster and journalist and writes for the *Independent*, *Sunday Times*, *Daily Mail* and *New Statesman*.

Richard Dawkins is Charles Simonyi Professor of the Public Understanding of Science at Oxford University, and a Fellow of New College. His awards include the International Cosmos Award (1997) and the Michael Faraday Award of the Royal Society (1990). He has written five books on aspects of Darwinian evolution, including *The Selfish Gene*, *The Blind Watchmaker* and *Climbing Mount Improbable*. His latest book is *Unweaving the Rainbow*.

Len Deighton began his writing career with *The Ipcress File*, which became a classic film. He has written many works of fiction and non-fiction, including spy stories and war novels such as *Goodbye Mickey Mouse* and *Bomber*, and his acclaimed history of the Second World War *Blood, Tears and Folly*. He is co-author with Max Hastings of *The Battle of Britain*.

Sally Dugan is a writer and teacher. She has written for *The Times* and the *Radio Times* and two books in collaboration with Windfall Films: *Measure for Measure* and *The Day the World Took Off*, the latter co-authored with her husband David Dugan to accompany the Channel 4 series on the Industrial Revolution.

Richard Dunwoody rode over 1700 winners during his career as a jockey, including in the Grand National and Cheltenham Gold Cup. He was five times voted National Hunt Jockey of the Year and was awarded an MBE in 1993. He writes for the *Daily Telegraph* and co-presents *BBC Racing*; his publications include *Hell for Leather* and *Hands and Heels*.

John Elliott is Regius Professor Emeritus of Modern History at the University of Oxford, where he was a Fellow of Oriel

College and held the Regius Chair of Modern History until 1997. He has written extensively on 16th- and 17th-century Spanish and European history, and his books include *Imperial Spain, 1469–1716* and *Europe Divided, 1559–1598*.

Jane Fearnley-Whittingstall works as a garden designer and consultant in Britain and overseas. She is a gold medal winner for gardens exhibited at Chelsea Flower Show and has lectured and broadcast on radio and TV in Britain and the US. Her books include the bestselling *Gardening Made Easy* and her most recent work *Peonies – the Imperial Flower*.

Paul Ferris was born in Swansea. His biography of Dylan Thomas, the standard work, and his edition of Thomas' letters have both recently been revised and reissued. His other books include lives of Caitlin Thomas and Sigmund Freud, and his latest novel *Infidelity*.

Fergus Fleming worked in publishing for six years before becoming a freelance writer in 1991. He is the author of *Barrow's Boys*, a history of 19th-century British exploration, and *Killing Dragons: the Conquest of the Alps*.

Paul Fox worked in television for more than 40 years, both in the BBC, where he was Editor of *Panorama* (1961–63), Controller of BBC1 (1967–73) and Managing Director (1988–91), and in ITV, where he was Director of Programmes (1973–84) and Managing Director Yorkshire Television (1977–88). He was Chairman of ITN (1986–88).

Frances Fyfield is an award-winning crime novelist; her most recent book is *Blind Date*. She is also a lawyer who has worked for many years with the Metropolitan Police and the Director of Public Prosecutions.

John Gillingham is a specialist in the medieval period, with a particular interest in Geoffrey of Monmouth, relations between English and Celtic peoples, and Richard the Lionheart. He is now Emeritus Professor at the London School of Economics and Political Science.

David Gilmour's books include the prizewinning biographies *Curzon* and *The Last Leopard: a Life of Giuseppe di Lampedusa* and several works on contemporary Spanish and Middle Eastern history.

Andrew Graham-Dixon was chief art critic of the *Independent* from 1986–98; he received the BP Arts Journalism Award three years running and the Hawthorden Prize for Arts Criticism in 1991. His books include the bestselling *History of British Art* and *Renaissance*, which he also presented as a TV series.

John Gribbin has been Visiting Fellow in astronomy at the University of Sussex since 1993, and previously wrote for *New Scientist* and *Nature*, receiving the National Award of the Association of British Science Writers for his work on climate change. His many books include *In Search of Schrödinger's Cat*, *In Search of the Double Helix* and *In Search of the Big Bang*.

John Grigg is a historian and author of three volumes in a life of Lloyd George, the second of which was awarded the Whitbread Prize and the third the Wolfson Prize. He has also written a life of Nancy Astor, a book on the Second World War (*1943: the Victory that Never Was*), and Volume VI in the official history of *The Times* (*The Thomson Years*).

Robert Hardy is an actor and writer. He has appeared in numerous leading roles on stage, in the cinema and on TV, most recently playing Winston Churchill (in French) in the play *Celui qui a dit non* at the Palais des Congrès in Paris. He has been a consultant to the Mary Rose Trust since 1979, and his book *Longbow* is recognised as a standard work.

John Harris has written extensively on architecture and gardening. He is Curator Emeritus of the Drawings Collection, Royal Institute of British Architects, and Honorary Life President of the International Confederation of Architectural Museums.

Edward Heath was Prime Minister of the UK from 1970–74 and Leader of the Conservative Party from 1965–75; the longest-serving MP (since 1950), he has the honorary title 'Father of the House of Commons'. A keen yachtsman, he won the Sydney to Hobart Race (1969) and captained Britain's winning Admiral's Cup team (1971). His publications include works on politics, sailing and music, and his autobiography *The Course of My Life*.

Simon Heffer was educated at Corpus Christi College, Cambridge, where he read English. In the course of nearly 20 years as a writer and broadcaster, he has been Deputy Editor of both the *Spectator* and the *Daily Telegraph*, and is now a columnist for the *Daily Mail*. He has written five books, mainly on historical and political subjects, including *Like the Roman*, the definitive biography of Enoch Powell.

Anthony Holden is the biographer of Tchaikovsky, Laurence Olivier and Prince Charles, as well as of William Shakespeare. He has also published *Big Deal*, an account of a year as a professional poker-player, and translations of works from Greek tragedy to Mozart operas.

Will Hutton is Chief Executive of the Industrial Society and was Editor and Editor-in-Chief of the *Observer* (1996–2000). His books include *The State We're In*, *The State to Come*, and *The Stakeholding Society*. He was nominated political journalist of the year by *What the Papers Say* in 1993.

Howard Jacobson was a lecturer in England and Australia before becoming a full-time novelist and critic. His novels include *Coming from Behind*, *Peeping Tom*, *Redback*, *The Very Model of a Man*, *No More Mister Nice Guy* and *The Mighty Walzer*. He has also written four works of non-fiction, including *Seriously Funny: an Argument for Comedy*.

Simon Jenkins is a columnist for *The Times* and the London *Evening Standard*. He has edited both papers and was also political editor of the *Economist* (1979–86). He was voted Journalist of the Year in 1988 and Columnist of the Year in 1993. His publications include books on politics and the history and architecture of London, and most recently *England's Thousand Best Churches*.

Terry Jones was part of the *Monty Python* team from 1969–74 and directed the films *Monty Python's Life of Brian* and *The Meaning of Life*, which he also co-wrote and co-starred in. His other directorial credits include *Personal Services*, *Erik the Viking* and *Asterix and Obelix*. His publications include *Chaucer's Knight*, *The Crusades* (co-written with Alan Ereira), *The Knight and the Squire* and books for children.

Michael Kennedy has been a music critic since 1950 and for the past decade has written for the *Sunday Telegraph*. His books include a history of the Hallé Orchestra and biographical studies of Elgar, Vaughan Williams, Britten and Walton, as well as of Sir John Barbirolli and Sir Adrian Boult. He wrote the *Oxford Dictionary of Music* and is a frequent lecturer and broadcaster.

Neil Kinnock is a former Leader of the Labour Party and currently Vice President of the European Commission. He was MP for Bedwellty and Islwyn (1970–95) and is an Honorary Fellow of University College, Cardiff. His publications include *Making Our Way – Investing in Britain's Future* and *Thorns and Roses*. Born and raised in Tredegar, he has been singing since his schooldays and threatens to return to male voice choir membership when he retires.

Robin Knox-Johnston went to sea at 17 and in 1968–69 became the first person to sail single-handed non-stop around the world. He also set a new record for an around-the-world voyage in 1994. Author of 14 books, in 1989 he crossed the Atlantic following Columbus and using Renaissance navigation methods and was awarded the Royal Institute of Navigation's Gold Medal.

David Kynaston was educated at New College, Oxford, and the London School of Economics and has been a professional historian since 1973. Since the late 1970s his main focus has been the City of London. The first three volumes of his history of the City, 1815–2000, came out in the 1990s; the final volume is due to appear in 2001.

Andrew Lambert is Professor of Naval History in the Department of War Studies, King's College, London. He is Honorary Secretary of the Navy Records Society, Vice President of the British Commission for Maritime History and a Fellow of the Royal Historical Society. His books include *The Last Sailing Battlefleet: Maintaining Naval Mastery 1815–1850* and *War at Sea in the Age of Sail (1650–1850)*.

Kevin McCloud is best known as the presenter of *Grand Designs* (Channel 4) and *Don't Look Down* (BBC2). His company McCloud Lighting produces decorative and contemporary lighting, and his publications cover a range of architectural areas, including home decoration, colour, lighting and self-build design and construction.

Charles MacLean is a writer specialising in Scotch whisky, on which he has published eight books, including the standard work *Scotch Whisky* and *Malt Whisky*. He is Editor of *Whisky Magazine* and Chair of the Scotch Malt Whisky Society's Nosing Panel.

Stirling Moss is Britain's best-known racing driver. In a career that ran from 1948–62, he entered nearly 500 competitive races and finished first, second or third in more than 300 of them. He competed in every major motor racing event apart from the Indianapolis 500.

Brian Moynahan is the author of *The British Century* and has recently finished writing *The Faith*, a history of Christianity, which will be published in 2001. He was for many years a foreign correspondent with the *Sunday Times*.

James Naughtie co-presents the *Today* programme on BBC Radio 4. He also introduces music on BBC radio and television and is the host of BBC Radio 4's *Bookclub*. He is a former chief political correspondent of the *Guardian* and the *Scotsman*, and writes for many newspapers and magazines.

Nigel Nicolson, the younger son of Vita Sackville-West and Harold Nicolson, lives at Sissinghurst Castle in Kent. He served in the Second World War in Italy and Africa, where he first avidly read the novels of Jane Austen. He is the author of numerous books, including *Great Houses of Britain*, *Two Roads to Dodge City*, *Portrait of a Marriage*, *The World of Jane Austen* and *Virginia Woolf*.

Ruth Padel is a poet, journalist and scholar. She writes the *Independent on Sunday*'s column 'The Sunday Poem' and has published four collections of poetry (most recently *Rembrandt Would Have Loved You*, shortlisted for the T S Eliot Prize). She has won the National Poetry Competition and is a Fellow of the Royal Society of Literature. She is the author of *I'm a Man: Sex, Gods and Rock 'n' Roll*.

Michael Palin was part of the *Monty Python* team that made the TV series and five films, including *Monty Python and the Holy Grail*, *Monty Python's Life of Brian* and *The Meaning of Life*. His other film acting credits include *Time Bandits*, *A Private Function* and *A Fish Called Wanda*. He has written and appeared in numerous TV programmes, including *Around the World in 80 Days*, *Pole to Pole* and *Full Circle*, and is the author of the bestselling books *Hemingway's Chair* and *Michael Palin's Hemingway Adventure*.

Rowan Pelling was educated at Oxford and is Editor of the *Erotic Review*, a columnist for *GQ* and a regular contributor to the *Spectator* and *New Statesman*.

Shyama Perera is of Sri Lankan descent. Born in Moscow, she arrived in Paddington, West London, in 1962, aged four. A writer and broadcaster, she took British citizenship in 1990.

Jane Pettigrew is a consultant, lecturer and writer on tea, and has published seven books on the subject, including *Jane*

Pettigrew's Tea-time. She has also written on food, table style and social history.

Brian Pippard has been in Cambridge since 1945, and was Cavendish Professor of Physics (1971–82) and President of Clare Hall (1966–73). He was President of the Institute of Physics (1974–76) and became a Fellow of the Royal Society in 1956.

Mary Quant is a designer and Chairman of Mary Quant Ltd and Director of the Mary Quant Group of Companies since 1955. She was awarded the OBE in 1966 and is an Honorary Fellow of the Royal Society of Arts and Goldsmith University. Her publications include *Quant by Quant, Colour by Quant* and *Quant on Make-up*.

Ian Rankin was educated at the University of Edinburgh. His first Inspector Rebus novel *Knots and Crosses* was published in 1987. His other novels include *Black and Blue*, which won the CWA Macallan Gold Dagger for Fiction, and *Hanging Garden*; both were televised. *Dead Souls* was shortlisted for the CWA Macallan Gold Dagger Award in 1999.

Frederic Raphael was educated at Charterhouse and St John's College, Cambridge, where he was a major scholar in classics. His publications include 19 novels, biographies of Somerset Maugham and Byron, screenplays and translations from Aeschylus and Catullus (with Kenneth McLeish). He won the Royal Television Society's Writer of the Year Award for his TV plays *The Glittering Prizes* and is a Fellow of the Royal Society of Literature.

Andrew Roberts is a writer and historian, whose books include *The Holy Fox, Eminent Churchillians* and *Salisbury: Victorian Titan*, which won the Wolfson History Prize and the James Stern Silver Pen Award for Non-Fiction. He appears regularly on TV and radio, writes for the *Sunday Telegraph*, and is a regular contributor to the *Spectator, Literary Review, Mail on Sunday* and *Daily Telegraph*.

Hugh Sebag-Montefiore is the author of *Enigma: the Battle for the Code*. A barrister before becoming a journalist and author, he has written for the *Sunday Times*, the *Sunday Telegraph*, the *Observer*, the *Independent on Sunday* and the *Mail on Sunday*. He is also the author of *Kings on the Catwalk*.

Ned Sherrin has worked in radio, TV, film and theatre, and co-wrote many novels and plays with Caryl Brahms. His publications include *Theatrical Anecdotes* and the novel *Scratch an Actor*. In TV he is principally associated with *TW3*, and in films with *The Virgin Soldiers*. He directed the play *Jeffrey Bernard is Unwell* and *Side by Side with Sondheim*, in which he also appeared in the West End and on Broadway. His radio programme *Loose Ends* is in its 15th season on BBC Radio 4.

David Steel was leader of the Liberal Party from 1976–1988, when he co-founded the Liberal Democrats with the SDP, and was Foreign Affairs Spokesman for the Liberal Democrats until 1994. He was created a life peer in 1997

and became Presiding Officer of the Scottish Parliament in 1999. His publications include *A House Divided* and his autobiography *Against Goliath*.

Rick Stein and his wife Jill run the internationally renowned Seafood Restaurant in Padstow, whose many awards include Egon Ronay's Restaurant of the Year (1996). His publications include *Taste of the Sea, Fruits of the Sea* and *Rick Stein's Seafood Odyssey*, all based on his award-winning TV series. He was *AA Guide* Chefs' Chef of the Year 1999–2000.

Thomas Stuttaford has been a GP, MP, occupational health physician and genito-urinary physician. He has worked in TV, radio and the print media for nearly 40 years, and has been *The Times* doctor for 19 of these. He is the author of *To Your Good Health, In Your Right Mind* and, in conjunction with Alistair Service and Dr John Dunwoody, *A Birth Control Plan for Britain*.

Hugh Thomas was Professor of History at the University of Reading (1966–76) and Chairman of the Centre for Policy Studies (1979–89). He was created a life peer in 1981. His books include *The Spanish Civil War*, which won the Somerset Maugham Prize, and *An Unfinished History of the World*, which won the Arts Council's prize for history in its National Book Awards. He is also the author of *The Slave Trade*.

Stephen Venables is a writer, lecturer and broadcaster, specialising in outdoor adventure. His six books include *Painted Mountains*, which won the Boardman-Tasker Prize for mountain literature. He was the first Briton to climb Everest without supplementary oxygen, reaching the summit alone by a new route. His most recent trip was to South Georgia to take part in an IMAX film about Sir Ernest Shackleton.

Alexander Walker has been the London *Evening Standard*'s film critic since 1960, and was three times named Critic of the Year in the annual British Press Awards. He is the author of 22 books on Anglo-American and European cinema, including two definitive studies of the British film industry, biographies of film stars including Peter Sellers, Garbo and Elizabeth Taylor, and most recently *Stanley Kubrick, Director*.

Judith Watt is a fashion historian and writer and a visiting teacher in the history of fashion at Central St Martin's College of Art and Design. She is the editor of *The Penguin Book of Twentieth Century Fashion Writing*.

Neil Wenborn is a full-time author and publishing consultant. Co-editor of the *Companion to British History*, he has published biographies of Mozart, Haydn and, most recently, Stravinsky. His poetry has been published in Britain and the US and has been awarded a number of national prizes.

Simon Winchester, who for most of his career has been a foreign correspondent working almost everywhere in the world, is the author of the bestselling book about the birth of the *OED*, *The Surgeon of Crowthorne*. He is now completing a book on the 19th-century geologist William Smith.

First published in 2000 by Cassell & Co, Wellington House, 125 Strand, London WC2R 0BB

Commissioning Editor: Annabel Merullo *Design Director:* David Rowley
Assistant Editors: Tim Whiting and Stephen Guise *Design:* Pentagram
Consultant Editor: Neil Wenborn

Printed and bound in Italy
This book has been typeset in Monotype Baskerville (cut in 1923)

In his determination to improve the quality of English printing and typography, Birmingham-based craftsman John Baskerville designed the epitome of 'Transitional' typefaces. The font Baskerville marks the evolution of the 'old-style' Garalde into the 'modern' Didone faces that emerged in the 19th century. Although Baskerville gained little commercial recognition in 1754, his wide, generously proportioned characters have an elegance and legibility which make the font one of the most popular book faces of today. It remains an original British design of great distinction. – Angus Hyland

Acknowledgements

The publisher would like to thank the following people, museums, and photographic libraries for permission to reproduce their material. Every care has been taken to trace copyright holders. However, if we have omitted anyone we apologise and shall, if informed, make corrections in any future edition.

Page 9 Bridgeman Art Library; 12 Bridgeman Art Library; 15 Hulton Getty; 18 Kobal; 22–23 Humphrey Spender/Hulton Getty; 26 Kobal; 29 Art Archive; 32–33 Hulton Getty; 37 Corbis/Bettmann; 38 Art Archive; 42 Science Photo Library; 45 Public Record Office; 48 Norman Parkinson; 52–53 Robert Capa/Magnum Photographers; 57 Cartier-Bresson/Magnum Photographers; 59 Bridgeman Art Library; 61 by courtesy of The Dickens House Museum, London; 64–65 Kobal; 66 Still Moving Picture Library; 71 The Lebrecht Collection; 74–75 Hulton Getty; 78–79 Royal Geographical Society; 81 Kobal; 84 Art Archive; 87 Corbis/CG; 90–91 Canadian Centre for Architecture, Montreal; 93 Canadian Centre for Architecture, Montreal; 96–97 Bridgeman Art Library; 99 Bridgeman Art Library; 103 Kobal; 107 Hulton Getty; 108 London Transport Museum, London; 113 Hulton Getty; 115 Hulton Getty; 119 Kobal; 122 Art Archive; 125 Art Archive; 126 Art Archive; 131 Hulton Getty; 134–135 Royal Geographical Society; 137 Ronald Grant Archive; 140 Hulton Getty; 144–145 Hulton Getty; 147 Hulton Getty; 148 Hulton Getty; 152–153 Science Photo Library; 157 Bridgeman Art Library; 158 Oxford Picture Library; 163 OUP Archives; 165 Bridgeman Art Library; 168 Michael Holford; 171 Science Photo Library; 174–175 Jeffrey F. Morgan; 179 The Lebrecht Collection; 180 Robert Capa/Magnum Photographers; 185 Rex Features; 188–189 Hulton Getty; 191 Robert McLeod/Robert Harding Picture Library; 194 Kobal; 196 Bridgeman Art Library; 200 Robert Opie; 203 Sarah Fitch/Gieves and Hawkes; 206–208 Herbert Ponting/Popperfoto; 210–211 Hulton Getty; 214 Hulton Getty; 217 Bridgeman Art Library; 220 both Science and Society Picture Library; 223 Hulton Getty; 226 Lebrecht Collection; 229 Bridgeman Art Library; 235 The Archives, Times Newspapers; 236–237 Bridgeman Art Library; 239 Ian Berry/Magnum Photographers; 243 Tate, London 2000; 246–247 London Transport Museum, London; 249 Christopher Pillitz/Network Photographers; 252–253 Hulton Getty; 257 Art Archive; 259 Art Archive.